RIDING
FOR THE
TEAM

Also by the USET Foundation

The U.S. Equestrian Team Book of Riding:
The First Quarter-Century of the USET
Edited by William Steinkraus, Foreword by Whitney Stone

Riding for America: The United States Equestrian Team
Edited by Nancy Jaffer, Foreword by John H. Fritz

RIDING
FOR THE
TEAM

Inspirational Stories from the
USA's Medal-Winning Equestrians
and Their Horses

THE UNITED STATES EQUESTRIAN TEAM FOUNDATION
Edited by Nancy Jaffer

TRAFALGAR SQUARE
North Pomfret, Vermont

First published in 2019 by
Trafalgar Square Books
North Pomfret, Vermont 05053

Disclaimer of Liability
The authors and publisher shall have neither liability nor responsibility to any person or entity with respect to any loss or damage caused or alleged to be caused directly or indirectly by the information contained in this book. While the book is as accurate as the authors can make it, there may be errors, omissions, and inaccuracies.

Trafalgar Square Books encourages the use of approved safety helmets in all equestrian sports and activities.

ISBN: 978-1-57076-872-9
Library of Congress Control Number: 2019946656

Book design by Lauryl Eddlemon
Cover design by RM Didier
Index by Michelle Guiliano, DPM (linebylineindexing.com)

Typefaces: Poppl-Pontifex; Gotham

Printed in China

10 9 8 7 6 5 4 3 2 1

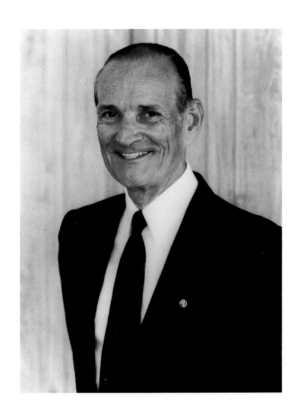

In Memoriam

*This book is dedicated to the memory of William C. Steinkraus,
U.S. Equestrian Team Foundation chairman emeritus. He was always
an inspiration: the country's first Olympic individual equestrian
gold medalist, an extraordinary sportsman, erudite author,
insightful editor, and accomplished musician.*

1925–2017

CONTENTS

INTRODUCTION

When the American flag flies high at international competitions, it's a sign that the United States Equestrian Team (USET) Foundation is succeeding in its mission—providing resources to ensure accomplishments in the global arena.

And what accomplishments U.S. teams have delivered: fantastic performances by horses and athletes representing the country in eight disciplines, earning scores of medals and the respect of the world for their prowess.

As the 70th anniversary of the USET's founding approaches, we remember the visionaries who ensured the country would be well-represented in the Olympics, Nations Cups, and other important competitions after the cavalry disbanded following World War II and the Army equestrian team was no more. Whitney Stone, the longtime USET chairman, and those foresighted pioneers who joined him, went to work on what it would take to put American equestrians atop podiums across the continents.

They could not, of course, envision the future specifics of the new organization's reach: there were no Pan American Games, World Championships, or World Cups in 1950. But they laid a masterful foundation that could be expanded as the need arose and the number of those participating in teams grew exponentially over the years to come.

In 2003, the USET became a foundation. Working in conjunction with the U.S. Equestrian Federation, the foundation is its philanthropic partner, supporting not only the competition, training, coaching, travel, and educational needs of America's top equestrian athletes and their horses, but also aiding in funding the pipeline of developing international high-performance competitors. These rising stars someday will have medals placed around their necks at the world's most important equestrian sporting events.

To understand what has been achieved over seven decades, it's important to recall the hundreds of athletes whom the USET Foundation and U.S. Equestrian Federation have helped to raise the flag. It's fascinating to learn the histories of dedicated equestrians competing at the highest level, no matter which discipline they pursue. While the details of their personal accounts may differ, every one of them shares a love of horses and their country. All have an engaging tale about their success and how they have overcome the inevitable complications along the way, giving the reader insight into what it takes to reach the top tier of the sport.

The compelling stories collected in this volume, as told by the athletes who have become part of equestrian history, demonstrate how to make dreams reality, while acknowledging sacrifice as the other side of achievement. Those who compete at the highest level share several characteristics in addition to the love and appreciation of the horse. All have demonstrated singular focus to achieve excellence, putting aside other pursuits as they strive to represent their country. While the book is called *Riding for the Team,* it is a general title that also includes the drivers and vaulters who are not in a saddle while competing.

This is the third volume in a series. The first, the U.S. Equestrian Team *Book of Riding,* was published to mark the organization's 25th anniversary in 1975. Edited by William Steinkraus, then the president of the USET, it offered training principles, riding pointers, and history lessons from those who became legends of the sport.

The second book, *Riding for America,* which I edited in 1990, was an update that included athletes and other key figures who made their mark during the generation after the USET's founding. While the first book dealt only with the Olympic disciplines of show jumping, dressage, and eventing, *Riding for America* also included the USET's newest discipline at that time, combined driving.

Nearly three decades later, *Riding for the Team* continues the tradition while adding four other disciplines supported by the Foundation: vaulting, which is gymnastics on horseback; endurance; the Western sport of reining; and para-dressage. There's something for everyone on the roster of international horse sports these days.

The athletes who share the inside story of their achievements in these pages are only a small sampling of the worthy competitors who have represented the country since 1990 and brought honor to the effort. Because so many people were candidates to be part of *Riding for the Team,* we are not including anyone who was in the 1975 or 1990 books, even if they are playing a different role in the current era. The stories listed in the table of contents offer simply a sampling of the many outstanding individuals who have contributed to an impressive equestrian record for America over the last 30 years in the Olympics and FEI World Equestrian Games, a multi-discipline World Championships format that debuted in 1990. This book would have to be many times its current size to include each of them.

We are grateful to everyone who has given their all, not only by riding for the Team, but also by supporting it in so many different capacities, from the veterinarians to the coaches, grooms, volunteers, sponsors, and contributors, to the athletes' families who have shared a dream and helped make it come true. The officers and staffs of the USET Foundation and the U.S. Equestrian Federation, the governing body of American horse sport, also play instrumental roles in the sporting triumphs that make a nation proud.

On a personal note, over the last half-century I have known most of those whose stories appear in these books. Some I have followed since their days in equitation, interviewing them after they won those championships and then again, years later, once they stepped down from the podium after the Olympic medal ceremonies. From the sidelines at nine Olympics, all eight World Equestrian Games, and dozens of World Cup finals, I've had a ringside seat from which to follow triumph and tragedy, victory and loss, all of which play their role in the vibrant panorama that is equestrian sport today. It's been a privilege.

Nancy Jaffer
Gladstone, New Jersey

Special thanks to Sara Ike of the U.S. Equestrian Team Foundation, who was kept busy obtaining and organizing the many photos in this book.

In addition to the USET Foundation, the organizations referred to in this book are:

- The U.S. Equestrian Federation (USEF): The governing body of horse shows in the United States, as well as an umbrella group for a variety of breeds and disciplines, it is an official member of the FEI (see below) and the U.S. Olympic Committee (USOC).

- The American Horse Shows Association (AHSA): The original U.S. governing body of horse shows, a predecessor of the USEF.

- The Fédération Equestre Internationale (FEI): Based in Switzerland, it is the governing body of international equestrian sport and formulates its rules.

- National Reining Horse Association (NRHA): Dedicated to the promotion of the reining horse, it serves as the standard-setting body for the sport of reining, while promoting public interest in agriculture and ranching through reining horse shows and programs.

- American Endurance Ride Conference (AERC): The organization that sanctions endurance riding in North America, it also promotes the establishment, maintenance, and preservation of trails.

SHOW JUMPING

SHOW JUMPING IS THE MOST POPULAR OF THE OLYMPIC EQUESTRIAN sports, with the greatest number of participants and spectators. Its roots are in fox hunting, stemming from the era when fences were constructed around previously open fields in Britain and the jumping horse became a necessary and desirable mount.

Competition naturally followed, and the discipline became a fixture at shows in the late nineteenth century. It grew increasingly more sophisticated as the years passed. The Olympics included show jumping starting in 1912. At the time, participants were limited to members of the military, but that changed after 1948, following mechanization of the armies.

Show jumping at the international level today involves obstacles of up to 1.60 meters in height, including brightly painted rails, faux stone walls, gates, and water jumps. They are arranged differently for every competition, requiring not only power on the part of the horse but also technical expertise on the part of the rider.

Some classes are one round against the clock; others require jumping an initial round within the time allowed, which is followed by a jump-off over a shorter course among those who are tied, with time deciding the winner for those tied with an equal number of penalties. Entries are penalized for knockdowns, refusals, and exceeding the time allowed.

BEEZIE MADDEN

A Focus on Excellence

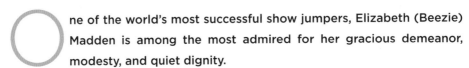

One of the world's most successful show jumpers, Elizabeth (Beezie) Madden is among the most admired for her gracious demeanor, modesty, and quiet dignity.

Her accomplishments are many, with Olympic team gold medals from Athens 2004 and Beijing/Hong Kong 2008, where she also earned individual bronze. She was on the silver medal U.S. teams at the 2016 Rio Olympics and at the 2006 World Equestrian Games in Aachen, Germany, winning individual silver there as well. She took individual bronze at the 2014 WEG in Normandy, France, where she also was part of the bronze medal team. Beezie twice has won the FEI World Cup finals and four times has been the U.S. Equestrian Federation's Equestrian of the Year.

Beezie accounts for many firsts: She was the first woman to earn more than $1 million in show jumping, as well as the first American and the first woman to reach the top three on the world ranking list.

Her horses have included such stars as Northern Magic, Authentic, Judgement, Coral Reef Via Volo, Simon, Cortes C, and Breitling. She is based at John Madden Sales in Cazenovia, New York, with her husband, a former FEI vice president who has managed her career and works with sponsors and owners, as well as teaching and supervising the barn.

A believer in giving back to her sport, Beezie serves on the boards of the U.S. Equestrian Federation and the U.S. Equestrian Team Foundation.

At the 2008 Olympics in Hong Kong, Beezie Madden guided Authentic to team gold and an individual bronze four years after riding him to team gold at the Athens Games.

My parents, Kathy and Joseph Patton, had hunters, so I basically grew up in the stable. I've loved horses since I can remember. I was five years old when my brother, Stewart, and I got our first Shetland ponies, Flicka and her dam, Fudge, along with their bridles—but no saddles.

I jumped and did everything with my pony bareback. I would ride so much that my parents would tell me when Flicka had had enough, because otherwise, I would have ridden her all day.

They didn't have pony classes at the shows in Wisconsin at that time. So at a couple of shows, we had to ask them to just lower the fences for us. I trained with Michael Henaghan and didn't show a jumper until my last junior year, when we converted my junior hunter, Storytime, to a junior jumper. I only competed in the equitation finals during my last two junior years. My best finish was eighth in the hunt seat Medal on a borrowed horse.

But I got more from equitation than a brown ribbon. Equitation teaches you to ride technical courses smoothly, which I think is important, because our sport is a game of concentration on the part of both horse and rider. The more effective you can be while still being smooth is critical because the horse has to concentrate on his job as well.

One of my best qualities is being able to focus and block out distractions. When people say there was a big crowd for a class I was in, I say, "I couldn't tell you, I didn't notice."

When I feel like I'm under pressure and have the honor of being on the team and riding for my country, I approach it one round at a time. You can't think of a multi-day show or a championship as a whole. I think of that competition and that course. I want to do it to the best of my ability in that round. You're behind the eight ball if you worry about making a mistake; you've just got to show them how good you are.

After my junior career, I went to Southern Seminary College in Virginia for two years because Russ Walther, who headed the riding program, wanted me there. I was on the intercollegiate team and won the 1984 Cacchione Cup, the most prestigious award at the Intercollegiate Horse Shows Association's national show.

Intercollegiate competition was a fun experience, hopping on strange horses and having to get it done (as I would do decades later in the Final Four at two World Championships). It also was a valuable experience because I learned to work with a team. When you do that, it's not all about you and your success.

I graduated as valedictorian and was accepted to the University of Virginia, where I had been turned down when I first applied for college. But then trainer Katie Monahan offered me a job and I had to decide whether I would go to school or work with her. My parents said they would support

me in college, or if I didn't go, they would support me while I was training with Katie for a couple more years. So I went with her.

While riding with Katie, I discovered many things that were new to me. I learned so much from her about riding. From Pancho Lopez, who ran her barn, I absorbed a lot of valuable information about being a horseman.

My nature is not real aggressive, so Katie was my switch from equitation and hunters into jumpers. Every kid who goes through that needs to learn to be a little more aggressive and effective. It's not all about smoothness. Sometimes you just have to get it done.

John Madden, who had worked for Katie, was transitioning out to start his own business as I was transitioning in. He moved to Wisconsin and one day he saw my mom at a show, telling her, "I wish I could get someone like Beezie to ride for me." My mother replied, "Why don't you ask her?" So he did. We worked well together for 10 years and in 1998, we got married.

My first time on a team was in 1988 in Guadalajara, Mexico, where I rode Northern Magic. Rodney Jenkins was supposed to be on the team and serve as Chef d'Equipe, but he pulled out and I went in. John was asked to be Chef. I was only supposed to be the fifth person, but after I won a class, John sought advice about who to put on the team from Bertalan de Nemethy, the former U.S. coach, who was there as an official.

Bert told John I should be part of the Nations Cup squad. I went double-clear and we won. That was a milestone in my career. I never imagined being good enough to ride for the Team. I was a kid from the Midwest who did seven or eight shows a year until my last junior year. I wasn't on anyone's radar, including my own.

Northern Magic was my first good horse. We went to Europe with him the next year. It was quite an experience. In those days, not so many

Beezie and her husband, John Madden, a former FEI first vice president who has guided her career through Olympic, World Championships, and Pan American Games medals, as well as FEI World Cup finals victories.

Beezie Madden raised the FEI Longines World Cup Finals™ followed up that victory with another in 2018.

Americans wanted to go to Europe to compete. If you were going, you went on an official team or with a private stable's tour–Hunterdon, which was George Morris' stable, and Sandron, run by Joe Fargis and Conrad Homfeld, were the two operations that were doing that. We went on our own, and knew we had to win enough money to get back home!

It isn't easy to get invitations to compete in Europe when you're starting out, but we had help from Johan Heins, a Dutch horse dealer, the man through whom we buy our horses. On our 1989 tour, we hooked up with Conrad, Joe, and Katie to form a squad for the Rome show. The fact that I was

naïve helped me. I was able to go in there thinking, "I can do this." I still have a copy of the Italian newspaper that came out the day after the Nations Cup; it had a photo of me, jumping the headlines.

This was kind of a storybook tour. Next, I got picked for the team at Aachen. When we walked the course the first day, John asked, "Do you think our horses can jump this?" I told him, "I hope so."

In those days, the American Invitational was in Tampa Stadium, so my horses were used to being in a stadium like the one they had at Aachen, and since it was the same feeling, that helped us.

We won money in Rome and I was Leading Lady Rider at Wiesbaden. We were able to pay our

One of Beezie Madden's busiest mounts in 2014 and 2015, the Dutch-bred Simon, did everything from Nations Cups to the World Cup Finals.

And when I had one bad round, I was out. It was discouraging. But I felt I was close enough and it kept me hungry.

My first FEI World Equestrian Games was Jerez, Spain, in 2002. Michael Matz, who had the ride on Judgement, recommended me to the horse's owner, Iron Spring Farm, after he retired, and that meant a lot. The first time I jumped Judgement, I was impressed and told John, "We don't have any horses in our barn that feel like this."

To do your first championship is amazing. The scope of the WEG is almost more overwhelming than the Olympic venue, because so much is going on at the same time. The first day I was there I watched eventing; it was a real team atmosphere.

I didn't handle the pressure at the WEG as well as I would have wanted. It was a wake-up call, because I was trying to do everything too perfectly instead of going in there and riding—doing what I did best every day.

A friend of John's, Ed Huber, had a farm in upstate Cazenovia, New York, and John started his business there. Ed would let him have stalls and when he sold a horse, John would pay him. Eventually, John found a farm that he liked in the area, but it was beyond his means. When it became affordable, we bought it, and now we own more than 300 acres where we also have based a horse-retirement business that has attracted a group of famous former showring stars.

way home and had proved it could be done. We got the fever, after having a good experience the first time.

The main goal for both John and me is to represent the United States—for me to be on teams and win medals for the country (and obviously, for ourselves, too). We've been lucky with our owners, because that's been their main goal, too. They have been people who were really in it for the team and the country, and included my parents, Carol Hofmann Thompson and her sister, Judy Richter, the Jacobs family, Mary Alice Malone, Gwendolyn Meyer, Elizabeth Busch Burke, and Abigail Wexner.

I tried to make the teams for the 1992, 1996, and 2000 Olympics, but they were all chosen objectively following a 1990 lawsuit over team selection.

For the trials for the 2004 Athens Olympics, Authentic pulled through on the last day when my other horse, DeSilvio, got hurt after he was leading the standings. I ended up in the top four.

We got Authentic when Elizabeth Busch Burke wanted to buy a horse, and she liked the Thoroughbred type, so he was a perfect choice for her—especially since he was winning six-year-old classes right and left. He didn't jump in classic form, he had a bit of a "drapey" front end, but the feeling on him was better than it looked. You couldn't get him too close to the fences, he was too careful. He had a cool personality; he was very cocky.

Being in Greece was exciting. None of us on the team—McLain Ward, Chris Kappler, Peter Wylde, and myself, as well as alternate Alison Robitaille—had ever been to the Olympics. I don't think any of us were actually friends before this, but we had respect for each other. We were all excited to be there and we ended up doing a lot together; it was a great feeling.

That is, until Authentic colicked badly the day of the jog. They wouldn't let us compete if we gave him any medication, and it was looking as if he'd need surgery and we'd be out of the Games. Then we let him roll, and that did the trick. Frank Chapot was Chef d'Equipe and he made me the anchor after I was able to go clear in the individual qualifier, despite everything we had just been through with the horse. We were all pretty equal going in, so I was honored and excited, and I thrive off the confidence of others. That kind of inspired me.

When you think about it, we were four rookies with two nine-year-old horses, Authentic and McLain's Sapphire, on the team. We won silver behind the Germans and were on the podium with wreaths of olive branches on our heads. But as it happens, that wasn't the last time we were on the podium.

A German horse tested positive for a banned substance at the Games. That eventually dropped them out of first place and moved us up. Eighteen months after the closing ceremonies in Athens, we were presented with the gold medal during a brief ceremony in Florida.

The 2006 WEG in Aachen was amazing. We got team silver and I won individual silver in the Final Four ride-off, where we all switched horses. After the team medal ceremonies, we did the victory lap at a walk. McLain turned to me and said, "I don't think we'll ever experience anything like this in our lives again."

But he was wrong. We won team gold two years later in the next Olympics, in Hong Kong, where the venue was fantastic and the skyscrapers formed a dramatic backdrop for the arena. We beat Canada in a jump-off, so it was all North American on the highest levels of the podium.

The individual medal competition in Hong Kong was a great example of a team effort. McLain was in the jump-off and he found a shortcut by jumping over some bushes in the ring to save time against the clock. I was able to follow suit and win the individual bronze. Bronze was also my color at the 2014 WEG, where I was on the bronze medal team and took the individual bronze in what would be the last Final Four ride-off before the FEI came up with a more conventional way for deciding the individual WEG medals.

I love riding on teams, but know I can't do it forever. So John and I planned what we should do after that. When I step back, I'll continue riding and developing special young horses. We would also like to have students with goals of riding for the U.S. Equestrian Team. That would be exciting for us, too, and a new focus, while continuing our dedication to seeing the United States represented well internationally.

ROBERT RIDLAND

A Californian Comes to Gladstone

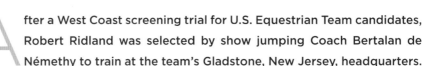

After a West Coast screening trial for U.S. Equestrian Team candidates, Robert Ridland was selected by show jumping Coach Bertalan de Némethy to train at the team's Gladstone, New Jersey, headquarters. Bert was a graduate of the Hungarian cavalry school and had served in World War II, so everything was done with military precision and according to impeccable standards at the historic stables when Robert rode there in the 1970s. The facility was recognized worldwide as the base for such renowned riders as team captain William Steinkraus, Frank Chapot (who would succeed Bert as coach), Kathy Kusner, and George Morris.

Robert was the reserve rider at the 1972 Olympics in Munich and rode on the 1976 fourth-place Montreal Olympic team, as well as winning Nations Cup teams at Lucerne in 1976 and in Rotterdam and Toronto in 1978. In 2012, Robert became coach of the U.S. Show Jumping Team, with a stellar record that includes team and individual bronze medals at the 2014 FEI World Equestrian Games, team bronze and individual gold and bronze at the 2015 Pan American Games, team silver at the 2016 Olympics, and team gold at the 2018 WEG—the first gold for the U.S. team at a World Championships in 32 years.

The president of show management company Blenheim EquiSports, Robert has served as a member of the U.S. Equestrian Federation board of directors and the FEI Jumping Committee. An international course designer who also has been a World Cup finals technical delegate, the Yale University graduate has run the Las Vegas World Cup finals and was co-manager of the Washington International Horse Show.

Robert and his wife, Hillary, who live in California, have two children, Peyton and McKenna.

The few of us left who once were part of the old U.S. Equestrian Team, the original concept, can look at show jumping with a unique perspective to compare it with where the sport is today. So much time has passed that there are not that many current riders who are familiar with where the sport came from and the circumstances that led to what it has become.

Having Coach Bertalan de Némethy go around the country to select riders with potential was a totally different system than what we have now. Another difference was the fact that we didn't have private owners to the degree that we do today. The top horses in the country were owned by the USET or loaned to the team, and we got matched with the ones we were going to ride.

When I got to team headquarters in Gladstone, I was young, only 18, and already enrolled at Yale. I was well prepared by my riding and competition experience to that point and had ridden at shows in the East. Even so, there was a bit of culture shock.

The first time I met Bert was when he was in California for the screening trials. Bert was Hungarian nobility and very old world; I was very West Coast and didn't leave my California ways at home. It was quite a proving ground.

U.S. Equestrian Team Coach Bertalan de Némethy with (left to right) Robert Ridland, Dennis Murphy, Michael Matz, and Buddy Brown after winning the 1978 Nations Cup in Rotterdam.

Robert Ridland guided the United States to two bronze medals in his first world championships coaching gig at the 2014 FEI World Equestrian Games.

The riders in training lived in rooms over the team stables. One of the many requirements involved always dressing appropriately in boots and breeches. It also meant making sure they were clean. A few times, we had to have the washer and dryers working on our breeches at the last minute before we got on the horses in the morning.

I wasn't really prepared for winter, having grown up with California's sunny version of the season. I will never forget a particularly cold morning when there was only time to wash the breeches, not dry them. And that was a problem, because at the time, I had just one pair of breeches (something I rectified soon after).

Once we got outside, my breeches basically froze. We were riding on the flat in the indoor ring. Bert was there in front of this jet engine of a heater that was blasting at him! He was wearing this

heavy overcoat and looked as if he could survive the Arctic, while I was practically shivering.

George Simmons, the barn manager, had been in the military and ran the place like a Marine sergeant. He gave us all lessons in tack cleaning. I had thought I was pretty good at it—that is, until I ran into George at Gladstone. And Dennis Haley, one of the grooms there, also was meticulous about making sure we cleaned our tack according to the team's requirements.

I was lucky enough to be taken under the wing of our team captain, Bill Steinkraus, the Olympic individual gold medalist who was one of the greatest riders of all time. When I first rode on the team, Billy was my mentor in so many ways. He needed someone to go golfing with, so he taught me how to play on our off days.

That gave us a lot of time to talk, and I was

always watching how he approached the sport. I remember my first couple of shows in Europe when I joined the team. We got to Lucerne, Switzerland, which was the third one. As we were sitting on the Volkswagen bus being driven to the showgrounds, Billy turned around to us and said, "Ladies and gentlemen, now we start."

I'll never forget that because I thought we had started two weeks earlier. But Lucerne was the important Nations Cup, with the honor of our country riding on our performance.

Billy was all the things that everyone said about him—the class he brought to the sport, the sense of perfectionism. Billy never compromised on anything. He *was* the sport.

The thing that impresses me in retrospect about my experience at Gladstone is how young we all were at the time. I rode on my first international team when I was 19 years old. A couple of years later, Buddy Brown rode on his first team when he was 18 and won the Grand Prix at Dublin. Michael Matz was my age as well.

After my years with the team, however, there seemed to be a trend, not just in the United States, but in other countries as well, to have older riders—and the same riders—constantly on their team. The British, before they turned things around and won gold at the 2012 London Olympics, fielded lots of squads with riders who were older, and that was detrimental.

When I came in as U.S. coach, I said, "We're going to use the riders who were our age when we started competing." There's no reason in the world why you would have to wait until you were in your late twenties or early thirties to bring something to the table from the point of view of international competitions.

While the USET ran things at the international end of the sport for America when I was riding, having stepped in to replace the cavalry after World War II, today everyone, in effect, has his or

her own private professional team. That means we don't just select the rider, we embrace not only the rider, but also the owners, and all the support staff behind the horses.

These teams operate the same way Gladstone did in its heyday. An example is Beezie Madden, the Olympic and WEG medalist, who works with her husband, John. He grew up in Gladstone just like I did, except that he was a groom there. He started his career from the bottom up, which is why he is so good at what he does. He was immersed in Bert's program—his system, his standards—from the very beginning...from polishing the brass to cleaning the tack.

Bert would come downstairs for inspection and all of us were there to make sure the horses were turned out appropriately and everything was done right. John took that knowledge and the other knowledge he gained through his career to establish with Beezie what they have today at their business in New York State. It's a mini-Gladstone that didn't just develop out of thin air. Bert's

At the 2012 Olympics, Robert Ridland consulted with Beezie Madden as he was learning the ropes.

system lives on, even though it's not all under one roof in New Jersey.

It was a big change when we went from the team structure of my era to the professional sport we have today, but in many ways, it's the same at the top level. Our top professional riders have the same degree of perfection and control of the details that Bert oversaw in Gladstone.

Since that job already is taken care of by our top riders, I don't have to look over their shoulders and micro-manage every single professional. What I have to do is manage the chess pieces, and that's a completely different job. I have to make sure what the objectives are, as well as how we get there and how each rider has the priorities for reaching that goal. Those priorities are, of course, different from the priorities of individual riders and owners. My job is to mesh the two together.

While I may lead the way, I'm not going solo on this. The U.S. Equestrian Federation in effect also has its own team, from Lizzy Chesson, the Managing Director of Show Jumping, to my Assistant Coach, Olympic medalist Anne Kursinski, and Young Rider Chef d'Equipe DiAnn Langer, as well as members of the USEF committees who work on behalf of the sport's best interests.

From the horse side, some things haven't changed. Over-competing and not adhering to a strict schedule of long-term goals and long-term scheduling still will be detrimental. Bert knew what our schedule was in the beginning of the year, as well as when the training sessions would be. He knew when we would select the team for Europe, when we would prepare for Europe, what shows we would do in Europe, which Nations Cups we were going to compete in, what the fall circuit would be. He was always 12 months ahead of time in his planning.

I do the same thing, but I do it with each individual rider instead of with a group. Unless our objectives are very clear about what our priorities

are, it's too easy to add a little too much to the schedule because the world is so much different in our sport from Bert's time.

The opportunities to compete in big money Grands Prix have proliferated. Even in our own country, the number of FEI events has ballooned. It's really crucial that the riders who are part of this program, who we feel can really contribute to the team's important goals and markers we have for the year, stick to the plan and the schedule. That's what I do in the early weeks of each year at the winter circuits in Florida and California, getting together with each rider to develop the plans so we can stick with them. I have always stressed that I will defer to sound horsemanship and long-term planning over short-term results.

What has made a huge difference for my job is technology. I can monitor the riders and watch their Grands Prix performances from my office. I'm seeing live-stream Grands Prix from Europe and all over the world from there. That helps me spend more time at home than I would have if I were doing this job in the 1970s or '80s.

At competitions, we go in there one horse at a time, one rider at a time, and it's our course to do. What I pay attention to is how we can be our best and lay down as many clean rounds as we can. If we do that, we'll be in a good position—it doesn't really matter who we're up against.

We have had a situation where it was felt that in order to really compete, you had to be in Europe. For us to be and remain competitive for the next 20 years, we need to truly level the playing field so people don't feel they have to go to Europe in order to compete at the highest level. While I like to see the best competitors spending more time riding in the United States, that doesn't mean we should never show in Europe. But if the top riders are always in Europe, it means they are not in the U.S., inspiring a new generation of riders and generating star power for the discipline.

MCLAIN WARD

The Pathfinder Becomes
the Anchor Rider

The son of professional equestrians Barney and Kris Ward, McLain rode before he could walk. Born and trained to be a top show jumper, McLain began fulfilling his destiny early. At age 14, he was the youngest person ever to win the USET Medal Finals East (now the USEF Talent Search Finals East) while taking the team's Talent Derby in the same year.

At the time he said, "I've had so many experiences most 14-year-olds haven't had. If it continues, I'll be ahead of the game." He was right. Those early victories foreshadowed enormous show jumping success. At the age of 24, he became the youngest rider to earn $1 million in his discipline. Eventually, he would rank as number one in the world—an Olympic, World Equestrian Games, and Pan American Games multi-medalist. McLain's persistence is as legendary as his ability—he took the 2017 FEI World Cup Finals on his seventeenth try at the title.

His horses have included more than a few superstars, including Sapphire—after whom the Grand Prix of Devon is named; Rothchild; his winning World Cup mount, HH Azur; and his 2018 WEG team gold medal anchor ride, Clinta. McLain, his wife, Lauren, and their daughter, Lilly Kristine, live where he grew up, at Castle Hill Farm in Brewster, New York.

When I first began competing on the team at championships, Beezie Madden was the anchor rider. That was appropriate, since she is older than I am and had a little more experience at the time. Our international championship careers basically coincided for 15 years. I generally was the lead-off rider and everybody was very comfortable with me as the pathfinder. We were very successful for a long time with Beezie and myself in those roles. I had ridden anchor on a few teams, though not very often.

In 2016, however, there was a transition and I became the anchor and kind of remained in that spot. The qualities you need to go first and those you need to be the anchor rider are sometimes a little bit different, but the order in which you ride for the team is heavily determined by the horse you're riding. Some horses fill one of those spots better than the other, but you have to be very cool and have a great amount of experience, so that you've been in most situations you encounter as part of the team—wherever you ride in the order.

You're always going to be more successful in the long run if you've been in a situation before and can figure out how to handle it. Either way, you understand your job is to jump two clear rounds. That's all that you are responsible for. You can't get distracted by other things, and need to be as prepared and ready to go as possible to do that job.

Most people would say there's more pressure for an anchor rider than a lead-off rider because you understand the consequences of any penalties you accumulate pretty clearly and know what has to be done. You've been put in that position because they're expecting a certain performance from you. The pressure is greater for the anchor rider, but someone who has more experience and been in more positions can bring that to the table. You're using all that knowledge to be mentally and physically in the right place.

The Rio Olympics was a huge moment. We went into the 2016 Games thinking that with four faults or better in the Nations Cup overall, we would win the gold medal. It seemed logical. And then France had what I considered an out-of-body experience that day. Roger Yves Bost went right before me and jumped a clear round to clinch the gold medal.

So there I was, the U.S. anchor rider, walking down the ramp with a focus 100 percent on jumping that clean round and winning that gold medal. Then all of a sudden, that wasn't possible. It was a blow, but I had only 45 seconds to digest that information and realize that if I had one fence down, there'd be no medal at all. That would have been a very disappointing Olympics for us.

After I went into the ring, I pulled up HH Azur and took a moment to tell myself, "Okay, it's a little bit disappointing. But now there's a job to be done, and I have to focus on the things I can control and let the bigger outcome sort itself out."

The mission had become bringing home the silver, compared to the possibility of no medal and a fifth-place finish. For me, what happened there is a moment I'm very proud of. We delivered and made it happen, and it ended up being a phenomenally successful Olympic Games.

At the 2018 WEG, the pressure was really on. We thought the formula for determining the team medals would preclude a jump-off, so everyone was surprised when after the second round, Sweden and the United States had the same score, 20.59 penalties. That triggered the first team gold medal jump-off in the history of the WEG. How close was it? After four members of the Swedish team had gone, and three members of ours, it was all down to me and my mare Clinta. The Swedes had three clear rounds; we had two to that point, so I needed not only to be clear, but also fast.

I'd dropped a rail during the afternoon, which set up the need for the tiebreaker. In a situation

A joyous and relieved McLain Ward raised his arms in triumph after a ride on Clinta under pressure to clinch team gold at the 2018 FEI World Equestrian Games.

McLain Ward went for his second straight Olympic team gold medal in 2008 on the remarkable mare Sapphire, in front of a crowd of 18,000 at Sha Tin Stadium in Hong Kong.

up the first one earlier in the day and I figured it was on my throat for the second one. I knew what the time was I needed to beat and I knew I had a super-careful horse. She did it, and she was brilliant. We got the gold. All the horses were brilliant all week. Our team, our staff behind us, all of the owners—this is an army that produces this gold medal on our home turf. It was a very emotional moment for all of us.

How do I withstand pressure like that? I've had a lot of practice coming back from some really difficult times, whether they are personal or family situations, good and bad, my own regrets and missteps.

What am I proudest of in my career? It's not an individual win or individual moment, though I'm proud of those. They do, however, become a blur.

Instead, I'd say, when those difficult times are public, I'm proudest of being able to deal with and face them, to be able to find the right course—that doesn't mean whether I was at fault or not at fault—to always move toward being a better rider, a better horseman, a better person.

I do it all against the backdrop of the many changes in show jumping that have taken place during my career. It's evolved as all sports have,

like that, I'll get tunnel vision. I'll get into a little bit of a zone before a jump-off where that focus is pretty hard to cut through. As I've matured, before getting on a horse in a tough situation, I'm a little more loose than I used to be. I talk with people I'm comfortable with. There are people over the years you've learned to rely on and you trust what they have to say. They're not the sort of people who say the wrong thing in the wrong moment. I'm more relaxed before getting on because I understand the job better than I used to. When I'm in game mode, I don't notice a lot of what's going on around me.

At the WEG, I had two chances. I had messed

and all businesses, for that matter. We certainly have gotten more and more away from the nature of the sport—it's become more of an arena sport. That's to do with public relations and selling our sport and making it interesting for people to follow. At the highest levels, the sport is being done better than it's ever been done. You realize it when you sit in Barcelona for the Longines FEI Nations Cup Final and see rider after rider from a pretty wide number of regions of the world come in with almost perfect form.

For sure, there are things lost in the evolution of the sport, which is being done at a higher and more intense level than ever. We've gotten further away from nature and riding just for the sake of riding. We've lost the beauty of simply interacting with the horse on a daily basis to some degree. But when you weigh one against the other, it's really phenomenal at the highest level.

I was very blessed to have people who helped me and saw the way forward. My father believed in taking the U.S. Equestrian Team concept and making it accessible to the masses. That's what has changed in our country. Everybody has a chance for this now. That's a beautiful evolution.

I remember Billy Steinkraus, the Olympic individual show jumping gold medalist and chairman emeritus of the USET, used to say that in his time, the old guys told him the sport wasn't as good as it was at the turn of the twentieth century. Billy said, "I can't do anything about that. I live in my moment."

So you take the sport you have and try to be the best at it you can be. That puts you in a position where you can try to leave the sport better than you found it. That gives you influence. When I look at my time in the sport, we've lost some good things, but we've gained so much more. We're in a much better place for the horse and entertainment factor, for the level of the sport, for the opportunity for people. Even though it's so much more expensive, there is more opportunity in some ways. Forty

At the 2016 Hampton Classic, McLain Ward turned his focus to lifting his delighted toddler daughter, Lilly Kristine, into the air after the awards ceremony.

or fifty years ago, a lot of people couldn't even imagine riding for the team. Now there's a route to get there.

In order for that to happen, the riders that were from the wrong side of the tracks had to get to the level where they were beating the people from the right side of the tracks. My father saw it was the way forward, and maybe it wasn't accessible to him, but it would be accessible to me. I was the crossover where subjectivity has given me the benefit of the doubt at every turn. You see it from both sides.

The best compliment I ever received from trainer George Morris was this: "You're a perfect blend of your father and Billy." That happened for two reasons—because my father was a great rider

Team silver medalist McLain Ward at the 2016 Rio Olympics on HH Azur, who also was his mount for victory in the 2017 FEI World Cup Finals.

with a super feeling for a horse, a great athlete but a little rough around the edges. And Billy was open-minded enough to accept someone from my background when he saw a difference in what I was.

What I want to define my career and my life is my ability to rise, no matter what happened; to learn from it, be better for it, and become what I am today and what I hope to be tomorrow. For me, that's the greatest accomplishment. You're trying every day to be the best you can be. You become more educated and get better experience.

Someone who isn't flawed and has not had to face challenges hasn't accomplished very much because he or she isn't putting it on the line. Since I was 14, I've been putting it on the line in every way. There have been some bad moments for a variety of reasons. But to be able to face those challenges, to be able to be where we are, *that's* the accomplishment.

RICH FELLERS

It Pays to Be Flexible

Rich Fellers began his show jumping career at age 11 when he received a two-year-old Appaloosa, Sure Chic, for his birthday and then taught him to jump up to World Cup qualifier level. Rich has had many successes since, including a team bronze medal at the 1991 Pan American Games on El Mirasol, and two U.S. Equestrian Federation Grand Prix Horse of the Year honors with McGuinness and Stealth Sprenger. But he is most closely identified with Flexible, the USEF's International Horse of the Year in 2012. Flexible and Rich were the top-placed American combination in the London Olympics, finishing eighth. Four months earlier, they won the 2012 FEI World Cup Final, the first time in a quarter-century that the title finally came back to the United States. Affectionately known as Flexi, the Irish stallion competed in a record eight World Cup Finals. Flexi and Rich also were members of the winning U.S. Nations Cup teams at the Spruce Meadows Masters in 2008 and 2010. Flexi was the individual winner of many major Grands Prix over his long career, including the 2015 $126,000 Longines FEI World Cup™ North American League qualifier at Thunderbird Show Park in Langley, British Columbia, when he was 19.

Rich and his wife, Shelley, are the parents of a daughter, Savannah, and a son, Chris. He helps them operate the Rich Fellers Stable out of Timberline Meadows Farm in Oregon.

I t started out as a gamble in 1989 when we took Harry and Mollie Chapman up on their invitation for my wife, Shelley, and me to work privately for their Oregon stable. It meant leaving a good business and a prime opportunity in Southern California. But we saw it as an offer we shouldn't refuse and made the move. It was fortunate that Harry and Mollie came along to partner with us, because that really changed our lives in a big way.

Both Shelley and I had grown up in rural areas: I was from Oregon and she was from Kentucky, so while thinking of starting a family we wanted to raise our kids in a similar type of region rather than bustling Southern California. I knew Harry for years; he and his daughter competed on a local Northwest show circuit during my youth and he ran the store where I used to buy my tack.

Harry always referred to "the pipeline": he had to have a pipeline of horses coming along. During the early 1990s, Irish bloodstock agent Dermot Forde met Mollie in the VIP area of the La Silla

show in Monterrey, Mexico, and that led to years of horse shopping in Ireland. In 2002, we were looking for a horse in Cavan and saw Flexible in the young horse competition. He was a jumping machine, the only six-year-old in the finals of a competition for six- and seven-year-old horses, where he finished second. Edward Doyle did a phenomenal job producing him.

We bought him, and he spent 30 days in stallion quarantine at the University of California at Davis. Then he had to be trucked up to Oregon, so he wasn't at his best when he arrived. As he stepped off the van, I said, "Wow, he's so much smaller than I thought." Flexi had been a stout, muscular 16 hands when I tried him, but he'd lost muscle tone, grown some hair, wasn't shod, and looked like a little fat pony.

George Morris was teaching a clinic at Harry and Mollie's the day our horse came to his new home, so we took him to see Flexible. George looked at him and looked at me and didn't know what to say. Harry wasn't so impressed either. But that all kind of changed when Flexi showed us what he could do.

I had some concerns, but I knew what I'd seen and what I'd felt when I tried him. Shelley and I were both confident he would be really competitive. Actually, he already was competitive and we'd watched him in action.

Since he was very much a blood horse with lots of energy, we figured Flexi would shine in

The 2012 London Olympics was the realization of a long-held ambition for Rich Fellers and the brave little stallion Flexible. The combination was the highest placed on the U.S. team at those Games, finishing eighth.

Rich Fellers' victory gallop on Flexible at the 2012 FEI World Cup Show Jumping Finals was the first for a U.S. rider at that competition in 25 years.

When Rich Fellers took the offer from Harry Chapman to ride for his stable in Oregon, it changed his life. He and his wife, Shelley, were very close to Harry, who died in 2018, and his wife, Mollie.

speed classes. He was by Cruising out of a mare named Flex who won the 1995 Irish National Championships (defeating Cruising while she was in foal to him!). From a bloodline perspective, Flexi is basically three-quarters Irish Thoroughbred. He started competing in Florida as a seven-year-old. I jumped him in a 1.30-meter class in the indoor ring in Tampa. John Madden was standing there and he wanted that horse. He picked him out right away.

Harry and Mollie said, "No, he's not for sale." They did that many times, and I really respect that. I was always very good about letting them know when someone was interested, and they were always polite about saying no.

At the end of Flexi's seven-year-old year in 2004, he had a vein blockage in his right foreleg and was out for almost two years. In 2007, when he was getting back into the sport, I had a very unlucky year. My two top Grand Prix horses, McGuinness and Gyro, suffered injuries. My "number three" horse at the time was Flexible, who was healthy again and had won a big speed class that summer at Spruce Meadows.

After Gyro was sidelined, we said, "Okay, let's see if Flexible's ready to start jumping some bigger classes." That fall, he jumped in his first World Cup qualifier in the Equidome at the Los Angeles National Horse Show. He won, which was a bit shocking, not only to me, Harry and Mollie, my crew, and my wife, but I think the other competitors, as well.

He won several World Cup qualifiers in 2008, definitely making the transition from a speed horse to a Grand Prix horse. He went to his first World Cup final in the spring of 2008 in Gothenburg, Sweden, where he was fourth the first day in the speed round and we were very impressed. Even at 1.50 meters, the jumps looked quite large at that stage, especially since on the West Coast, World Cup qualifiers were a bit light. The second round of the final looked un-jumpable when Shelley and I walked the course. But Flexible just flew right around, and I had the winning time in the jump-off, although we had the last rail down.

I was shocked and amazed at how well Flexible was doing. On Sunday, I had four faults in the first round and going into the final round, I was still in good shape. There weren't too many clear there. The last round, I remember people walking the final line over and over again—the whole track was very big and the final line was big and technical. But Flexi handled it.

I wound up second to Meredith Michaels-Beerbaum of Germany and her sensational Shutterfly. It was quite a thrill and a surprise for our whole team. That really launched Flexible's spectacular career. He went to the World Cup finals every year after, 2008 through 2016, with the exception of 2014 (because he had major blood clots in his right hind leg in 2013).

In 2012, we were involved in trying to get on the London Olympic team. After the initial trials, we were third, but with some subjective adjustments, we were dropped down to seventh, and I found myself on the outside looking in.

I went to the World Cup finals in the Netherlands that spring before the Olympics with a bit of a chip on my shoulder and something to prove. We weren't helped by transportation problems from a cancelled flight that meant a 20-hour trailer ride to Los Angeles and a re-routed flight that got us to s'Hertogenbosch much later than we planned.

We were concerned Flexi would be wrung out, but it didn't seem to affect him. He won the speed round. In the big jump-off on Friday, there was a tricky combination that caught a lot of people. I had a fence down but so did several others. Even so, I went into the final two rounds on the Sunday within a rail of the lead. After the second round that day, Steve Guerdat of Switzerland and I were tied, which meant a jump-off.

George Morris, the U.S. team coach, asked me what I wanted to jump in the warm-up and I told him I didn't want to jump. He looked a bit stunned and said, "That's great." I did walk/trot transitions as Steve was getting his superstar, Nino des Buissonets, ready to go in the jump-off.

When Steve headed to the ring I followed him and stepped up to watch him go as the groom held my horse. Steve was blazing fast and his horse, which Meredith told me was the fastest in Europe, jumped super. (Nino and Steve would go on four months later to win individual gold at the Olympics.) The crowd roared and I hopped on little Flexible.

I said I could ride the same track and do the same numbers. There was an option to leave out a stride in the last line. I felt if I tried to match Steve's track, that Flexible would be faster because he's quick across the ground and he wasn't a big overjumper. I left out the stride, as Steve did, and made neat turns. That was obviously enough to bring the World Cup trophy back to the United States for the first time since 1987.

After I won the World Cup finals, I was feeling like, "Okay, the ball is in the (Olympic) selectors' court."

The next target was the observation trials. We went to Del Mar a couple of weeks after the World Cup and Flexible was still on fire. We won both of those trials. Then we headed to Calgary. We rested him, so he was fresh, sound, and still feeling very young at 16. I didn't jump any extra classes with him. It was a very difficult track for the first class, with only two clear, myself and Beezie Madden on Coral Reef Via Volo. He won that. Later that week was the final trial and then the team would be picked. Flexible was still fresh as a daisy.

I never jumped a fence to prep for any of those jump-offs at Del Mar or Calgary. I would just do flatwork and keep him on the aids. I followed Kent Farrington in the ring for the tiebreaker in that final trial. He was riding Uceko and really fast. That particular jump-off track had one place where you jumped a vertical and then you landed and made a left loop around an oxer. I thought, "I can jump this vertical on an extreme angle, right to left, and could pull Flexible left and turn back right to this oxer." It was very awkward but definitely a shorter track moving around to that oxer. I told my son, Chris, who walked the course with me, that it was doable for Flexible.

I said, "I want to win and make sure I make the team, and I'm going to make that kind of awkward, funny turn there." The whole crowd oohed and aahed when I jumped the vertical on that super angle. Someone who was videoing asked, "Is he lost? He's going the wrong way." But I wasn't. I couldn't do anything wrong, and that sealed the deal as far as team selection. It pays to be Flexible! I was super-proud of Flexi and happy with my performance.

That's how I made the squad for the London Olympics and realized a lifetime ambition by competing there. Although I ended up eighth individually, the highest-placed American, as a team we didn't finish where we would have liked to and were out of the medals. Even so, it was a great experience and Flexi came through for the country.

That wasn't anywhere near the end of Flexi's competitive career, which continued until November of his twentieth year. By that point, though, he wasn't jumping as consistently as he had in the past, so I didn't think there was any reason to go on showing with him. He felt good, but he would just make a mistake at some point, and a lot of times, it was later in the course. That wasn't his style. The pattern was obvious to me and those of us who knew him. He was losing some of his athleticism and endurance, which is natural when you get older.

We started to get him ready for Thermal in 2017, but finally said, "It's time, he has nothing more to prove." There was no indicator he would be better at 21 than 20, so we made the decision to retire him after a marvelous career.

Flexi now has babies in the United States and around Europe. I'm hoping someday I can train one of them and enjoy the type of fulfillment and success I've had working with this very special stallion, small of stature but large of heart.

WILL SIMPSON

Clinching the Gold

Although he wanted to ride Western when his relationship with horses began, Will changed his mind after he saw jumpers flying over enormous obstacles, horses and riders working together in harmony to clear them.

One of six children who grew up in Springfield, Illinois, he signed up for lessons at age 11 and rode with the Sangamon Pony Club. Will, who went on to work for Rodney Jenkins, gained fame early by setting an outdoor high-jump record of seven feet, nine inches on Jolly Good in 1985 in Cincinnati.

A five-time FEI World Cup finalist, he has won more than 75 Grands Prix, including the Del Mar International for four straight years, before clinching a team gold medal for the United States on El Campeon Farm's Carlsson vom Dach at the 2008 Olympics in Hong Kong.

Will also gives back to the sport. From 1998 through 2008, he served as President of the West Coast Active Riders organization. He also was on the board of the North American Riders Group, and chaired the U.S. Equestrian Federation's High Performance show jumping committee. Will served on the board of the Compton Junior Posse, coaching inner city children.

Based in California, Will has two children, his son, Ty, and daughter, Sophie, who made her mark as a champion equestrian on the junior scene in her teens.

Will Simpson always looked for his kids after he finished a round at the Olympics, wanting to tip his hat to his son, but he had a bit of a search after the final round in Hong Kong because he didn't know where they were sitting.

After my first round in the Nations Cup at the 2008 Olympics, where Carlsson vom Dach had a foot in the water, and the second round, where I had the last jump down, the officials added everything up and called us back in for a jump-off against Canada for the gold medal. It all happened so fast, and next thing, you're called back on your horse. It was basically going from "You're finished," to "Here you go again."

I was a little disappointed following my second round. If there had to be a jump-off, I wanted to seal it so badly. And I got my chance.

I wasn't concerned that Carlsson vom Dach was out of gas. He was the type of horse suited to that hot, humid climate. I had plenty of horse left. When it was my turn to go, I didn't have to worry about the clock. Coach George Morris and my teammate McLain Ward came running up in the schooling area as I was finishing getting ready and said, "Now, Will, all you have to do is go clear."

A sense of panic came over me. "All you have to do is go clear" in a jump-off in the Olympic Games? The jumps are huge. Anything can happen. It's late at night in Hong Kong, with a crowd of 18,000 people in Sha Tin Stadium watching every move. But here we go.

And then, immediately, I felt a sense of calm. My favorite part of show jumping is the jump-off. We have a saying, "The sport's no fun unless you get in the jump-off." And here we were, going into the jump-off! I thought, "Okay, I've got this. This is what we do. This horse loves to jump off." It was time to show the world how well this horse could jump.

So I went in with a peaceful feeling that came over me. We came to the combination on course—we had a slight rub, nothing even close to knocking a rail down. No problem. The last jump seemed to be a mile away…it was at the other end of the ring, a big oxer. I wondered, "Am I going to get in a fight with this horse right here?" But he just got

Despite running into all kinds of problems on the day of the final selection trial in the United States for the 2008 Olympic team, Will Simpson was able to keep smiling.

into a groove and I let him go his speed, which is a little fast, and he got right to the base of the jump and fired up over it—way up over the front rail. He soared right over the fence.

After that, the announcer yelled, "Gold for the United States!" What a feeling.

It was a lifetime body of work that came down to a successful moment right then. Both McLain and George were on the kiss-and-cry podium. There was a debate about how fast I was going—some people thought it was way too fast; George thought it was just right. I felt it was the horse's natural pace, and I wanted his body and his mind working at the same rate. It was a really fun debate…although it would have been a terrible debate if I hadn't jumped that clean round! But it worked out perfectly, and our anchor rider, Beezie Madden, didn't even have to jump again.

It was a thrill. Then I was in a little bit of a panic. Ever since we had a double clear in Rome, when my son, Ty, was there, I would tip my hat to him after I crossed the finish. My kids had seats in different sections every day. It took me about an hour to get back and forth from the security area to the public area.

I hadn't had the time to go see my kids that night, so I had no idea where they were. I had to tip my hat as I went by each individual section and know that somewhere along the line, I would connect. That became my trademark—the whole thing was a like a surreal dream, I was so preoccupied making sure I tipped my hat to Ty as I brought the horse down to a walk and headed toward the out gate.

We rode back in the ring for the awards ceremony. It was great being with my teammates, Beezie and Laura Kraut, as well as McLain, all walking out there. It had been a long journey, about 13 months from the time we bought Carlsson and nine months since we left California, tried out for the team, made the team, and went to Europe.

I started riding Carlsson in 2007 for the Gonda family's El Campeon Farm. Eva Gonda and I saw this 11-year-old Holsteiner when I was showing in Europe. The horse was quick, light, brave, careful, and a little bit hard to ride. We knew he'd be a superstar in California. Trainer Gilbert Boeckmann had recommended the horse, who was ridden by Christian Seimer. Christian treated Carlsson like a pet. As we were vetting the horse, we didn't need a lead rope; he followed Christian around as if he was a dog.

Carlsson was a little aggressive to the jumps; you had to finesse this horse. You couldn't *make* him do anything. If you kind of let him do it his way, he was a beautiful jumper. I rode him in a loose ring snaffle because I didn't want to discourage him with too much bit. We kept on going up through the ranks and were pointing toward the 2008 Olympics. While the main body of the Olympics was in Beijing, the equestrian competition was in Hong Kong because of quarantine issues on the mainland.

We had a conversation with the whole Gonda family about whether it would be worth it to go to Florida for the Olympic trials. In the end, the Gondas as usual were, like, "Hey, if you want to give it a try, let's give it a try."

We decided our program at the beginning of 2008 would mean staying right at home at El Campeon, where we knew the footing. It wasn't worth taking a chance on new footing in Thermal, where the winter circuit had just moved from Indio.

At the same time, I didn't want to show up in Florida too early and peak too early. So we trained for three or four weeks in the indoor ring at El Campeon, doing gymnastics, then we went to the outdoor sand ring and jumped little courses. After that, we headed for what we called the grass field, which was like a sand ring with grass coming out of it.

I set the jumps there bigger than I had ever jumped at home; I set the oxers wider than they ever were before, knowing that's how they would be in Florida. Then we made the trek east.

I spent one week doing little classes in the de Némethy ring at the Palm Beach International Equestrian Center, rather than going into the big International Arena right away.

The first trial was on a Sunday night. It was very hot during the day in Wellington, and I wasn't used to the humidity. Carlsson would lather everywhere where his skin made contact with his tack. I thought, "Wow, I'm over-cooking this horse."

So on the day of the first trial, I hand-walked Carlsson, then put him away and came back for the class at night. But meanwhile, a cold front came in and it became freezing. Carlsson was going around the first Olympic trial with his tail over his back, snorting, and really running away, so we had three down.

A fault-free trip in the jump-off by Will Simpson on Carlsson vom Dach clinched gold for the U.S. team at the Olympics in Hong Kong, "a lifetime body of work that came down to a successful moment right then."

Then we had to wait four days until Wednesday for the next trial. All my buddies were saying, "How are you enjoying your vacation?" But it wasn't much of a vacation, because we had to score in order to participate in the prize money. We needed to be first, second, or third in the second trial to go on. Otherwise, "It's lights out, we're going home."

I don't know how it happened but we won the second leg of the trials. That gave us enough prize money and we qualified for the rest of the trials. After we had won three in a row, it was all heading in the right direction.

That was, until early on the morning of the last trial, when I got a call from Roger Solis, who was taking care of Carlsson. He told me he went to feed the horse and he wouldn't eat. I was up even before the phone rang, awakened by the loudest thunder I had ever heard. When I got to the venue, I went right to Carlsson's stall to see what was going on.

I noticed when you put the food up to his mouth he would eat, but he couldn't move his neck. So no one really knew what happened, but my theory was he freaked out at the thunder and tweaked his neck and was totally out of whack.

We had 12 hours before the night class, and it was spent with everyone—chiropractors, veterinarians, acupuncturists—working on the horse.

We actually got him to where I could ride him. George Morris and Frank Chapot, who had also served as Chef d'Equipe, came out to watch Carlsson jump. They said I could go in the last trial, but I disagreed.

I said, "I can't, the horse is exhausted. He never rides that easy. He cantered around like a regular working hunter. That's not him. He's sound, he's healthy, but he's exhausted from all this treatment."

They told me, "You're giving up your spot if you don't go."

Yet when we went the next morning to the riders' meeting where they named the top 10, it was decided we would be in that group after they looked at our results and saw that Carlsson was back sound. That's what got me to Europe.

After that meeting, we walked the horse down the street from the showgrounds to a nearby farm and rested him, turning him out and rehabbing him for the rest of our stay in Florida. By the time we got to Europe, he was in jumping shape again and ready to carve out his spot on the team.

The group of 10 finalists got split up, with half going to La Baule in France, St. Gallen in Switzerland, and Rome. The other half did Aachen, Germany, and Rotterdam in the Netherlands. You get to know people quite well when you're riding with them on a daily basis, as we did in Europe, then in Hong Kong.

When you've finally been named to the team, as the Games get closer, you start thinking you should walk around in bubble wrap. You've got all these things going through your head. Your horse could wake up on the wrong side of the stall. You're on pins and needles the whole way through. Then, finally, you're riding in the ring with your teammates after all is said and done, and you got the job done. *That's* an amazing ride…

and then to dismount and get on the podium and hear the national anthem and the medal is around your neck, it's a once-in-a-lifetime feeling that you're in exactly the right spot. There's no better place to be. There we were, back in the ring with our teammates after such an accomplishment.

I remember the moment when it first occurred to us that we could win. Our horses were jumping great, right from the beginning. We knew we just had to stay the course. When that feeling of realization set in, it was incredible. Just to be able to go to the Olympics was a big step. But when that feeling came over all five of us (my teammates and George) and then somehow, it all came together at the right time, it was an amazing thing.

When I got home to El Campeon, they had a big banner across the road greeting us, a whole welcoming party. Carlsson was sold after the Games, and he had a succession of riders, but none of them clicked with him. He was just that kind of a special horse.

In the end, it all worked out when he retired at Summer Wind Farm in Kentucky with Karen Bailey, who is also a wildlife rehabilitator. I visit him when I'm in Kentucky, and so does Christian Seimer, who had loved him so much. Carlsson wound up with an incredible spot for the rest of his life and couldn't be in a better place.

MARGIE GOLDSTEIN ENGLE

"Can't" Never Crossed My Mind

She's only five feet, one inch tall, but the biggest horses and the tallest jumps are no match for this determined champion, who rarely says no to a challenge. Even injuries can't keep Margie down; she simply rides through adversity, complete with the plates, screws, and rods needed to fix whatever went wrong. "Most of the pain I've kind of learned to tune out," she says.

Over three decades, she won more than 200 Grands Prix. Her career includes a tenth-place finish as the highest-ranked U.S. rider at the 2000 Olympics, a World Equestrian Games team medal, three Pan American Games team medals and an individual medal, as well as 10 American Grand Prix Association Rider of the Year titles.

The 1991 American Horse Shows Association Equestrian of the Year, Margie in 1992 was named the Rolex/National Grand Prix League Rider of the Year, repeating that honor in 1993.

She became a co-recipient of the 2012 USEF National Show Jumping Championship, her third national title. In her off-hours, the fun-loving rider, who has a ready roster of jokes plays a mean hand of poker with her horse show friends. Margie lives in Wellington, Florida, with her husband, veterinarian Steve Engle.

My parents were very nervous when I first wanted to ride, not only because of my petite size, but also because they knew I was kind of a daredevil. My father, Irvin, an accountant, and my mother, Mona, a school principal, didn't know anything about horses, so it took a long time for me to talk them into letting me take riding lessons.

At Gladewinds, the Miami stable where I started riding, someone fell off while jumping and was paralyzed from the neck down. So my parents said I could ride on the flat but they didn't want me to jump. I finally talked them into letting me jump, but the deal was that I could only ride until I got hurt.

Naturally, the first time I hurt my shoulder, I didn't want to tell them. It was my fault, because I was goofing around. A friend and I were riding double on a pony. I pushed her and when she fell, her foot swung around and knocked me off, and she landed on top of me. It would turn out I had an impacted fracture of my shoulder, but I kept saying I was fine because I had a lesson that day and I didn't want to miss it, since I only got one lesson a week.

I could move my lower arm but couldn't move my shoulder. I thought I could will it away. When I got home, my parents kept asking what was wrong with my shoulder. After almost a week, my parents told me, "You have to get an X-ray." Unfortunately, the doctor who treated me told my parents how dangerous horseback riding is. He said if I had waited much longer, I would have had to have surgery.

Everything I didn't want him to say, he said, and wrapped me like a mummy so I couldn't move the shoulder. Growing up with two older brothers, I learned I had to be kind of tough if I wanted to play football or tennis with them, and that attitude carried over into my riding. In hindsight, most of my accidents could have been prevented if I had more of a sense of self-preservation and stayed away from some of the difficult horses.

I didn't own a horse until I got part of Daydream

Even at age five, Margie Goldstein looked at home on a pony and showed signs of emerging as the crowd pleaser she would become during her stellar career.

Still in jodhpurs and paddock boots, a 12-year-old Margie Goldstein showed prowess in the hunters with great form on Gladewinds Angelwings in 1973.

Describing the stallion Royce, Margie Goldstein Engle compared him to "an overgrown puppy dog. He grabs a broom if it's by his stall and starts sweeping. Everything's a game for him, even when he's jumping the jumps."

when I was 25. I did a lot of catch riding, and most of the rides I got—because I wasn't a big name yet—were the stoppers and rearers…the ones people didn't want to ride. For me, it was a challenge. The more they told me the horse couldn't be fixed, the more I wanted to try.

Discussing my show jumping aspirations, people told me, "You're not going to be able to do this. Financially, you don't have enough backing."

It's not like we were poor, but my parents were putting both my brothers through college. (Mark became a doctor and Ed is an actuary.) Show jumping really is a sport for people who have a lot of money. They never thought it was anything you could make a good living from.

Aside from that, technically, I wasn't built for it—especially for riding big-barreled Warmbloods with

my rather short legs. People kept trying to steer me into being a jockey. I did gallop some racehorses, but I didn't like the atmosphere at the track. They didn't treat the horses the same way we did. I also didn't love running around in a big circle. Dorothy and Robert Kramer, who owned Gladewinds and were like second parents, felt "the racetrack is not a good atmosphere for a young lady."

Growing up, I was part of a group of kids that practically lived at the barn. We slept on hay bales during slumber parties, and we'd have birthday parties for the ponies. Many of us who grew up at the stable are still friendly with the Kramers' daughter, Robin, and I named my own business after Gladewinds.

I worked there to earn extra rides, starting out by cleaning dog pens at their kennels and moving

Margie Goldstein Engle with American Grand Prix Association founder Gene Mische and one of the 10 coolers she won as AGA Rider of the Year.

on to mucking stalls until they gave me a job breaking their ponies. Whichever ponies were the most difficult, those were the ones I wanted to ride. When no one else liked them, I liked them all the more.

I did some equitation, and won the South Florida finals with Alabama, loaned to me by Phil DeVita, Sr. I qualified for the Medal and Maclay finals but never had the horses I could ride in those championships, so I didn't go.

The trainers at Gladewinds were great. I learned a great deal from Penny Fires and Bibby Farmer. A big influence was Karen Harnden Smith, who also taught there. She was giving a lesson one day to someone who told her, "I can't do that." I overheard Karen when she replied, "Take 'can't' out of your vocabulary. If you're riding, that shouldn't cross your mind."

It stuck with me, and I did believe anything was possible. The Kramers gave me projects, horses other people had given up on, which was

good for me to learn about getting into horses' heads and figure out what worked with them. A lot was trial and error. I've had to learn to be more careful. When you're younger, you think you're invincible. Then you start figuring out that if you get hurt, you're out for a period of time. I missed quite a few things by getting hurt, but I was bad at saying "No" to people who asked me to ride.

Once I started getting better horses, it made me appreciate them so much more. The dealer who had Daydream saw me riding Puck W, whose head was bigger than my whole body. He figured anyone desperate enough to ride that horse and get him around as well as I did would like to ride some of his horses.

My parents had a hard time watching when they used to come to the horse shows. Actually, my mom would not watch at all, and she nearly bruised my father's arm, holding him so tight. Once I started riding better horses, she could watch a little more. But when I tried to break the indoor high jump record on Daydream, she asked me, "Why do you have to do those things?"

She did come around, and actually wrote a book about me, *No Hurdle Too High*, with the proceeds going to the U.S. Equestrian Team.

Riding for the team was always my goal, and I achieved it in 1989 with a double-clear as the anchor rider on Saluut at Toronto's Royal Winter Fair, where we won the Nations Cup. It's a special feeling to ride for your country. You get a sense of pride from representing the place where you grew up, and our country is special because it offers everyone amazing opportunities.

Since the United States had such depth in riders and horses, it was a great honor to be selected for a team. I was very proud whenever Chef d'Equipe Frank Chapot used me as the anchor in the Nations Cups. The frosting on top for 1989 was winning the American Grand Prix Association Rider of the Year title.

One of my favorite team experiences was the Rome show in the 1997 Samsung Nations Cup series, where I won the Grand Prix. I rode Hidden Creek's Laurel, Hidden Creek's Gypsy, and Hidden Creek's Alvaretto there. It was one of the strongest teams I've ever been on. Riding with me were McLain Ward on Twist du Valon, Anne Kursinski with Eros, and Allison Firestone with Gustl P. The riders and grooms all got along so well, which really enhanced the experience. On top of that, we got a bonus at the end because we were all clean in the Nations Cup, and the bonus paid for our trip.

For my first time going to Europe, it was very exciting. Hidden Creek's Alvaretto won in Arnheim and I was leading rider at St. Gallen, so that really helped give my career a boost. The experience became even more special when I got back to the States and *Sports Illustrated* published a big article on me. Even in my wildest dreams, I never imagined being on the cover of that magazine, and there I was. My mother still has a copy of it to this day.

Hidden Creek's Perin won the Olympic trials for the 2000 Games in Sydney, but he had only been jumping Grands Prix for three or four months. He just did everything out of sheer scope and ability because he had such a huge heart. Although he was very, very green, he got better and better during the Olympics. I was the anchor for the Olympic Nations Cup and finished in the top 10 individually, the highest-placed U.S. rider at the Games.

Although I was focused on my business, I did what my parents wanted and got a degree from Florida International University. I liked being a student, whether of equestrian sport or at school. I started out taking a complete schedule of courses at the university while working part-time but ended up getting mononucleosis. I was in school from 7:00 a.m. to noon, then went straight to the barn. After that, I came home to do my studies and grabbed what little sleep I could.

The last few years at the university, I took fewer credits so I could work full time. My parents didn't know this was something at which you could make a living, so they wanted to make sure I had a backup plan with an education.

A lot of what is involved in having a show stable is running the business end of it—that's the hard part: organizing the help, managing entries, the hay, the feed, and the billing. Having a father who was a certified public accountant certainly helped.

People always ask me, "How did you get through injuries?" I don't think about it, you work through it. When I was young, whatever I did, I tended to overdo, whether it was practicing throwing a baseball through a tire, or swatting a tennis ball against the garage door for hours. So everyone would have to tell me to back down when I did physical therapy. Whatever I'm told to do, I'll go home and do it double the time they specify. Like me, most riders just do whatever they have to do to get back riding as soon as possible. Of course, it's more important for me to work out now that I'm older. When I was younger, I rode 60 or 70 rounds in a day and did the hunters as well as the jumpers.

A lot of kids who get scared when they fall off write to me and wonder, "How do you get over it?" I answer as many of those letters as I can.

I think you almost *learn* to fall off and then you're not afraid of it. Most of the people who have the worst injuries are those who never fall off. At Gladewinds, when I started riding, the trainers taught all of us kids about emergency dismounts, which helped us to learn to land better when coming off a horse or pony. I think the more anxiety people have about falling off, the more it works against them, so when they do come off, they are not sure how to land.

When people ask me about retirement, I say that won't come until I'm not competitive and it isn't fun anymore. But whatever happens, horses will always be part of my life.

KENT FARRINGTON

From Pony Racer to World Show Jumping Number One

Always ambitious and a goal-setter, Kent is a top-notch manager of both people and horses. As a kid, he got involved in pony racing, and his love of speed is reflected today in winning jump-offs, motorcycles, and fast sports cars.

"I don't know that you'll meet another person in the world who can plan and execute better than Kent Farrington. He's so smart," said Laura Kraut, who has ridden with Kent on Nations Cup teams.

Kent's first instructor, Nancy Whitehead, took him to a George Morris clinic, where that master trainer saw his talent and loaned him horses to ride in Florida. During Kent's equitation days, when he won the 1998 hunt seat Medal finals and the championship at the Washington International Horse Show, he worked with trainer Andre Dignelli. Kent earned team gold in the North American Young Riders Championship, then turned down offers of college scholarships to apprentice with Olympic medalists Tim Grubb and Leslie Howard before starting his own business.

Although horses are his profession, he is multi-faceted. While he has no formal training in architecture, Kent has bought, designed, and sold a number of equestrian properties, in addition to laying out his own much-admired farm in Wellington, Florida.

Kent earned a berth on the United States' 2014 FEI World Equestrian Games Team, where he was part of the bronze medal effort with Voyeur. In 2016, he realized his long-held dream of competing at the Olympics, where he rode the same horse to a team silver medal and finished fifth individually.

Someone of Kent's determination can handle whatever comes his way. When he broke his leg in a fall from a horse during the 2018 Winter Equestrian Festival, he made recovery his mission and worked out rigorously to come back and be competitive three months later.

A master of "diversified risk," Kent has assembled a string of horses with different owners, so he isn't reliant on one or two. His mounts over the years have included Madison, the 2005 American Grand Prix Association Horse of the Year, Up Chiqui; Gazelle, Uceko, Creedance, and many more. His propensity for planning paid off in a big way when he became the number-one-ranked show jumper in the world in 2017, earning the Longines FEI World's Best Jumping Rider Award.

Opportunities to be with horses were few where I grew up in Chicago, so I started riding at a carriage horse stable after I was inspired by a photo of my mother, Lynda, riding a horse in Wisconsin. We soon moved my riding activities to a farm outside the city where my sister, Kim, and I got our first pony, Samantha, on Christmas. I was thinking about the Olympics even then.

After joining Pony Club, I got involved in pony racing. I wanted to be a jockey at first, but when I got too big for that, I focused on equitation and show jumping. My mother traded three used computers for my first horse, MVP No. 4.

Although my father wanted me to go to college, I'm doing what I want to be doing. I don't think I'd be happy sitting behind a desk. I worked with Tim Grubb and Leslie Howard after graduating from high school. After 18 months with Leslie, she encouraged me to start my own business. She told me she thought I had a lot of talent...but that I wasn't a great employee!

It was a little sooner than I expected. I was only 21, but you have to take the opportunities you have, make the most of them, and step up to the plate. It's one thing to question what you're doing. It's another to question yourself. I try not to do that too much.

Even from his pony racing days, Kent Farrington was determined to be a winner and let nothing stand in the way of an ambition that eventually would take him to the world Number One ranking.

Whenever anybody asks about my most significant Grand Prix victory, I always say that it was winning my first five-star in 2006 with Madison. It was the final Grand Prix in Wellington that season and the only five-star show at that time in America. That was sort of a catalyst for my career. I brought Madison up from when she was young, and she also was the first horse I rode on the U.S. team.

It was important for me after Madison that I was able to follow her with another top horse. That would be Up Chiqui, who won many classes. The best show jumpers in the world are consistently riding different horses. That's a sign of somebody who can do the sport and isn't a one-horse wonder.

I'm trying to be at the top of my game at all times. A lot of things have to come together to win a particular event. For me, what I do is more about being consistent at the top of the sport. Over time, your number is going to come up, and it's going to be your day to win. To focus solely on one particular event is a difficult way to approach our sport, because so many things are out of your control.

What *is* under your control is managing the horses and having people around you to support them. What you have to do is plan on being ready for opportunity when it comes your way.

I always own at least a piece of my horses. I'm a big believer in investing in yourself. No one wants it more than me. It says a lot when I'm going to put everything I have into my own career. I make my plan with what I think is best for the horses I have at that time and what I can do to win the most. I've tried to do that my whole career.

At the 2014 FEI World Equestrian Games in Normandy, France, Kent Farrington was part of the bronze medal squad with Voyeur on his first global championship team.

Kent Farrington's vision of riding for an Olympic medal came true at the Rio Games in 2016, when he and Voyeur were on the silver medal team, and he came close to an individual medal, finishing fifth.

There are two things I try not to do—be boastful or live in regret—because they're both a waste of time. I take the positive and go forward; learn from the experience of what *did* go well, recognize what didn't, and keep moving. I have an interest in making something that functions well, and going to shows around the world is a dream for me.

Recovering from a broken leg in 2018 made me stronger and more confident in the decisions I make about what I want and don't want to do with my career. I really realized how much I wanted to ride and love my sport. When you're away from what you like to do for a long time, you dream about it all the time, and you realize how much you miss it.

In any sport, you raise your level of competitiveness by competing against the best people in the world on a consistent basis. Your skills are only going to rise as high as your competitors force them to rise. By constantly challenging yourself against the best, you're going to improve. When I have a question, I go to the professional who I think would be most helpful in that particular area. I try to ask someone who has a lot more experience than I do, someone like an Ian Millar, who has done the sport at a high level for more than 40 years. He's been everywhere and seen everything more than once.

McLain Ward is a good friend. Because I didn't have McLain's professional horse background (both McLain's parents were in the industry) he was always someone I had to catch up with. That's been the challenge for me since I was a kid, starting way behind from where he started. As you get older, the age gap narrows; we've become good friends, and we rely on each other for insight or if we have a question about training or a course. That's part of what makes great competition. You want your friends and everybody to go at their best.

We've ridden on a bunch of teams together. We have a similar competitive mindset. I'm always happy when he does well, and he's always happy when I do well. I think we both take it from a very professional angle. We try to leave no stone unturned. We lose sometimes because we're trying to beat each other and not paying attention to what some of the others are doing. But it's a great rivalry; it makes us both better.

These days, there's a lot more money in the sport than there used to be, and I think that's great. It obviously draws more attention and raises the level of sport from what used to be a sort of hobby sport into a professional sport.

To be number one at least once in my career is great; more for my team than for everybody else. They work really hard, long hours. It's a job of passion more than a job for a salary. To know we made it to a place where we were at the top of the world at one time is a great thing for team morale, more than anything else.

LAURA KRAUT

It All Started with Simba Run

A real horsewoman who was never afraid to get her hands dirty, Laura came up through the ranks after grooming and taking care of her own horses before becoming a professional.

She has represented the United States at three Olympic Games, winning a gold medal in Hong Kong in 2008. She was a member of the silver medal WEG team at Aachen, Germany, in 2006, and the 2018 gold medal WEG squad in Tryon, North Carolina. Her resume includes numerous World Cup Finals and stints on many Nations Cup teams. She also is a highly sought-after coach whose students have included Grand Prix rider Jessica Springsteen.

While Simba Run is her best-known mount and the one that kicked off her international career, she has had many other top horses including Anthem, Liberty, Cedric, and Zeremonie.

Laura, whose son, Bobby, is an aspiring show jumper, divides her time between Wellington, Florida, and the farm in England that belongs to her partner, Olympic double-gold-medalist Nick Skelton.

On a summer day in 1990, we were at a show in Germantown, Tennessee, where it was 105 blistering degrees. Geoff Sutton, who was the owner/rider of an interesting Thoroughbred show jumper, Simba Run, said to me, "I can't deal with this heat. Would you ride my horse? I've been thinking about stopping doing this."

I took Simba in the Grand Prix and that was the beginning of a beautiful relationship with the former racehorse who took me to the Olympics and earned more than $300,000 in prize money during his show ring career.

When I met Simba, all I'd ever ridden were Thoroughbreds, so for me, he wasn't unusual. He was hot, he liked to root the reins out of your hands, he was very brave—nothing ever spooked him. He would jump anything you pointed him toward. In the 10 years I competed him, I don't think he ever stopped at a fence. The more you

Laura and Zeremonie were on the 2018 FEI World Equestrian Games team in Tryon, North Carolina, where they had to compete in a jump-off to secure the team gold. It was the first time the United States had won a show jumping World Championships gold since 1986.

did, the more he revved up. So a lot of riding him was learning how to do very little. He had the most unbelievable amount of scope. He made my career and taught me all about how to do this.

My sister, Mary Elizabeth, and I started riding because my mother, Carol, was obsessed with horses. When I was five, I got a $250 cart pony. He couldn't canter because all he had done was pull a cart and trot. I spent the better part of a year falling off trying to get him to canter. Then I had another pony who was a stopper. The last pony we had, Plain 'n' Fancy, came from an Indian reservation. She was white with one brown ear and the pony of my dreams, because she didn't stop or run away. She won a lot, even though the only thing that was fancy about her was her name.

She and I made an impression on trainers Kathy Paxson and Ann Kenan, who ran Hunter Hill Farm in Atlanta. When I was 12, they called my mother and asked if I would ride their very fancy ponies. That turned into basically a job that lasted until the end of my junior career.

I rode their ponies and horses, but I also worked hard out of the saddle. Back then, you did everything—riding was only 10 percent of what we did with the horses. We groomed them, iced their legs, cleaned stalls, rode them bareback in the field with no halter or bridle. We'd take them swimming. As I got older, I drove the truck and trailer. We learned every aspect of management, which made you appreciate the horses, not just the competition. And that's important. In our world, you're lucky if you have a one-percent win ratio.

I spent one semester at college before I told my father I thought it was crazy that we were going into debt for me to continue, since my future was horses. He told me, "That's fine, but you're on your own."

It didn't occur to me I wouldn't make it. I went to work for Judy and Roger Young because my family had moved to Camden, South Carolina, and I lived at home. Then Mary Elizabeth and I moved

Simba Run, an off-the-track Thoroughbred, jump-started Laura Kraut's career in the big time. They finished in the top 10 in the 1992 FEI World Cup Finals and were the reserve combination for the Barcelona Olympics a few months later. That gave Laura an opportunity to observe a Games close-up without the pressure of competing, as she would go on to do in 2000 and 2008.

into our own place. She was a really talented rider, but the competition end of it made her nervous. Now she manages our whole operation, horses and staff; she also teaches and rides on the flat.

Actually, she was the rider for the Youngs when I was just grooming and braiding at their barn. During that time, I had a jumper I rode at Motor City and Charlotte. After nine months, I left

Going for the gold, Laura and valiant little Cedric were fault-free in the tie-breaker to help secure the top prize for the United States at the 2008 Olympics in Hong Kong.

to start a business and began working with Rodney Bross, a big dealer and a really good horseman. In the mid-1980s, I would catch ride anything for anyone. I started to ride for Judy Helder, who had a horse named Night Magic, related to Good Twist, Gem Twist's sire. I won the Pennsylvania Big Jump at Harrisburg with that horse, which was my first big victory. George Morris even came over and wanted to know about the horse.

I was riding 40 or 50 horses. Then I met Bob Kraut, married him after eight months, and moved to his family's farm in Wisconsin. From 50 horses, I went down to two. I took Night Magic to Germantown. That's where it started with Simba.

I didn't know Simba had potential to be an international horse, because I had no idea what an international horse was. In 1992, the Olympic year, we had finished in the top 10 of the World Cup finals in California. Then we headed for the Olympic trials, which were purely objective. I think we jumped 10 rounds with no drop score. It was survival of the fittest. But we did well in the trials and we made the team for the Barcelona Olympics, where I was the alternate. I didn't even have a passport because I had never left the country. I had to go to Chicago and sit and wait all day for my passport on an emergency basis.

When I walked the course at the Olympics, I

was thinking, "Thank goodness I'm the alternate." Our trials had been numerous, but they were in familiar locations. Barcelona had one of the biggest Olympic courses, and the jumps were all different than what we were used to.

It had been hammered into me that the objective system—where selections were made by the numbers—was wrong and I shouldn't have been there, that Greg Best and Gem Twist should have been there. Gem had won team and individual silver medals with Greg at the 1988 Olympics, but a refusal at Devon during the 1992 trials put him out of the running for Barcelona. A lawsuit over team selection for the 1990 World Equestrian Games had resulted in a purely objective selection system for years thereafter, and in 1992, no drop score was allowed.

I didn't understand what was really happening because I'd never been part of the sport in this way. I learned it wasn't just about getting there—you wanted to get there and win. Through the trials, though, it was just about making the team. No one thought about going and winning. I was beginning to understand I was possibly a fine choice for the squad's fifth person, but Greg obviously would have been better and should have been on the team.

Although I didn't ride in the Games with the team of Anne Kursinski, Michael Matz, Lisa Jacquin, and Norman Dello Joio (who wound up with the individual bronze), just being there told me the Olympics—my first international show—was my future.

"I've got to do this," I thought. "This is the ultimate."

I went to the opening ceremonies and it was great. I became determined to figure out how to get my business going so I could head in that direction again.

My next international show was the 1994 World Cup finals in Holland, but Simba tied up

there, so it didn't work out. I didn't go to another show in Europe until the year 2000. I was busy buying horses, getting clients, teaching, making money.

I had talked to Anne Kursinski a bit about forming syndicates. It took me a while to figure out how to do it. I had a client from Minnesota who was Dutch, and he saw an ad for a horse at Stal Hendrix. When I flew over to Holland in 1998, I met the owners, brothers Emile and Paul Hendrix, who have since been instrumental in my success. I told them that if they ever saw a horse they thought would have potential for me, to let me know. That's how I got Liberty.

She was only seven, but I told people she was an Olympic horse. To make that happen in 2000 was a miracle. I lost a year by having my son, Bobby, but I made up for the gap when Katie Monahan Prudent came to me and said she thought Liberty could go to the 2000 Olympics in Sydney, Australia, if we had some international mileage.

She put together a team to go to Europe for a tour of three shows. It was Francie Steinwedell, Elise Haas, Katie, and me. She sold me by saying if I came back to America after that and did the trials, Liberty and I would have the experience and mileage to go to the Olympics.

It was quite a trip, which ended after I became leading rider at the Rome show. Then we had to go to U.S. Equestrian Team headquarters in Gladstone, New Jersey, for the Olympic trials.

Katie gave me a plan, and I executed it and won the first trial at Gladstone. Having spent so many years on my own, she took the pressure off by telling me what to do. After the Eastern trials, the top 10 went to California for the rest of the series.

It wasn't the way to build a team, with a lot of drama in the selection process. If someone promised me I would be on the next Olympic team, but the trials process would be like they were then, I wouldn't go. However, I learned a lot, and it was a valuable experience, and I got to compete, along with Lauren Hough, Margie Engle, and Nona Garson. Libby (Liberty) tried her heart out. We didn't medal, but having Katie there was fun.

I knew an Olympic team could have cohesiveness, and that's why 2008, with a different trial process that allowed for subjectivity, was better. In 2005, I bought Cedric, my mount for the 2008 Olympics, just because I thought he was cute and he jumped high. He was 15.3 hands at the most, really narrow, and short from nose to tail. There was nothing big about him, apart from his heart.

Cedric didn't like walls, but he knew when he had to perform, and he didn't put a foot wrong the whole Games. It was great. We were in Hong Kong while the other sports were in Beijing because China was unable to establish equine disease-free zones on the mainland.

George Morris was Chef d'Equipe, and my teammates McLain Ward, Beezie Madden, and Will Simpson all got along great. Having McLain's special mare, Sapphire, and Beezie's terrific ride, Authentic, on our side was like a security blanket. I had confidence Cedric could jump anything. But would he jump everything?

The thing about the Olympics is you're there to do a job. Sometimes you win, sometimes you lose, sometimes you're fifth. This time we took gold. I try to be a good team player. You have to be. That's the whole point of it—being supportive of the others, pulling your weight, not being a bad sport.

I've been fortunate that pretty much all my teammates have been great. Everyone brings his or her own element. It's fun to get to know them and see how they do things. I would never name a bad team member, but I don't think I've run across anyone like that. Once you reach that level, there's a certain amount of professionalism and sportsmanship that is a part of you. Otherwise, you wouldn't make it that far.

Since 2000, I've gotten to do what I wanted to do. My greatest influences were the Hendrix brothers, George, Katie, and Nick Skelton, the Olympic double-gold medalist who is my partner. Being around a horseman and a rider like Nick has been key. His influence on my riding has been one of the things that helped me get to the next level, along with his attention to detail. He's meticulous about everything: tack, cleanliness, preparation, presentation. If you go to his stable in England, you can eat off the floor.

I've been lucky enough to enjoy tremendous support from so many people—friends, owners, staff, associates, students, and family. That is what has enabled me to achieve what I have done. I had the determination, but without them—and Simba Run—I wouldn't have made it.

PETER WYLDE

Letting the Team Decide

Peter Wylde's ability to make a name for himself in the most important equestrian competitions manifested itself early while riding with trainers Fran and Joe Dotoli. The native of Massachusetts won the National Horse Show's 1982 ASPCA Maclay hunt seat horsemanship championship in Madison Square Garden. He then went on to take the Intercollegiate Horse Shows Association's prestigious Cacchione Cup while a student at Tufts University. After becoming a show jumping professional, Peter rose to even greater heights, earning the individual bronze at the 2002 FEI World Equestrian Games on Fein Cera and being part of the U.S. gold medal team on the same mare at the 2004 Olympics. He also is known as a mentor to up-and-coming young riders, having served for years as the lead clinician at the U.S. Hunter Jumper Association's Emerging Athletes Program national finals. Peter's training and sales operation is based in Millbrook, New York.

I am fortunate to have won many awards during my riding career, but one that has a very special meaning came my way during a ceremony at the 2003 FEI World Cup final in Las Vegas.

As U.S. Equestrian Team President Frank Lloyd presented me with the Whitney Stone Cup, he said I was receiving it not only for my performance at the 2002 FEI World Equestrian Games, where I won the individual bronze medal on Fein Cera, but also because of the way I handled a difficult moment before the WEG began.

Here's what happened. When Fein Cera arrived

for the WEG, she had fallen down on the plane during the landing in Jerez, Spain, and bruised her tailbone. It was so swollen, causing pressure on her hind end, that it made her sore when she moved. For 24 hours, it was touch and go as to whether I should ride. Her veterinarians and my groom did everything they could to bring the swelling down and make her comfortable.

But while the question of whether she would be ready to compete hung in the balance, I sat down alone and burst into tears. At this stage of my life, I had given up everything—my house and my business—to base myself in Europe to train and try to make the WEG. Then I flew Fein Cera to America to do the WEG selection trials, financing it myself and giving up all the horses I had in Europe. I'd finally made a championship team with a horse that really was great. So when I thought I might not be able to achieve the goal for which I worked so hard, out poured all my anxiety.

Fein Cera had come to me in 2000 as a sales horse from Allison Firestone. I showed the mare in some 1.45- and 1.50-meter classes as I focused on making the 2001 World Cup finals with Macanudo de Niro, who won two qualifiers.

Then foot-and-mouth disease swept around

Even relaxing at his Florida home with his dog, Amy, Peter is always reminded of his international show jumping triumphs by the portrait of Fein Cera, his mount for the 2002 WEG individual bronze and the 2004 Olympic team gold.

Europe, closing the borders and cancelling all the shows. By the time we went to the World Cup finals in Gothenburg, Sweden, Macanudo de Niro hadn't been able to go to a show for six weeks. That was a disaster for a super-spooky horse. On the second day of the Cup, in the jump-off class, he spooked going into a double and landed on the back pole of an oxer coming out. He sustained a cut, and it looked as if I wouldn't finish the finals.

I did have Fein Cera there to do smaller classes and Sally Ike, the U.S. managing director of show jumping, suggested that the mare could do the final day of the Cup. One problem was that I'd only jumped her in one 1.50-meter class. On top of that, she hadn't competed in a qualifying class as required. But there had been a notice that if a horse was entered at the s'Hertogenbosch, Holland, show, which was cancelled because of foot-and-mouth, he or she would be eligible to compete in the finals. Fein Cera had been entered and Sally petitioned the ground jury to accept us. We were in.

Fein Cera was my kind of horse, with so much power and scope. She beautifully handled the challenge of the massive courses on the Cup's final day, with one rail down in the first round and a clean trip in the second. That moved me from eleventh place to a tie for sixth. Any horse that jumps 4 and 0 in the final in Gothenburg is a championship horse. I said, "I have to get the money to buy this horse."

I got on the phone and called everybody I knew. I raised half of the funding I needed but still fell short. A friend I'd called who couldn't help me did find someone who was interested. I got in touch with a Swiss enthusiast, Pierette Schlettwein, who had seen me ride but never met me, and she came through so I could keep competing on Fein Cera.

There was a lot riding on the WEG, not just for me, but also for my investors who had faith in me and the mare. Luckily, the tailbone problem subsided and she came around. When I was able

The 2002 FEI World Equestrian Games was a big moment for Peter Wylde, who won the individual bronze in Jerez, Spain. The difficult format was the Final Four (discontinued after the 2014 WEG) in which the top four riders rode each other's horses over the same course. He is pictured here on his mount, Fein Cera.

to ride in the warm-up, I jumped six fences and she felt great. I thought, "Here we go, it's going to happen."

But first, there was a question as to whether I should be replaced on the team by the alternate, Laura Kraut, on Anthem. Chef d'Equipe Frank Chapot was visibly torn about having to make that decision. After all, he'd been put in that difficult position at previous championships.

I had basically won the trials. So do you allow a horse that has a crisis issue to go, or do you go with the alternate?

I took the reins into my own hands on this one and called a meeting of the team on behalf of Frank Chapot. He, Laura, and my other teammates, Beezie Madden (Judgement), Nicole Shahinian Simpson (El Campeon Cirka Z), and Leslie Howard (Priobert de Kalverie) were the only ones there. I wanted to make sure if I was the one chosen to ride on the team, that my teammates were 100 percent with that decision.

My instinct told me this horse was going to be great and that being in the competition wasn't going to hurt her. The question was, would she be able to perform the way she had been performing? I was pretty sure that she was going to, based on the way she did the warm-up.

I said to my teammates and Frank, "I want to ride, but I want everyone on this team to say right now they are behind this." And they were. Even Laura, who would have taken my place if I dropped out, wanted me to ride. You could see the relief on

The 2004 U.S. gold medal team of *(left to right)* Chris Kappler, Peter Wylde, Beezie Madden, and McLain Ward wore traditional laurel wreaths on the podium in Athens.

Frank's face. It took the pressure off him. It wasn't his decision; it was our decision.

It all worked out. Although the team did not medal, winding up sixth of 21 nations, I had a double-clear in the Nations Cup before winning the individual bronze medal. Fein Cera was named best individual horse of the finals, where the top four riders switched horses and rode the same course.

The Whitney Stone Cup, named after the man who stepped up as founder of the USET for international competition after the cavalry was disbanded, is given to "the active competitor who displays consistent excellence in international competition and high standards of sportsmanlike conduct, while serving as an ambassador for the United States and equestrian sport and exemplifying the team's highest ideals and traditions." I felt incredibly honored to receive this trophy, and not just for the obvious reasons. Whitney Stone and his wife, Anne, were close friends of my grandmother, Mary Ryan, and actually introduced her to my grandfather, Joe Ryan. For years, every Thanksgiving we would go to Morven, the Stones' estate in Charlottesville, Virginia, where we got a tour of the stable from Anne Stone and saw Shuvee, their famous racing mare who was by Nashua. My grandmother would have been so proud if she knew her grandson won the Whitney Stone trophy.

My point in writing about this is to illustrate how competition and being in a sport puts us in situations where we do things we might not otherwise want to do. I was very proud about that moment when I got my teammates together. The Whitney Stone Cup reminded me of the whole experience at the WEG and what it was about: teamwork and horsemanship, and that horse being there, and my knowing she was at the peak moment of her career.

My speed round with her was such a perfect round: every distance, every stride, I almost never had to touch the reins. I was fifth—top six is a good result. After she jumped double-clear in the Nations Cup, I was in first place. I thought, "Wow, that's really cool." That was a moment in which I was consumed with pride.

The thing that struck me the most about the Final Four was how proud I was that Fein Cera was named Best Horse. That's such a special thing. I had worked with this mare for the 18 months prior, and she was beautifully schooled and looked so good. And what an experience to ride all those other horses. They each were incredible...and so different. It was fun. But do I believe that format legitimately picked the World Champion? Definitely not, and the FEI has agreed. Starting with the 2018 WEG, the Final Four concept was dropped. I feel strongly about the bond and experience between a horse and rider. It's not the rider that wins the medal; it's the horse-and-rider combination. I totally think changing horses doesn't belong. Five rounds are enough to decide the World Champion.

CHRIS KAPPLER

From 20ᵗʰ Century Gold to 21ˢᵗ Century Gold

Chris began riding in Illinois with his mother, Kay, and sister, Katie. He got his show career under way with Alex Jayne and continued his development with George Morris at Hunterdon, the legendary stable in Pittstown, New Jersey, which graduated many show ring stars. After earning top equitation results, including second in the ASPCA Maclay and USET Talent Search Finals, as well as third in the AHSA Medal Finals, he went on to national and international Grands Prix. Chris was named Midwest Rider of the Year in 1987, 1988, 1989, and 1991. In 1989, he received the USET's Lionel Guerrand-Hermes Trophy, awarded to the young rider who "exemplifies outstanding sportsmanship and horsemanship."

Chris is the winner of more than 100 Grands Prix, including the American Invitational and American Gold Cup, each three times. Internationally, he took team gold and individual silver with Royal Kaliber at the 2003 Pan American Games, and subsequently was named the U.S. Equestrian Federation's Equestrian of the Year. In 2004, Chris and Royal won team gold and individual silver at the Olympic Games in Athens. His other top horses included Seven Wonder, Concorde, and VDL Oranta.

Since retiring from competition in 2009, Chris has focused on training horses and riders. He is a founder and former president of the North American Riders Group, and has served on the USEF board of directors. Chris also has been a selector for U.S. show jumping teams.

Royal Kaliber jumped beautifully in the team competition at the 2004 Athens Olympics, the culmination of his career. Chris Kappler developed the stallion who contributed to the U.S. silver medal. The United States later was upgraded to gold after the winning German team was dropped in the rankings following a positive drug test for one of its horses.

As a member of the U.S. gold medal show jumping team at the Athens Olympics in 2004, I was struck by the similarities between our squad and the previous U.S. team that won gold at the Olympics, 20 years earlier in Los Angeles. It was almost an identical parallel in terms of the composition of the team, with an identical result.

In 1984, each horse on the team was amazing: Touch of Class with Joe Fargis, who won individual gold; Abdullah, Conrad Homfeld's individual silver medal ride; Calypso, the longtime mount of Melanie Smith, and Albany, ridden by Leslie Burr.

Then, if you advance two decades, you have four more superstar horses. Fein Cera was coming off an incredible 2002 World Equestrian Games, where Peter Wylde rode her to individual bronze. Then there was Sapphire with McLain Ward and Authentic, ridden by Beezie Madden. These two horses at the start of their stratospheric careers would go on to contribute to team gold again four years later in the Olympics held in Hong Kong, where Beezie also took the individual bronze.

My horse, Royal Kaliber, was in his absolute prime in 2003 and 2004. No horse at the time had won more in his career. Interestingly, I was the first person in 12 years to be subjectively selected, after complete objective selection had not always paid off.

When I was growing up, watching Conrad and

Abdullah, I dreamed of doing what they had done. Then to duplicate Conrad's 1984 results in Athens, home of the original Olympic Games, was, for me, a dream come true. Like Conrad, I won individual silver in a jump-off, even though, through a sad twist of fate, I did not finish my round after Royal got hurt in the process.

There was such a shift in the way America picked its equestrian teams after we went to objective selection following a 1990 lawsuit over who made the squad for the first World Equestrian Games. Between 1983 and 2004, there was a dramatic change. We had gone from Bert de Némethy, the longtime team coach, to Frank Chapot, who was team captain during his riding days. Bert handed over a team that was in a very good place, so in 1984, Frank was able to step in with a squad that could win all those medals over an innovative course designed by Bert. With that 1984 course, Bert set the style for tests that were much more technical and "careful," with related distances playing a major role. It was the beginning of an evolution to a more technical and difficult style of riding and training you needed to succeed over the courses. He also used lighter materials than were customary during the past in his courses, which asked as much of the rider as it did of the horse.

In my second-to-last junior year, we were at the Traders' Point Horse Show in Indianapolis, where we watched the fantastic win by the 1984 U.S. team on television. The whole thing was incredibly inspirational and made you want to be an Olympian. Later that year, George Morris was judging the AHSA Medal finals in Harrisburg and pinned this wet-behind-the-ears Midwest kid third. He told my mom that my style of riding was very much like Conrad's.

That became my visual. Riders often find someone they identify with and tend to watch, whether it's body shape, mentality, or riding style. With Conrad, I admired his body of work, what he was able to accomplish through his riding, his techniques, and his partnerships with his horses.

Frank was involved with restructuring over two decades to get the United States back on track where we duplicated our 1984 win in 2004, after some dramatic highs and lows; two Olympic silver medals in 1988 and 1996, but no Olympic team medals in 1992 and 2000, and no team medals at all in the World Equestrian Games from 1990 through 2002. The team underwent pretty tremendous turmoil with the 1990 lawsuit. So it was incredibly satisfying for Frank to be able to finish his time as coach with a gold medal 20 years later and hand the team off to the next coach, George Morris, in a position that allowed for a very structured format, including subjectivity.

I was traveling through Europe in 2000 when I tried Royal Kaliber as an eight-year-old in Henk Nooren's small indoor arena in Holland. We had a fantastic trial, so I went back to America and talked to Kathy and Hal Kamine about him. We had been discussing getting a horse together, but this was the first one that got me excited enough to want to work with them. They were very gracious and bought the horse for me, with the plan to try to develop to the highest international level that we could. Although Royal was not an approved stallion, he had really great old Dutch bloodlines. He was by Ramiro out of a Voltaire mother.

That year and the next, I really started to develop him. The old Cincinnati Horse Show was very much like the American Invitational. They always had a fantastic crowd, lots of atmosphere, and a course designed by Richard Jeffery. I wasn't sure what to expect, since Royal and I had jumped a Grand Prix together for the first time just the previous week. I decided to wing it in this big class, even though I knew it would be a stretch for him at the age of eight.

When he walked in the arena there, he grew six inches and was incredible when he jumped around.

Chris Kappler stepped forward to lead the North American Riders Group as its founding president in an effort to improve show jumping in North America. Beezie Madden and McLain Ward looked on during the inaugural meeting of the program. The organization succeeded by critiquing and rating shows, which prompted them to improve.

That night, he was double-clear and finished third. I had a special feeling about him from that day on.

When there was a big event, he always seemed to rise to the occasion. He immediately became an international success for me. We had our growing pains together a bit through the 2002 World Equestrian Games trials. We missed out on the WEG, but we had finishing to do and got that accomplished the rest of the year.

In 2003, I won the American Invitational, the AGA Championship, and Devon. I think Royal is the only horse who has done that in a single year. At the beginning of that season, Coach Frank came to me and asked about my plans for 2003, suggesting I should consider the Pan American Games in Santo Domingo. They were really important that year, because we needed to qualify for the 2004 Olympics based on our performance there. I realized I couldn't be a chooser and had to be part of the process if the United States was to go to the Olympics.

But Frank was able to secure for me the privilege of being the first rider since 1990 selected on subjective results. That enabled me to go to Europe to get some more finishing done on the horse instead of being involved in the selection trials. We were double-clear in the Nations Cup at Aachen and fourth in the Grand Prix. That took us through to the Pan Am Games, where the team

won gold and I took individual silver as we qualified for the Athens Olympics.

In 2004, I came in fifth in the Invitational and Frank said I was good to go, that I had shown the necessary form and I was set to be on the Olympic team without going in the trials. That enabled me to focus on my plan to get the horse to peak performance in the right place at the right time. It also reassured the selectors about the ability to make a subjective pick for the team again.

Although the Olympics had been in the back of my mind since 1984, I was so focused on myself and my horse and our training that I tried not to think about it. Instead of realizing an entire life's work was coming up to this one moment, I was obsessed with the riding, the training, and care of the horse, trying to keep focused on my process.

I knew there wasn't anything they could show me at the Olympics that we hadn't done already. I felt as prepared as we could possibly be. I loved Royal. He gave you everything every time you rode him. Whether you were just on the flat or doing a little school, he always gave you 100 percent. I

It was a moment in which tragedy and joy mingled, as Chris Kappler (right) earned the individual show jumping bronze medal at the 2004 Athens Olympics, where Rodrigo Pessoa of Brazil took silver and Cian O'Connor of Ireland got the gold. Chris pulled up in the jump-off for silver against Rodrigo after his mount, Royal Kaliber, injured himself. Weeks later, the stallion had to be put down. Chris eventually moved up to the silver after Cian lost the gold because of a positive test for a prohibited substance on his horse, Waterford Crystal.

owed it to him to give him my 100 percent in turn. He was just a special horse and a really close friend.

It was a great U.S. team in Athens, home of the first modern Olympics in 1896. I grew up in the Midwest with Beezie, McLain and I were close, and Peter Wylde was a top professional. It was strong and comforting all around, with four riders who knew their horses and had a good team behind them.

It was pretty hot in Athens that year, and because they could almost guarantee no rain, the competition was on grass instead of all-weather footing. The grass was not really 100 percent; a lot of people felt it wasn't what it should be for an event like that, and an investigation undertaken post-Olympics for the FEI confirmed this after several horses sustained injuries on that ground.

The Nations Cup had both rounds on the same day at the 2004 Games. The team competition started at nine in the morning, and it was an extremely long day. We got there early to ride, feed, and walk the course. After the first round was finished, with the United States in second place, we had a long stretch until the second round began after dark.

The day got even longer when we were tied with Sweden for the silver medal after Germany won. The jump-off was judged on faults and time. We got a break when McLain figured out a shortcut to the last fence by jumping a rock. There was a certain risk to it—the horses might balk at something that wasn't the kind of jump they were used to—but it was a risk we were willing to take because it was a tight jump-off.

McLain told me, "It's just like the equitation, six strides to the rock and six strides to the oxer." All my equitation days paid off right there. Beezie had put in a phenomenal effort in the second round, and she got paid back for her three previous clean rounds because she didn't have to go in the jump-off since McLain, Peter, and I were clear and fast to earn silver, and the format involved the best three out of four scores.

After the awards ceremony and drug testing I didn't get back to where I was staying until two in the morning. I had been up for nearly 24 hours! But there was an even longer wait before we got the team gold. In 2006, our team reassembled for a small ceremony in Florida as we were presented with the gold medal. A positive drug test for a banned substance from a German team member's horse had demoted that nation to fourth and put us first, 18 months after the Athens Games ended.

The day of the individual medal competition in Athens was really big jumping. I had a rail in both rounds, while Rodrigo Pessoa of Brazil had two rails in the first round with Baloubet du Rouet and was clean in the second. We were tied for silver with 8 penalties after Cian O'Connor of Ireland clinched gold on Waterford Crystal.

In the jump-off, Rodrigo had the last fence down; he was fast, but not so fast. I knew exactly what I had to do. But turning to the double vertical combination, Royal took a funny step. I thought maybe he just slipped. But then he stumbled between the two elements of the double vertical. I don't know how he left it up. I knew immediately on landing he was not right. I pulled up and jumped off.

Royal's well-being was number one for me. I could tell he was injured and in a lot of pain. They got the horse ambulance in there and took him away. Meanwhile, I had to get through the medal ceremony and drug testing. By the time I got back to visit Royal, Tim Ober, the team vet, had him settled as well as he possibly could. It was terribly distressing to see him like that...my horse.

I can't remember how soon the U.S. horses left for home, but we felt it wasn't in Royal's best interests to ship him right away. We wanted to get some stability so he could fly and get out of there. But there was a problem. He was so fit and used to moving that being idle put him into shutdown. He started to have enteritis; his colon became inflamed. We finally were able to get his situation stable enough to fly him to a clinic in Holland.

We flew over a team of vets put together by Dr. Ober, but his condition just kept deteriorating. We tried a surgery and that didn't help. We lost him.

It was an incredibly sad day for me because that horse was a great friend. For a stallion, he was so kind and so enjoyable to be around and ride. In a lot of ways, he ruined it for the horses who came after him—he was impossible to live up to.

Ironically, a drug violation also changed the results of the individual medals, nearly a year after the Games ended. A tribunal stripped Cian of his gold medal in the wake of his mount testing positive for two banned substances. So Rodrigo moved up to gold, and I got the silver. But the decision, announced after Royal's passing, was a hollow promotion for me. The framed medals and the dried laurel wreath I wore during the ceremonies in Athens pale in comparison to my time with Royal. I will always have this great memory of my horse, great photos, and a great painting of him. He was the horse who gave me what I wanted so much, and I thank him for it.

LUCY DAVIS
The Dream Comes True

---⚐---

Remarkably, Lucy was only 21 when she was named to the U.S. bronze medal team at the 2014 FEI World Equestrian Games, riding with McLain Ward, Beezie Madden, and Kent Farrington. She and her brilliant mount Barron rejoined those iconic riders at the 2016 Olympics, where the squad earned silver. U.S. Show Jumping Coach Robert Ridland believes in having a younger rider included with veterans on championship teams.

Before the WEG, he said of Lucy, "She's got nerves of steel. She knows what to expect. As I told her, `You're not the fourth rider. You're one of four riders.'"

A native of Los Angeles, Lucy came up through the ranks, making the equitation finals and earning double gold in the junior section of the North American Junior and Young Rider Championships in 2008, the same year she was Best Child Rider at the Pennsylvania National Horse Show. She returned several times to NAJYRC, winning individual silver in 2009 and taking gold with the Zone 10 team in 2010.

A multi-dimensional talent who graduated from Stanford University with a bachelor of science in engineering and a specialization in architectural design, Lucy also is the co-founder of The Pony App, a stable management and horse care application. Following the Olympics, she became a trainer at Old Salem Farm in Westchester County, New York, while continuing to focus on developing her own horses.

The 2014 FEI World Equestrian Games in Normandy was the first time Stanford University graduate Lucy Davis had ridden on a championship team. Coach Robert Ridland felt it was important to pair up-and-coming riders with veterans so they gained experience, and in this case, it worked out with a team bronze medal to which Lucy and her mount, Barron, contributed.

knew what I wanted. Almost as soon as I began taking riding lessons, I zeroed in on my future with horses. My dream since I was in kindergarten always was to be in the Olympics. When I made the team for the 2016 Olympics, my two best friends from kindergarten, Kellie Barnum and Christine Kanoff, came to Rio with their families to watch me ride. They joked that I gave them ample notice because I was already talking about it in kindergarten!

My grandfather, Robert Barron Frieze, was a jockey's agent until he was 75. He worked hard to get where he wanted to be, and became a huge role model for me. He knows a good horse when he sees one.

Because of what he did for a living, horses were very important in the life of my mother, Kelly Davis, and eventually in mine as well. She worked as a hot walker and did odd jobs at the racetrack in the summers. When my mother decided to take riding lessons at a local stable, she would bring me along. But whenever I had to leave the barn, I would scream, cry, and throw a tantrum. I started riding when I started walking, and my mother was involved with my riding and showing through my time in high school and college. We've sort of done it together. She's a good horsewoman. Even though I don't come from a true jumping family, I definitely come from a line of horse people. The exception was my father, George Davis, but he has become a dedicated follower of the sport. He's likely to start his Sunday mornings watching the live stream of Grands Prix from Europe and is always up on what's happening there.

Early in my career, I took the usual route through the equitation and the hunters. As I moved up to the jumpers, California trainer Archie Cox helped me. He is an amazing person and horseman, still a very special figure in my life.

When I was 17, I started working with German trainer and world-class rider Markus Beerbaum, which was an important shift, because I committed myself to my dream of being in the Olympics. Markus, a European Championships and WEG medalist, and his wife, Meredith Michaels-Beerbaum, an Olympic, WEG, and European Championships medalist who was a three-time FEI World Cup Finals champion, both know what it's like to compete at that level. Beyond their system of how they train the horses and take care of them, they always put together a whole program of preparation. We had a two-year plan, a one-year plan, and once I made the team, a three-month plan. It's all very detailed, something different than I had experienced previously when I was younger and in school.

Experience is helpful in our sport, almost above everything, but I always felt I was prepared, with a really good trainer, Markus, behind me, and my other teammates. I just wanted to go for it.

I knew U.S. Show Jumping coach Robert Ridland from California. I grew up riding at the Blenheim shows, of which he is president. He and I have a little West Coast vibe and have gotten along well because of that. Robert likes to give young people a chance, pairing them with older riders. He's given me a lot of opportunities. With Robert, if you deliver, you get rewarded.

I had some Nations Cup experience before the 2014 WEG, but the teams for those two types of competition are hugely different. The Nations Cup is always super special, because it's a team competition for your country. I've enjoyed that aspect of it.

The WEG, however, was on a whole other level. At training camp, you get to bond with your teammates. But when you are competing in a championship, there's no small talk or chitchat. It's high intensity. For the Rio Olympics, I was two years more mature in my riding, so that was hugely helpful. My teammates—Kent Farrington, Beezie Madden, and McLain Ward—were all, and continue to

Lucy Davis had been dreaming since kindergarten of riding in the Olympics, and when she made the silver medal squad in 2016 aboard Barron, several of her kindergarten classmates journeyed to Rio where they saw her make good on her childhood prediction.

be, great supporters. I went through the necessary steps to be on that team. They gave me the respect to do what I was doing to continue to be on a team with them. They instilled a lot of confidence in me and were nothing but encouraging.

Things came together for me to start making teams after I bought Barron as an eight-year-old. He had an unwieldy name, so when 25 members of my family were around that Christmas, we voted on a new name and Barron—after my grandfather—was the winner.

The process of bringing Barron along was rewarding. I could feel he had the ability. Whether he had the brain, the stamina, and the heart could only be proven over time, but luckily, he did.

Actually, Barron has a weird brain—he goes from lazy to crazy; he doesn't spook at a jump, but he's frightened of a squirrel on the side of the ring.

The 2016 Olympic silver medal team of *(left to right)* Lucy Davis, Kent Farrington, McLain Ward, and Beezie Madden on the podium in Rio de Janeiro.

Any change of environment or weather or location always affects him. You have to see how he's feeling emotionally every morning; he's a very quirky horse. But in the ring he's the bravest, the most careful, and he fights for it.

At the 2013 World Cup Finals, I was clear in the Grand Prix, and after that, Robert gave me a chance to be on a team at Rotterdam, starting our Nations Cup career while riding with championships multi-medalists Beezie, Lauren Hough, and Laura Kraut. That kicked off our run to the 2014 WEG team.

But my most important ambition, the Olympics,

was no foregone conclusion, even after the WEG medal. I had a rough winter leading up to the 2016 Olympics and was in no position to qualify with points for the short list of 10 from which the Games team would be chosen. I feared I had crushed my Olympic dreams.

In Europe, I'd had a lot of bad results, forgetting how to actually ride and becoming over-analytical. The luckiest thing was that my horse was healthy. I was the one who was kind of sabotaging our performance, and it wasn't good timing. If I think too much about what I'm doing and question the program or the process, it definitely affects the way I ride. I kind of spiraled out of control. Every time one little thing went wrong, I made it into an issue. That's really easy to do when you work years for something and sacrifice a lot to get there. It's a very mental sport. You get to a position where you're so close and every small misstep or error becomes magnified. You can twist everything in your head. I was thinking each mistake meant all those sacrifices I had made over the years were going to amount to nothing.

As soon as I looked at both sides of the coin and accepted I might not make my dreams come true in 2016—or alternatively, that there was a chance I *could* get on the team—things were back in proportion. I told myself that whatever happened, the work hadn't been for nothing; that I've learned so much and experienced so many great things. Then I snapped out of it and started to do better.

Robert and the selection committee gave me the chance to prove Barron and myself again, and we ended up on the Olympic team. Once I was there, he said he expected as many clear rounds from me as from Beezie, McLain, and Kent. His comments obviously were very special and instilled a lot of confidence in me. I was able to hunker down and go on as an underdog again, something I do better than coming at it on top.

I'm lucky to have already achieved my two main goals in the sport, the WEG and the Olympics. Now I have to set new goals for myself, broader goals. Having experienced the magic of the Olympics, I don't think it ever will be easy for me to be watching it from the couch. I have to hold out for the Los Angeles 2028 Olympics because it's my hometown, and riding on the team there would be too good to be true. At some point, I'm sure I'll want to have a family and do everything that is part of that. At the moment, however, I'm pretty career-focused. I'm concentrating on setting myself up to establish a more professional business with the horses as well, not just with The Pony App, but also with my own riding. I'm working for support to sustain it and get some horses to develop.

The next step in my career is starting to train others. Old Salem Farm provided that opportunity. I never saw myself having a big training stable. I didn't think I had the patience for that, but in the past couple of years, I've taken on a few students and enjoyed those more than I anticipated.

Riding is my passion. I've been lucky to make it into my profession and do it in a way that works best for me. I've designed my life around these horses. I'm looking forward to continuing down that road. The nice thing is, you can do this sport for a long time, so I think my involvement will continue to evolve.

LAUREN HOUGH

The Journey to the Pink Coat

L auren was a champion from the start. She earned numerous titles with her small pony, Swan Song, before she went on to much success in the junior hunters and equitation divisions. As a junior jumper, Lauren rode on the 1993 gold medal Zone 10 team. The next year, at age 15, she won the USET Show Jumping Talent Search Finals East and secured the title of Pacific Coast Horseman's Association Grand Prix Rookie of the Year.

Partnered with Clasiko, Lauren first rode for the U.S. Equestrian Team at the 2000 Sydney Olympics. From there, she went on to a string of successes with the American flag on her saddle pad. In 2003, Lauren represented the United States on the gold medal Pan American Games squad in the Dominican Republic. And from 2004 through 2006, Lauren was a member of successful U.S contingents competing in the Samsung Super League, with the U.S. finishing first in 2005. Lauren was also a member of the 2007 Pan American Games bronze-medal-winning team in Rio de Janeiro, Brazil.

After stints on the winning Nations Cup teams in Rome, Italy, in 2009 and in Rotterdam, the Netherlands, the following year, the Wellington, Florida, resident also competed on the U.S. squad at the 2010 World Equestrian Games in Kentucky. At the Toronto Pan American Games in 2015, Lauren earned team and individual bronze medals with Ohlala.

In 2017, Lauren contributed to the Hermès U.S. show jumping teams that clinched Nations Cup gold in Sopot, Poland, Spruce Meadows, Canada, and Dublin, Ireland. In Ireland, an all-female squad earned the victory, forever marking a historic moment in equestrian sport.

Additional notable individual achievements for Lauren include winning the National Horse Show Grand Prix (twice), the Grand Prix of Ireland, and the

Saint-Lo Grand Prix in France. Lauren also earned the Leading Lady Rider Award for the 2014 Winter Equestrian Festival.

A highlight of Lauren's 2016 season was her victory in the $130,000 Longines FEI World Cup Jumping for the President's Cup at the Washington International Horse Show, where she was leading rider. In 2017, she and Ohlala won the Great American $1 Million at HITS Ocala.

Lauren Hough with her inspirational father, eventing Olympian Champ Hough, at a California horse show when she competed as a child.

When I was a child and someone asked me what I wanted to do with my life, I always said the same thing, "I'm going to ride in the Olympics."

I was fortunate that my father, Champ Hough, competed in the Helsinki Games in 1952 and won a team bronze medal in eventing. That was quite an inspiration for me. My first lessons were from my father and my mother, Linda Hough, a wonderful hunter rider who went on to be a sought-after judge.

I started my own business in 1998 when I was 21. I had a fantastic equestrian education. I was exposed to all the best with my family so involved in the industry that I felt ready. After putting together a syndicate, I went to Germany with Dutch trainer Henk Nooren and bought Clasiko and Windy City within 48 hours of each other on the same trip. Henk, whom I had met through Michele Grubb, helped me find all my horses throughout my career.

I told everyone in the Clasiko group that we were buying the horse so I could ride him in the Olympics. Did I believe it? Not really, but I thought it was a good selling point.

Clasiko was a beautiful horse with really good conformation. He was a powerhouse. I never sat on anything like that. When the jumps got big, he didn't even feel like he was making an effort. Although it felt as if they couldn't build the fences big enough to stump him, it took a while to learn to go fast with him and win a Grand Prix. When I found myself struggling with Clasiko during our early days together, Henk flew to Florida to help and advised, "You have to stick with it because he has a lot of talent."

Unfortunately, Clasiko sustained an injury in the middle of his eight-year-old year and didn't come back until he was 9. At that time, I had a student who wanted to ride in the Olympic trials, comprised of five rounds at the U.S. Equestrian Team training center in Gladstone, New Jersey, and five rounds in California. Since I would already be at the trials, I decided to enter Clasiko to give him mileage, thinking if he got in over his head, I'd simply withdraw.

I knew that I really needed a set of eyes on

Lauren Hough made the 2000 Olympic team with Clasiko after going through the selection trials without thinking she had a chance to be on the squad.

the ground for the trials. I always had the utmost respect and admiration for 1984 Olympic team gold and individual silver medalist Conrad Homfeld. At that time, he was focused on course building and had stopped training altogether. I called him in the winter of 2000 to see if he would consider helping me.

He said, "Thank you so much for asking, but I really want to give it some thought. What made you think of me?"

I told him, "I admire your calmness, and I don't want someone to come in and reinvent the wheel. I just want someone who will give me confidence and hold my hand to go through this process." At the time, of course, I wasn't thinking we would make it all the way to Sydney.

Conrad, who also won team gold and individual silver in the 1986 World Championships, did accept my invitation. He was an invaluable and instrumental part of a key time in my career, and he traveled around the world for me. Conrad never charged me a dime and wouldn't let me pay his expenses. I am eternally grateful to him.

In the middle of the Gladstone trials, I had to fly home to California to be in my cousin's wedding. It was a very quick trip, so when I returned, I was completely stressed and running late, which led to a bad round on the two-round day. Under the selection criteria, you were only allowed one drop score, and that less-than-optimum tour of the course had to be it for me.

There was a break before the final round, so I pulled myself together, took a deep breath, and went out to do what I had to do. I jumped a clean round and made the cut for the final group of 12 that went to California.

The best five from there were to go to Sydney for the Olympics, and the second group would go to Spruce Meadows in Canada for that show's Nations Cup. Competing in the second set of trials worked for me because it gave me the opportunity

to return to California, where I grew up. I also figured I'd get to be on my first Nations Cup team at Spruce Meadows, never thinking I'd qualify for the Olympic squad. I just stayed really focused and didn't have the Olympics anywhere but the back of my mind as my horse kept getting better. The last day was comprised of two rounds, and after the first round, I was in fourth place. I remember going back and sitting in the stable, reminding myself to stay calm and keep doing what I had been doing.

After jumping a clear in that last round, I galloped through the timers and threw my hands up in the air. It was like, "*Oh my God, my dream actually just came true!*"

I was in absolute shock as I walked out of the ring thinking, *"This happened!"*

Obviously, there was a lot of criticism as to whether objective selection was the right thing to do in choosing the Games team. And in my case, it meant that the first Nations Cup I ever rode in would be at the Olympics. I knew, however, despite my lack of team experience, that I couldn't be taken off the squad under the system being used at the time.

Looking back on it, I don't think I was aware of what a big deal it was. I was just living in the moment. The horses had to go directly into quarantine in California and were there for about three weeks. Like the others who would be on the team, I traveled back and forth to attend to the rest of my business on the East Coast. That's when I formed a bond with Margie Goldstein Engle and Laura Kraut, who would be on the team with me. We spent a lot of time together.

I'll never forget when my treasured "Pink" coat arrived: the scarlet jacket with the USET crest—something that could only be worn by a rider representing the U.S. team. My last horse show before I left for Sydney was the Hampton Classic, and I rode in the coat there because someone told me, "You need to wear this once before the Olympics."

When we arrived in Sydney, the horses had to be in quarantine again. It was another 10 days before we started to compete. That meant we had an opportunity to do the opening ceremonies and to enjoy the whole Olympic experience. The people in Australia were so nice. I'd like to go back and visit.

I was there to do my job. But it was in a good way, and I wasn't overwhelmed by it all. From the outside, I'm sure people thought I was really under a lot of pressure. Looking back on it now, I just did the best job I could at the time. Not having experienced it before, I didn't know any better. I'm sure that if I had enjoyed a bit more mileage, I would have understood—as I do now—that, of course, you kick a little harder and pull a little more when you're jumping in a championship and fighting for your team.

Although my horse was also inexperienced, I really went in feeling quite confident because we'd already been through ten rounds of championship-level jumping. As a nine-year-old, my horse probably benefited from that. My situation was a bit unique in that he was at the best he'd ever been by the time he got to Australia.

I feel fortunate I had that experience and was able to finish tied for fifteenth individually. I haven't been to another Olympics yet, but I can't wait to do it again. While I appreciated what I learned the first time around, now I want to go back and win.

I have gained a lot of Nations Cup and championship mileage since my team debut in Sydney. I feel very honored to ride for the team. The donors, support staff, and people around us do their utmost, and we're very privileged to be able to represent our country.

My next championship after the Olympics was the 2003 Pan American Games in Santo Domingo, Dominican Republic. We had to win a gold or silver to qualify the United States to compete in the Athens Olympics, so it was a very important event.

I had broken my collarbone in Florida, and it was too early in the healing process for me to ride in the Pan Am trials in Lexington, Kentucky, so I requested a bye. Only one bye was available, however, and it went to Chris Kappler with Royal Kaliber. Despite the pain from my fracture, I rode Windy City to two clear rounds. No one else was fault-free, so the selectors and Chef d'Equipe Frank Chapot decided that I didn't have to do any more of the trials.

Every afternoon in Santo Domingo, you could pretty much set your clock by the storm you would see coming around two in the afternoon. There was no cover, and although they would stop the competition, I was already soaked by that time. When the rain finished, they'd say, "We'll start again in 20 minutes."

I had to borrow teammate Beezie Madden's saddle and change my clothes standing in the middle of the warm-up ring. Despite the problems and the pressure, Beezie, Chris, Margie, and I ended up winning team gold and getting the U.S. show jumping team a ticket to Athens for the 2004 Games, where that squad also won gold and Chris won individual silver.

At the Rio de Janeiro Pan Ams in 2007, I rode Casadora on the squad with Laura Chapot, Todd Minikus, and Cara Raether. We won bronze at the same venue where the 2016 Olympics would be held. At that time, however, they hadn't finished any of the roads leading to the site, so it was nearly an hour trip each way every day.

By going to the Pan Ams, we were also able to go to Athina Onassis' five-star show in Sao Paolo. There had been a lot of plane crashes in the region at that time, so we chartered a bus because we were afraid to fly. We saw a lot of beautiful country. I was second, and it was quite a bit of prize money, which made the extra time and expense in Brazil worthwhile.

In 2015, I did my third Pan Ams in Toronto.

Lauren Hough earned the first individual championship medal of her career at the 2015 Pan American Games in Toronto, where she took bronze on the 15.2-hand Ohlala, sharing the podium with Andres Rodriguez of Venezuela, silver, and her teammate, McLain Ward, gold.

I was riding Ohlala, and I felt I had a contender to win an individual medal, so she went to Europe in the spring, and I flew her back directly to Toronto.

On paper, we had a very good team that included Kent Farrington, McLain Ward, and Georgina Bloomberg. I think we were all a bit complacent and figured, "Of course we're going to win." Then, in the first round of the Nations Cup, every single one of us had a rail down.

When you're going into the second round with 12 faults, it's not good. We certainly didn't want to go home without a medal. That motivated us to put in three clean rounds, and we won the bronze.

For the individual medals, we started on a clean slate with no penalties. I ended up with a 4-fault round and a clear after two rounds. Then I jumped off with five others for the bronze. All I was thinking about was the four years of prequalification for all the Grands Prix around the world that I would have if I won an individual medal. I said to myself, "If I've gotten this far and don't walk out of here with a bronze medal, I'm going to be really angry with myself."

McLain was jumping off for the gold, and he gave me a bit of a kick in the tail, saying, "You better win this." I didn't take every risk, but Ohlala is a naturally fast horse, and I was the only clear in the tiebreaker. It was a really proud moment for me to stand on the podium with McLain, the gold medalist, and silver medalist Andres Rodriguez of Venezuela, who sadly is no longer with us. It was a big sense of accomplishment.

That experience has made me even hungrier for another individual medal. The team is the most important thing, but in addition, individually, I enjoyed the experience very much. And now I know I'm well prepared to handle the pressure and the expectations going into the next championship. It's always an honor to wear the pink coat, and I hope to do it—and my country—proud.

DRESSAGE

DRESSAGE, WHICH IS THE FRENCH WORD FOR "TRAINING," provides a firm basis for any horse's development. In competition, this discipline illuminates the horse's gymnastic ability, as well as his way of moving and obedience to subtle commands.

At the Olympic level, dressage tests include not only walk, trot, and canter, but also lengthening and shortening of stride, and several special movements: They are the one- and two-tempis (flying changes of lead every one and two strides); piaffe (a kind of trotting in place); the passage (a cadenced, ground-covering trot); and the pirouette (where the hindquarters remain on the spot, moving slightly, while the front legs are elevated as they go around a small circle).

In 1996, the Musical Freestyle, also known as the *Kur,* became part of the Olympic repertoire, in addition to the traditional Grand Prix and Grand Prix Special tests. The Freestyle has contributed to the popularity of dressage. Riders take great care in selecting their music and choreography, with judges taking into consideration both technical and artistic aspects of the performance in marking the competitors. Scores are based on a percentage of 100, which would be perfection. Marks in the 90s are the highest ever awarded.

LAURA GRAVES

The Making of Diddy

In her sixth-grade yearbook, Laura Graves wrote that her dream was to represent the United States in the Olympics. While the road from her sixth-grade classroom in Vermont to her Team USA bronze medal at the 2016 Olympic Games in Rio was a long one, Laura and Verdades eventually were able to make that dream reality.

The rider and her Dutch-bred horse known as "Diddy" gained international attention after a second place finish in the Grand Prix at the 2014 USEF Dressage Festival of Champions. Later that year, at the World Equestrian Games in Normandy, the pair was the highest placed U.S. duo, finishing fifth in the Grand Prix Freestyle. Laura and Diddy have gone on to a strong FEI World Cup finals record, with a fourth-place finish in Las Vegas in 2015, and a second place finish in 2017, 2018, and 2019.

Laura and Diddy were fourth individually in the Rio Olympics and second in the Grand Prix Special at the 2018 WEG, after anchoring the silver medal U.S. Team—the best U.S. Dressage Team finish in a global championship since 2002. In 2018, she became the first American dressage rider to be ranked Number One in the world.

Laura lives in Geneva, Florida, with her partner and Diddy's co-owner, Curt Maes, and is trained by US Dressage Technical Advisor Debbie McDonald.

We bought Verdades in 2002 after watching a videotape of a little bay foal from the Netherlands. The first time that my mom, Freddie, and I saw him in person was outside the quarantine center in Newburgh, New York.

My mom and I kept looking at each other as each bay horse came out of quarantine and headed for a trailer saying, "This must be him." So then, when it wasn't, we'd look at the next one and say, "No, *this* one must be him."

Finally, we saw a group of men come out with a little, rough-looking foal. This colt required more people than needed to deal with any of the bigger

Laura Graves, who developed Verdades from the time he was a weanling, was the first American to be ranked Number One in the world for dressage.

horses, but he went right onto the trailer, and we got him home to Vermont. He was so green that he hadn't even worn a halter until he was imported.

Once we got back to Vermont, Diddy got very sick right away, which can happen with foals who have to be quarantined after their long flight. He was not used to being handled and was very strong for his size, which became a problem when the veterinarian said he had to be on injectable antibiotics. This meant one of his first experiences with people involved being kept in a stall and stuck with needles. It was quite a difficult transition for a youngster who had just lived in the field with his mother. He needed injections, but since it took two of us to hold him down, there wasn't anyone to give him the shots. We didn't have enough hands on deck since it was just my mom and me, so he had to move to the clinic. We thought it would be necessary to save his life, but he was probably traumatized. He was so sick that they had to drill holes in his guttural pouches to drain the infection.

Once Diddy recovered, we started him in our program. We focused on horse care—spending a lot of time working with all our horses on the ground.

They got a thorough grooming every day with currycombs and elbow grease.

Diddy was petrified of basic things, such as fly spray and Velcro, and you couldn't get near him with clippers. If he had come to me as a three-year-old, I would say, "Poor thing, someone treated him badly when he was young." However, at six months, he hadn't even been handled. We found that if you lose his trust, he's not quick to forget. We were in way over our heads.

Of course, we asked for help. Everyone knows a good cowboy or two, and we found one who started working with him, long-lining, and even training with tarps. Diddy began making some good progress...until they started umbrella work.

Our cowboy called and said, "You need to come and get your horse. I started umbrella work and haven't been able to catch him in the field since."

Diddy had decided he was not going to let that guy near him ever again! Even today, you cannot push him to accept opening an umbrella near him.

I broke Diddy to ride myself, with professionals on the ground helping. Sitting on his back wasn't

Curt Maes and Laura Graves, co-owners of Verdades, with Laura's parents, Freddie and Ron Graves.

an issue, but putting the saddle pad and saddle on him caused a ton of stress. We didn't have an arena, so I'd ride him up and down the road until he got scared and wanted to go home. I was a teenager at the time, and started to wonder, "What fun is this?"

I had a trainer and started bringing him to her place, but I was anxious about taking him anywhere because he was so unpredictable. Was he going to freak out or hurt himself? We then made the tough decision to leave him with this trainer and get him sold.

I was raised to believe that when you have a pet, they're your responsibility for life. There are few animals that came into our home who have not lived their entire lives with us. The idea of selling this horse wasn't in order to make a profit. It was more because he was young and didn't need to sit in a field. I knew we would be picky about who he'd go to.

After we dropped him off at my trainer's place, she called less than a week later; she couldn't believe I'd been walking and trotting Diddy under saddle. He wouldn't even let her on him. She told us that if people couldn't ride him, he couldn't be sold.

Little by little, she was able to sit on him. I kept riding him, too, and he bucked me off a few times. I dislocated my jaw in one fall. Then, while we were trying to break him to the spur, I was foolish and popped him one. He launched me, and that's when I broke two vertebrae. While I knew I had to go to the hospital as soon as I got up off the ground, I also knew someone had to get back on him.

I hung around the barn until my trainer got on, and then my mom drove me to the emergency room. I was supposed to be in bed for six weeks, but I didn't last that long. As soon as the pain felt manageable, I got back on my horse.

Even after Diddy turned five, he was still difficult about the saddle pad and saddles, not to mention snow falling off the roof of the indoor arena. On the other hand, when we were riding,

In 2019, for the third time in a row, Laura Graves finished second on Verdades in the FEI World Cup Dressage Finals.

roundness, steering, and moving off the leg were not even second thoughts for him. If I thought it, he did it. This horse seemed to have two completely different minds. Our riding was always the thing that made sense to him. He wanted someone to be close to him. When you sat on his back, it is like he felt you were hugging him.

When I rode with Madeline Austin, Liz Austin's mom, who breeds Dutch horses in Vermont, she said, "You know, this is an international quality horse."

I had no idea and was totally surprised. It took four hours to get Diddy on the trailer to go back home. I thought, "There's no way this one is *the one*. I should still sell him."

I left Vermont and went to cosmetology school. I enjoyed it, but it was my backup plan, and I reached the point where I thought, "If I'm going to do this, now's the time."

I searched online for "horse trainers, Florida." Any names I recognized, I applied for a working student position. I didn't hear back from many of them, but Anne Gribbons, a five-star judge, responded, and I went to her place near Orlando for an interview.

I was ill-equipped, with just a video of me riding Diddy at home. I didn't think she was impressed, but she said, "You certainly couldn't afford this horse now." Anne offered me an unpaid working student spot—even after she sat me on a bunch of Grand Prix horses, and I couldn't get them to trot.

I showed up at her farm with Diddy in early 2009. It was a huge turning point for me. We stayed for three years, and I learned many things—about training horses, hard work, and running a barn.

When it came to showing, I had horrible nerves, to the point where I would get physically sick before competing. Growing up, I had so many bad show experiences, from getting dragged around the horse show by our two ponies, to a Quarter Horse who would buck and carry on as soon as we entered the show ring. So showing had never been a super fun experience for me...until I took Diddy to a show at Jim Brandon Equestrian Center in Wellington, Florida. We went in there to compete at Third Level, and I'm thinking, "I'm going to have my hands full." But it was as if he had been doing it all his life.

He seemed to realize, "Hey, this is cool, all these people, all these carrots." After that show, I no longer had nerves; there was something about how much *he* enjoyed it that helped *me* learn to enjoy it.

If we hadn't ended up in this sport and we hadn't ended up training at such a high level, I think daily life would have been a big struggle for Diddy. He has always lacked confidence, and he can be so fearful. None of the naughty stuff he did

The 2016 U.S. bronze medal Olympic team of *(left to right)* Allison Brock, Laura Graves, Kasey Perry-Glass, and Steffen Peters.

came from a place where he had a temper. It was concern and fear. Having a job he could feel proud of and confident about changed his whole life.

In 2010, Anne Gribbons became the technical advisor for the U.S. team and didn't spend much time in Florida. My parents said they would help me for one year, but after that, I would have to figure it out—and I didn't have any money.

I decided to go home to Vermont and keep Diddy in the barn at my parents' place. I taught a little and was working promotions for a liquor company. Then, that summer, Anne was conducting a talent search at U.S. Equestrian Team Foundation headquarters in Gladstone, New Jersey, with developing dressage coach Debbie McDonald. She suggested I come and Debbie selected me to ride in the elite clinic that weekend.

By that fall, I was back in Florida, starting work at the barn every day at 6:30 a.m, but I also needed a paying job, so I went on Craigslist and applied for everything. The best fit was restaurant work, which I could do after I left the barn at four each afternoon. I started as a waitress and within the first year, I was asked to bartend. That's how I was able to earn the money so I could move off the farm into my own apartment.

In the fall of 2011, Diddy broke his jaw in a stable accident, and it mangled his face. To this day, he's either asleep or getting into trouble. Thank goodness there was a veterinarian at the barn doing dental work on some other horses who was able to sedate him and give him antibiotics right away. I sat with him all night and took him to surgery the next day. It was horrifying. The thought of Diddy not being rideable again didn't occur to me; I only cared that he would recover and be comfortable.

After the operation, it was like he had braces. They wrapped pins with wires around the molars and across the front teeth, covering them with acrylic so the wires didn't cut through his gums. I'm sure it was similar to what happened when I got my own braces—an incredible amount of pressure and pain. It was at least three weeks before he was able to pull grass out of the ground.

Going through all this had left him exhausted from fear. I could see he was broken-hearted and that broke my own heart. He's so unusually reasonable in human terms. If you pause and tell him in English what's going on, it's like he understands you. Unfortunately, sometimes a veterinarian's nature is to be physical with horses; he doesn't respond to that at all.

I wondered whether we could ever put a bit in his mouth again. Diddy and I have been through a lot together, and he knows I would never get him into trouble. Throughout all of this, he never said no to me. He trusts that I will ask him only to do things that are best for him.

I slept outside his stall for probably five days because I was worried he was going to stop breathing. His comfort was always a priority. As he was recovering, he was starting to get a little rambunctious, and I said, "He needs a job."

I put his regular bit on and took the noseband off, and we just hacked on the buckle everywhere. He started to rehab by thinking he had a little bit of a job to do. By January 2012, he was training again. He was still sensitive about it, but he had always been so nice in the hand that it wasn't really an issue. We have been lucky because he likes to do his job. He was schooling Small Tour and just getting fit again.

After Anne and I went our separate ways, my partner, Curt Maes, and I had a little six-stall barn in the Orlando area, and I needed a trainer. Because of the training session at Gladstone, I thought of Debbie.

Once I started training with Debbie, it was as if I had been missing one of my arms and riding with Debbie was my other arm. It was so natural. We ended up making some significant changes in Diddy's bitting, which changed his comfort level and way of going immensely.

I signed up to have my Grand Prix officially observed by Debbie, the developing dressage coach, and Robert Dover, who was the U.S. Dressage technical advisor, while they were looking for horses for the 2014 FEI World Equestrian Games. I rode on a Sunday afternoon at the Adequan Global Dressage Festival, and there was not a soul around during our ride.

After we had finished, I figured I hadn't been observed and walked back to the barn almost in tears. I was so frustrated and certain that I was just never going to crack into the top tier of the sport. During that weekend I kept comparing Diddy to other horses I'd seen and wondering, "Why am I not scoring better? He's nicer than these other horses."

I was done at that point, and I decided I would do something else, a career that at the end of the day was rewarding.

And then Debbie came running down to the stabling to talk to me.

"Laura, we just watched your ride," she said. "We've been watching Grand Prix horses all weekend. The potential we see in your horse is so much higher than what we've seen. You tell me when you want a lesson, and I'll be there for you."

All of a sudden, the fact that I was broke and scoring 64 percent didn't matter. I knew our path wasn't going to be a straight shot, but I knew this was the right path for me.

I was that kid who couldn't afford, who couldn't do, who couldn't have. That's where you're going to find the next top star. What is the best advice you can give someone like that? I'm sure they're looking for something like "work hard" or "seize opportunities." The best advice I can give, however, is to learn how to succeed at failing. Learn the way to get back on your feet. If you don't fail well, you're not going to make it very far.

There are going to be a lot of people who may not purposely want to hold you down, but not everybody is here to give you a leg up. You have to make it happen for yourself.

KASEY PERRY-GLASS

Saying Goodbye to My Comfort Zone

Kasey's spectacular dressage success is based on support from her family. Calling themselves "Team Believe," the group includes her mother, Diane Perry; her father, Robert Perry, a retired psychologist; five siblings; her grandparents; and her husband, Dana Glass.

They got behind her ambition to compete in the Olympics and helped her make it come true with an outstanding equine partner, Dublet. After winning team bronze at the 2016 Olympics in Rio, Kasey kept going, placing in the 2017 FEI World Cup Finals in Omaha and being part of the U.S. effort at the 2018 FEI World Equestrian Games in Tryon, North Carolina, where the dressage team claimed a silver medal for the first time in 16 years.

I just did not want to leave my home in Sacramento, California.

As a child, I wasn't interested in going to summer camp and would hide in the back of my parents' car. If I went to a slumber party at a friend's house, I'd call my mother when my friends got ready to go to bed and ask her to pick me up. I went to college at Sacramento State University, which enabled me to live at home. And then everything changed.

My dressage trainer, Christophe Theallet, a graduate of the French cavalry school at Saumur, moved to Spokane, Washington, six months after I started riding with him. I really liked his program and when he told me he was leaving, I was faced with a choice. There weren't any trainers around my area that would be a good match for me and my horse. So I decided to move to Spokane, beginning with a "trial," during what was a very scary month for me.

My parents were in shock. "You're going to leave?" they asked in disbelief.

Yes, indeed. I realized that if I really wanted to do what I said I wanted to do, I had to be out of my comfort zone. The next thing I knew, I had moved up to Spokane full time. It was a big change—actually, the start of a complete life shift.

Now I'm never home!

I was in Spokane for three years, splitting the time with winters in Florida. Christophe introduced me to the Adequan Global Dressage Festival, telling me, "If you're going to make it, you've got to go to Wellington."

I had come a long way since my involvement with riding started when my mother wanted to find a way to get me and my siblings out of the house. I had four sisters and a brother, so you can understand her thinking. There was a barn down the street where my mother and my sisters rode, and it was there that I got on a Western pony at age five. Eventually, I noticed the difference between Western and the English riding my sisters and mother did, so I switched saddles.

My sister, Holly, who now grooms for me, and I got into Pony Club and were introduced to trainer Carmela Richards. I grew up at her barn in a kid-friendly atmosphere with summer camp, lessons, and all kinds of activities. Carmela was into eventing, which meant I ended up being involved with it, too. I rode at Preliminary Level and was close to Intermediate, but the fences were getting really big. And at that time, dressage became my main interest.

The emphasis with Carmela was on our fundamentals and flatwork. She brought in dressage trainer Gina Duran when I was about 14, and I started riding with her. I loved the beauty and technicality of dressage, which she helped bring out in me during the eight years I worked with her.

I got really lucky as a kid. I grew up around some amazing women who instilled in me the importance of good horsemanship and the love of the horse, as well as his happiness. I was never in a situation where horses were abused or used as a

They wear different headgear, but dressage rider Kasey Perry-Glass and her husband, Dana Glass, a former working cowboy, have a business together. It's appropriately named Two Worlds Equestrian.

tool. They were all very well loved and cared for. That was a big part of who I was while growing up and who I am today.

We bought a horse in Europe sight unseen; that was probably the biggest mistake we've ever made. The horse was way over my head. I couldn't ride the horse without coaching every day, and Gina was two hours away in the Bay Area near San Francisco, so she helped me find a trainer in Sacramento. That was Christophe.

I never meshed well with my "Internet Horse." I didn't like riding him. He just wasn't for me, so it worked out when Christophe bought the horse for his wife.

Being in Spokane with Christophe, however, brought me together with Dana Glass, the man who would become my husband. When my family went on a 60-mile roundup of horses in Colorado,

Dana was the head wrangler. I thought he was a hot cowboy, and probably too hot for me, but he stayed good friends with my sister, Holly.

Eight years later, he was going to take a job in Spokane, so my sister told him to call me. We became really good friends over the phone and much more than that after he moved to Washington.

Soon I was asking him to marry me every week, and you know how that turned out.

Dana is an expert at groundwork, great at training horses (he has worked with Buck Brannaman), and we have started a business together, Two Worlds Equestrian LLC.

In order to fulfill my goal of riding in the Olympics, a new horse and intensive training were needed, and that was going to cost money I didn't have. My parents are my main sponsors, but I required more funding, so I decided to approach my grandparents, Joyce and Jim Teel. They are in the grocery business, Raley's Supermarkets, a terrific company founded by my great-grandfather. It's still family-owned, and my grandparents are philanthropists involved in the music and art community, as well as a Food for Families program.

I needed to make my request in a formal manner. I have 30 cousins, which meant I had to explain to my grandparents why I was the one who deserved the money. They wanted to help every single one of us, not just one grandchild. I ended up writing a business plan, showing what it would take for me to go to the Olympics. It was two weeks before my grandparents said they would assist with the expenses involved in my quest. I was on my way.

I took a lot of flak from my siblings. They didn't get it until I made it to the Olympics, and then they realized, "Oh, wow, this really *is* something you could do."

You have to respect people's money. It's a lot to put considerable amounts into a person and horse when you don't know what's going to happen. The money wouldn't be there if I weren't doing as well as I am or didn't make it to my goal. It's a lot of pressure—pressure I was putting on myself because it was something I wanted to do.

After my grandparents said they would help us financially with a horse, the next step involved heading to Europe, where we went to see one specific equine prospect. My mom wanted us to try other horses so we weren't going to Europe for just one horse, but none were the caliber we wanted. At least, that was the case…until we arrived at Andreas Helgstrand's farm in Denmark.

If you go there, you ride at least 20 horses in a day, all different sizes, breeds, and potential. When he brought out Dublet. I said, "I don't want to get on him." He reminded me of my "Internet Horse"—the one I didn't like that we bought from Europe a couple of years earlier. My mother insisted I try him, and within one lap around the arena, I looked at Christophe and said, "You need to get your breeches on and get on this horse. He is amazing."

I knew Dublet was something special, and I had an instant connection with him. But my mother insisted we go to Norway and try the horse we had originally come over to see. We got to that barn and walked up to the horse. I was in shock about how tall he was. He was at least 18 hands, and if you have ever been next to me, you know I am short. Christophe got on him first, for maybe five minutes.

He dismounted and said to me, "Good luck with that one." He was so strong I couldn't do anything with him. There was no contest between that horse and Dublet. Therefore, the purchase of Dublet was made.

Eventually, we got five-star judge and former U.S. Dressage Team Technical Advisor Anne Gribbons into the mix by bringing her in for clinics. I ended up training at her barn in Orlando for a season with my horses and trailering from her place to Wellington. I was there within a year after Laura Graves, who would be my 2016 Olympic teammate, had left that job.

When she rode in the 2016 Olympics in Rio, Kasey Perry-Glass made believers of those who were skeptical about her ambition to compete in the Games.

Anne and U.S. Developing Dressage Coach Debbie McDonald had watched Dublet at a show in Del Mar, California, so we sat down with them, looking for more information about how to get us noticed.

Dublet knew the Grand Prix, but I wasn't educated enough in it; he had some holes in his training and was a lot to handle. Therefore, we decided to start out in Small Tour so we could get to know each other in the show ring. In April 2013, Dublet and I won our first Small Tour CDI at Rancho Murieta in my hometown.

Debbie and Anne also suggested I get a horse that could be a schoolmaster to teach me the ropes in the Grand Prix ring. We called Andreas, who brought in Scarlett. She was so much fun—she knew everything and had so much energy. She was the one I would show in Grand Prix during the Wellington season while Dublet got more training.

Scarlett got me into the Grand Prix mix, starting in February 2014 in Wellington, so I could get experience. That was a big thing. She did everything I wanted her to do. In 2015, I went to Europe with her and was able to compete on the Grand Prix circuit there.

Meanwhile, I was putting pressure on myself about the 2016 Olympics, because it was something I wanted to do that was only a little more than 18 months away. I heard a lot of naysayers, people commenting, "It's not possible," or "That horse is way over her head." I felt as if I were on this cycle of constantly pushing for the Olympics, so when I made it, the whole thing didn't feel real until we actually got to Rio de Janeiro and I was in the opening ceremonies. My entire family, including my grandparents, came to Brazil to see me.

The opening ceremonies were my "aha moment" when I realized that I really made the Olympic team, but then we got to the venue and I had to focus. You can lose that excitement through the competition, and we needed a medal, so I had

to gear up. One of the ways I focus is by braiding my own horse. That gets me into the zone.

To be on a podium in general is awesome, but standing there with people you truly care about and grew a partnership with was so amazing. Being in the ceremonies with Laura, Allie Brock, and Steffen Peters, people with whom I was so close, seemed unreal. I still get emotional talking about it. I care about all of them so much.

I went through a depression after the Olympics, though. I had been fighting for that spot for a long time. I was so focused on what I wanted and the hard work I was putting in that when I got through with it, I was kind of confused about where I was supposed to be in my life.

Following the Olympics, we didn't show again until the five-star competition in Wellington, where we won the Grand Prix Special in February 2017. Next up was the FEI World Cup Finals in Omaha, Nebraska, where we were seventh, and then another European tour, finishing ninth in the Grand Prix Special at Aachen.

After that, I gave Dublet eight months off from showing and lots of pasture time. I wasn't sure what the future would hold, or even if we would try for the 2018 FEI World Equestrian Games. I also took a big break, started talking to a sports psychologist and getting my mind right again. Mentally, I was not prepared for getting shot up into the high performance world. It's really important to be mentally strong, but I also learned you can still hold on to that emotional side of you. It's important to stay true to yourself, and take care of your horse and your mind.

We didn't compete again until the end of March 2018, when we won the Grand Prix and the Freestyle in Wellington. We made it to the WEG less than seven weeks after finishing second in the Grand Prix Freestyle at Aachen. We were proud to be sixth individually in the Grand Prix Special at the WEG in Tryon, North Carolina, but so sorry

Kasey Perry-Glass was thrilled with Dublet's performance throughout her first FEI World Equestrian Games.

that weather problems meant the Freestyle was cancelled. The best part of WEG, though, was the team silver medal and being on the podium again with two of my Rio Olympic teammates, Steffen and Laura. We were joined at the championship by Adrienne Lyle, who is a good friend. I am so happy she was able to be on that team with us for her first World Championships medal.

Like Laura and me, Adrienne is a student of Debbie McDonald, who became the U.S. Dressage Team's technical advisor in 2018. I have trained with Debbie since 2015 and know she is a master. She can pinpoint anything in the test where you can get extra points and is able to work through almost any complication. She's very dedicated and compassionate.

I have discovered so much over the last few years, not just about riding, but about how to prepare for what I have to do. The more organized I can stay in my daily life and my routine, the better I am. I'm an over-thinker, so I try to simplify my life in any way that I can. Taking a breath and prioritizing what's going on is important. When I'm at a show, after my warm-up I feel pretty secure. I trust my training, I trust my coach, and she sends me in having full confidence.

DEBBIE MCDONALD

From Riding to Teaching— and More

Brentina and Debbie McDonald were not only the stars of U.S. dressage during their competitive heyday from 1999 to 2006, they also were acclaimed internationally. Highlights of their career include double gold at the 1999 Pan American Games and leading the way to team silver at the 2002 FEI World Equestrian Games—the best finish ever at that time for a civilian U.S. dressage team in a global championships.

Debbie and Brentina became the first American entry to win the FEI World Cup finals, played a key role in securing the bronze medal for the United States at the 2004 Olympic Games, and were also on the bronze medal team at the 2006 WEG.

When Debbie retired from riding and turned her efforts to teaching, her students soared under her guidance. Adrienne Lyle, who began as Debbie's working student, competed in the 2012 Olympics, the 2014 WEG, and the 2018 WEG where she was part of the silver medal team, replicating her mentor's accomplishment in 2002. Two other students of Debbie's contributed to that WEG silver in Tryon, North Carolina: Kasey Perry-Glass and Laura Graves (who also earned individual silver).

After serving as U.S. Equestrian Federation Dressage Development Coach, Debbie became USEF Technical Advisor at the end of 2018.

Debbie and her husband, Bob, live in Wellington, Florida, and Idaho where their son, Ryan, and granddaughter, Maris, also reside.

Brentina's style and willing attitude always put a smile on Debbie McDonald's face.

ressage has changed around the world since I began competing in international championships with my special partner, Brentina, at the end of the twentieth century. We've been seeing horses display much more movement than they did during the days when I was riding in the FEI World Cup, the FEI World Equestrian Games, and the Olympics.

There always have been great horses over history, but there were two horses, between the years 2010 and 2016, who changed everyone's perspective.

The sensational Dutch-bred Totilas, who won all three gold medals at the 2010 World Equestrian Games with Edward Gal, was a model for the change. There have been some great horses other than Totilas, but he was the one who made everybody go, "Wow!" This black stallion inspired people to start looking for the big, elastic mover, although his scope, the way he moved, and the suppleness he displayed in his range of motion is very rare.

Valegro, the next big star, was a power horse, but he was absolutely correct in everything he did, and so accurately ridden by Charlotte Dujardin for Great Britain that you could not deny him being the world's number one horse. He truly was unbelievable. The British were not in the equation of global dressage for most of the modern competition era. But led by Valegro and masterminded by Charlotte's mentor, trainer Carl Hester, who rode

Debbie McDonald with Brentina, taking a pasture break next to a statue of the mare at River Grove Farm in Idaho, which was their base during their competition days.

Debbie McDonald's training made an enormous difference for riders such as Laura Graves, so it was a seamless transition for Debbie to go from competitor to the U.S. dressage development rider coach and then technical advisor/chef d'equipe.

Uthopia, the Brits took the team gold at the London 2012 Games, with Charlotte winning individual gold. It served notice that the British not only had arrived, they also now dominated. Britain continued to be a factor through the 2018 FEI World Equestrian Games, where Charlotte rode a new horse, Mount St. John Freestyle, to earn individual bronze in the Grand Prix Special, and Carl was aboard Hawtins Delicato as they took team bronze.

After Totilas and Valegro, the perspective of everyone in the discipline became different. We saw what was possible and we started going after it. In the United States, our program changed as we became so much more focused on training and the progression from young horses through the elite ranks. The super horses also made the sport more popular with spectators who understood the excitement they generated. For us, it also had the benefit of bringing more riders into the lower ranks who could eventually rise to the elite level.

Meanwhile, however, prices have gone up along with the quality of horses. Average people can't afford to buy into a horse with much training, but they can if they get a syndicate together. That presents its own problems, such as who gets the owner's pass at a championship, so you need to get the right people involved. It's an amazing experience for a group of good people who love the sport and feel something for the rider they are sponsoring.

My advice to a rider is that if you work hard every day, show up on time, and give 100 percent to every single client, you will be surprised who jumps up to support you when the time comes that you have to find a way to stay with your horse as he becomes more valuable. Being approachable is important, and you have to show that the horse is not just a ticket for a medal but that you actually have an emotional connection with your horse. Prospective syndicate members understand that, and they want to be involved with good people. They look at what you're like on a day-to-day basis: Do you treat staff nicely? How well turned-out are your horses? Is your barn immaculate? Do you care about how it looks?

At the same time, as horses were developing in a different way, judging has changed, and keeps changing. The idea is for it to be more transparent for spectators, who began doing their own judging

Brentina's retirement ceremony at the 2009 FEI World Cup Finals in Las Vegas. With Debbie McDonald and her husband, Bob, are Brentina's owner, Peggy Thomas, Jane Thomas, and Peggy's husband, Parry Thomas, Debbie's longtime sponsor.

in 2014 with a special app. Although judges are often criticized, they are under intense pressure, and I believe they try to be honest and fair. It's not a job I would ever want to do, though.

I got into dressage in a backhanded way. I was a hunter/jumper rider in my early career, but after a life-threatening fall when a pre-green hunter fell on me as she took off over a jump, I switched to dressage at the suggestion of my husband, Bob.

"I thought you were dead," someone who had witnessed the accident told me.

I was the mother of Ryan, a five-year-old boy, and I couldn't take a chance that I would be

permanently injured riding over fences, so Bob's idea of finding an alternative to jumping made sense.

Getting oriented, I worked intensively with Olympic veteran Hilda Gurney, spending a lot of time on the longe line as she helped me develop my seat. I had to make up for lost time, although originally, it was just a way to earn a living with horses through buying and selling. I never dreamed that I would be riding internationally at the biggest competitions in the world.

My story is not typical as I celebrated my fiftieth birthday at my first Olympics in 2004, where the United States won team bronze. In our sport, age is not as much of a factor as it would be in track and field or volleyball—*if* you have the right horse and can keep yourself fit enough to compete.

I had an amazing career with my horse of a lifetime, Brentina. She was the one who put me on the map. We had 14 wonderful years competing together through the levels, with nine years at Grand Prix. I brought her along from First Level after my sponsors, Peggy and Parry Thomas, purchased her at the 1993 Verden, Germany, Hanoverian auction. On the day the Thomases bought Brentina, Bob told them, "This will be the best horse you ever own." And he was right.

After doing the basics at home and working with Steffen Peters, who would become my teammate on the U.S. squad, I went to Germany to work with then-U.S. Coach Klaus Balkenhol. Three months there improved my technique. My big breakthrough with Brentina came at the 1999 Pan American Games in Winnipeg, Canada, where we earned team gold and I took individual gold on this wonderful mare.

As the time drew closer for Brentina to retire at age 17, I was realistic about my own future. I decided to stop competing, seeing an opportunity to give back to the sport that had served me so well, and try to help younger riders get to the Grand Prix level. Of course, my dream was to produce Olympians who could ride for the team the way I did, and becoming the U.S. Equestrian Federation's developing dressage coach made it possible for me to achieve that aim. Moving up to be the team's technical advisor at the end of 2018 was the culmination of this process.

I feel as if I've become a better coach than I was a rider, but it's also more difficult in a way because when you're on the ground, you're not in control of the test. That's a different type of pressure than you feel when you're riding. My teaching style involves a lot of sympathy for the horse. You have to work with a horse's mind, not just the movements. It's important to keep him in a happy mindset, so he can enjoy his life as a Grand Prix horse. You can't do that if you're drilling all the time. I believe in mixing things up.

My approach involves trying to make the riders believe they can't fail by taking the pressure off and letting them do the best they can. You couldn't know the pressure they feel in that situation unless you'd been there. I wish someone had told me to get out of my head for a minute when I felt that pressure and, instead, think how far I'd come.

I have been extremely fortunate in my life, and the riders with whom I have worked are a big part of that. My coaching has enabled me to continue being part of the discipline and the international scene, but in a different way. I get the same pleasure I enjoyed while riding when I'm standing on the side at a show or championship, helping the riders have the same experience I did.

STEFFEN PETERS

My Heart Beats for the United States

A naturalized American citizen who grew up in Germany, three-time U.S. Equestrian Federation Horseman of the Year Steffen Peters is an Olympic, Pan American Games, and World Equestrian Games dressage multi-medalist. He has competed internationally with a distinguished roster of horses, including Udon, Lombardi, Floriano, Ravel, Rosamunde, Weltino's Magic, Legolas, and Suppenkasper, among others.

In 2009, he and Ravel, who was his best-known horse, became only the second American combination to win the FEI World Cup Dressage Finals. Later that year, they had the highest score in all three portions of the prestigious Aachen, Germany, show, making Steffen the first American to be named the Aachen Grand Prix Champion. It was even more memorable because he achieved the title in the country of his birth.

Ravel was the USEF's Horse of the Year for 2009. He retired after the 2012 Olympic Games, ending a career that included more than 40 Grand Prix wins, and was inducted into the U.S. Dressage Federation Hall of Fame.

Steffen and his wife, Shannon, operate Steffen Peters Dressage at Arroyo del Mar near San Diego.

When I was growing up in Germany, my sister, Anike, who was riding ponies, kept bugging me to come along. I finally gave in, and that's basically how everything started.

My father, Hans-Hermann, picked out our horse, the Dutch-bred Udon, as a three-year-old. He came from a farm near the pony club where my sister and I were riding. My dad purchased him for 3,000 guilders, which would be about $1,000 in 2019 dollars. While my father had a very good eye, we certainly didn't know at the time that Udon would someday be my first Olympic mount.

While I was growing up, we watched so many wonderful riders, which was both inspirational and educational. It was a golden era for the sport in Germany, with such names in the forefront as Reiner Klimke, Johann Hinnemann, Jan Bemelmans, Herbert Rehbein, and Harry Boldt. I don't remember ever missing a major show. My father

Udon, who took Steffen Peters to his first Olympics, was a special horse purchased by Steffen's father and imported to the United States.

and my mother, Doris, took us, and we always were quite fascinated with dressage.

After I turned 16, I had a chance to ride for Jo Hinnemann. At that time, Udon was only four or five years old and I came into Jo's barn highly intimidated. When I asked if I could board and train with him, I didn't hear from him for a couple of weeks, so I summoned my courage and called him. He said, "Yes, of course you can come."

At that time, however, his wife, Gisela, was a math teacher at our high school, and my uncle was the principal. So you can imagine that my wish to spend a lot more time at Jo Hinnemann's place rather than at the high school was not an option!

In 1983, I met San Diego-based trainer Laurie Falvo at Jo's barn, and she invited me to come over to the United States. Having learned about the American dream in our English classes at school, I was quite fascinated by the idea.

During my mandatory time serving in the German army, I took a week's vacation during early April 1984 to cross the Atlantic and work for Laurie. I fell in love with San Diego and decided when I was finished with my service in 1985, I would go straight back to the United States.

That's just what I did. Instead of taking the second week of vacation to which I was entitled, I got out of the service a week early. I was discharged August 1; by August 2, I was back in San Diego.

My parents were extremely generous and sent Udon with me. They were very supportive. My grandfather took a different view. Our six-generation family business was a clothing store, and in my grandfather's opinion, there should not even be a discussion about what I should do. As the first-born son, *of course* I would take over the business. My father, however, had a different opinion. He told me, "I didn't have a choice. I want my son to have a choice." I still appreciate those words today.

When I returned to California, I worked at a Swedish breeding farm, Sea Breeze, where I met Guenter Seidel, and I was training young horses, living in a $200-a-month garage apartment. I then worked for Guenter until 1991, when I started my own business.

It was risky. But I had such a great time during that first vacation in San Diego with the phenomenal weather and the laid-back California attitude, I knew if I was going to make it, I would want to make it in San Diego. It also was a matter of being in the right place at the right time because dressage was just starting to become a bit more popular in the United States and the California Dressage Society was growing.

Udon was at Fourth Level when he arrived in the States, and I didn't have a clue that he could possibly be a team horse. I sent Jo Hinnemann videos so he could track our progress and offer advice. Guenter was helpful, as were Dietrich von Hopffgarten's monthly clinics at Sea Breeze.

When Udon started the Grand Prix, I decided I wanted to change my citizenship and ride for the team. I became an American in 1992, and made the U.S. squad for the Atlanta Olympics in 1996.

The neat thing was that my dad got to see Udon's final performance at the Olympics in 1996. He knew the horse from the first day the saddle was put on him—when my sister and I started breaking him—until that day in Atlanta. The fact that a horse he "picked" made it to the Olympics was huge, especially since my father was diagnosed with a brain tumor shortly thereafter.

Udon had a very, very strong character. He was so set in his ways. I always knew he would give me 95 percent of what he was capable of, but if I pushed him for 100 percent, it simply wouldn't work. He would get too resistant and certainly would have a strong opinion about it. But as a team horse, he was incredible because you could usually count on him getting 70 to 72 percent, and in those days, that was a gigantic score. There's no doubt in my mind that without Udon being with me in the United States, my career wouldn't have been the same. You need a horse that puts your name out there. Of course, you have to work hard and ride a lot of horses and teach a bunch of clinics, but without a horse that gives you a certain reputation in the show arena, it is extremely difficult. Therefore, I am always thankful for Udon and certainly for the support from Mom and Dad. I also was grateful to have Lila Kommerstad become my first sponsor when she stepped up to purchase Udon in 1991.

At the Atlanta Olympics, reporters kept asking how I felt about riding for the United States. Instead of saying something, I wanted to show how I felt, so I carried a little American flag with me when I rode, then took it out and waved it after my final salute. The crowd loved it. I fondly remember that little flag poking me in my tailcoat during my ride. No one ever again asked how I felt about riding for America.

People also asked me whether I thought I could have ridden for Germany if I hadn't become a U.S. citizen. At that time, in 1996, Germany was so strong that it wasn't an option. Later on, however, when Ravel was at his prime in 2008, 2009, and 2010, I think he certainly would have been good enough to be on the German team, but of course, that never was a consideration. My heart beats for the United States.

My special relationship with Akiko Yamazaki and her husband, Jerry Yang, is well known. It's not just a sponsorship; it's a close family feeling that we enjoy. Through all the years we've worked together, we never had one single argument about anything. We have opinions that we share, but we don't argue about them. I'm one of those extremely lucky guys to have friends and sponsors such as Akiko and Jerry. People like them don't come around very often.

I met Akiko for the first time at a clinic in Santa Rosa in the 1990s, where she had a very

Steffen Peters performs a half-pass at the Rio Olympics in 2016 on Legolas, one of 10 horses he has ridden at the top level in international championships.

talented Thoroughbred-type horse. I took on Lombardi, another of Akiko's horses and told her, "I think we can make a nice Fourth Level/Prix St. Georges out of him. I think anything above that would be rather difficult."

I would have to say the horse had some talent, but also some serious character issues. If it hadn't

Peters had incredible results riding Ravel at the 2010 Alltech FEI World Equestrian Games in Kentucky, where he picked up two individual bronze medals.

Steffen Peters with Ravel and his longtime supporter Akiko Yamizaki.

been for Akiko, I wouldn't have taken Lombardi in training. Before we knew it, however, he got better and better. Lombardi wound up being an international dressage horse, won the national dressage championship, and was chosen as a replacement horse for me if I needed one for the 2008 Olympics.

What happened next was that in early 2006, because Akiko and Jerry were of Asian descent, they decided they would like to have a Grand Prix horse on the team for the 2008 Beijing Olympics, where the equestrian competitions were held in Hong Kong due to quarantine restrictions. That was when the search for Ravel began. We found him at Edward Gal's stable in the Netherlands and started training. He did his first Grand Prix with me in March 2008, only six months before the Olympics, so he wasn't the most experienced horse by the time we got to Hong Kong.

He turned out to be a star. The Grand Prix Special and Freestyle together counted for the individual medal there. Ravel was fourth in the Special and third in the Freestyle. We were only 0.3 percent behind the bronze medal. I just missed being the first American to win an individual dressage medal at the Olympics since 1932.

When I think about my time with Ravel, what stands out are the victory in the 2009 FEI World Cup finals in Las Vegas and the individual bronze medals in the Grand Prix Special and the Freestyle at the 2010 Alltech FEI World Equestrian Games in Kentucky.

Any time you can win a medal at home in a major championship, that is an incredible feeling, harking back to Atlanta in 1996. I still can't put into words what it feels like when the whole stadium goes nuts for you, and you know your horse did an incredible job and fought for you. Actually, I think translating that feeling into words almost degrades the experience a little bit. It is so incredible it is really hard to describe. Those are amazing memories no one can take away from you. Each was the moment of moments.

When Legolas earned 77 percent in the Grand Prix at the 2016 Rio Olympics—where the team won bronze—that was another special moment in my career, and for Akiko and Jerry as well.

There are horses that you ride perfectly who do a good job for you. With Legolas, it was always like rolling the dice a little bit. You could try to ride so perfectly, but that didn't mean he would do his one-tempis or wouldn't spook or act up a little bit. While I worried about whether he would be reliable for a team spot in the Olympic Games, the technical advisor and my former teammate Robert Dover was always optimistic. He was right. What that horse did in Rio for the Grand Prix meant just as much to me as the individual medals in Kentucky with Ravel.

Legolas was always that "little boy," and for him to deliver for the team and contribute to a bronze medal was extremely special. That came on the heels of winning the team and individual gold at the 2015 Pan American Games in Toronto, where the United States qualified for the Rio Olympics. And it followed double gold in the 2011 Pan Am Games with Jen and Bruce Hlavacek's Weltino's Magic. It was nice to repeat the accomplishment.

Legolas was the most nerve-wracking horse that I rode. I knew something could always set him off or distract him. He had this incredible talent for piaffe and passage, but when his attention wasn't there, all the talent in the world wouldn't help you.

After Rio, it was on to yet another chapter with a new horse, Suppenkasper. While I was still getting to know him, we competed in the 2018 FEI World Equestrian Games in Tryon, North Carolina, in front of another home crowd, and the squad

Steffen Peters flashes his characteristic smile and a salute after finishing his ride on Ravel at the London Olympics in 2012.

came through with the USA's first team silver dressage medal since the 2002 WEG.

It has been over 22 years since I first competed in a global championship for the United States, and looking back, I am so proud I could contribute to the sport and the country that I love.

GUENTER SEIDEL

The Horses in My Life

During the decade from 1996 through 2006, Guenter Seidel rode consecutively on three U.S. Olympic dressage teams and three World Equestrian Games teams aboard four different horses, contributing to four bronze medals, and one silver, and leading the way to a fourth-place finish for the American squad at the 1998 WEG in Rome.

Guenter is adept at picking up on the style of different horses to get the most out of them in competition. A native of Germany, he came to the United States in 1985 and fell in love with the California lifestyle, including surfing.

The naturalized American citizen's contributions to the sport have been recognized in many ways. The USET awarded him the Whitney Stone Cup for not only achieving a distinguished record in international competition, but also for his sportsmanship, serving as an ambassador for the organization and equestrian sports. As part of his service to dressage, he has been a member of the U.S. Equestrian Federation's Dressage Eligible Athletes Committee.

Guenter recovered from a devastating 2010 riding accident in which he fractured his pelvis and missed the trials for the 2010 WEG. After he healed, he went right back to competing. He trains and gives clinics across the country from his base in California.

Guenter Seidel had only six months to get to know the rather tricky Graf George before embarking on a successful quest to be chosen for the Atlanta Olympic team in 1996. "In some of the warm-ups, he almost bucked me off," Guenter reported.

From the time I was a child in Bavaria, I was always obsessed with horses.

My parents wanted me to have a career in something other than horses so I could earn more money, but I was determined to make riding my life. I did my *bereiter*, or apprenticeship, with Hertha Beck, a Bavarian lady who was very classical in her teaching and very strict. She called my parents after I finished a year of her three-year program and told them to pick me up, because I had no talent. I refused to go.

After I went to America and became a professional, we stayed in touch. She came to the Atlanta Olympics in 1996 to watch when I competed on the U.S. team. I still remember when I came out of the individual test with Graf George and was eighth, which was unbelievable; I was ecstatic. I had never competed in Europe or internationally before the Atlanta Olympics. Hertha came up and said, "It was pretty good, but you could have done this…."

She did shape my riding because she was so tough on us, on all the kids in her program. From this, I learned not to be discouraged when someone tells you that you can't do something or it's not going to work out with a horse because you have a bad day. You learn not to give up right away and stick with it to see where it goes. That paid off as I rode so many horses in my career, and persisted with the difficult ones until they came around and performed up to their potential.

I always wanted to go to the Olympics. Did I think it would happen that fast? No. There's always hard work and dedication, but there's also luck, you have to be in the right place at the right time.

I was at a major crossroads in my life when the resident trainer from the Rancho Riding Club in Rancho Santa Fe, California, told me she was moving to Oregon. The club was looking for a dressage trainer and she asked me if I wanted to do it. I got the job. One day, I was riding with Dick Brown, a club member, and we started talking. I told him about Numir, a horse I thought could take me to the big time, and he and his wife bought him for me.

Dick and his wife, Jane, became my sponsors for 23 years. Dick was very involved with the USET, serving as its treasurer, as well as co-chair of its National Endowment Fund and chairman of the finance committee. The main arena at the USET Foundation grounds in Gladstone, New Jersey, is dedicated to Dick and Jane.

Although Jane had nothing to do with horses when I met Dick, once the Browns bought Numir, Jane got involved. She educated herself and ended up knowing a lot. Jane organized things, ordered feed, coordinated transportation, packed for every trip to Europe, and put on horse shows.

The Browns were unbelievably supportive; they shaped my career. Nothing would have happened without them. I always have been thankful to them. They were great, great people. I appreciate everything they did for me and the horses. There was nothing spared for the welfare of the horse and giving me the best opportunities.

I never had my own horse. So all my life, I've ridden a lot of horses. That's where you gain experience.

The start of my international career came with Graf George. I showed him first in December 1995, the year before the Olympics in Atlanta. We had the trials early in 1996, and then the Games. So it basically was six months that I had to get to know him. He was very sensitive and hot, but quite experienced. Michael Poulin had ridden him on the bronze medal team in the 1992 Olympics. I'm kind of slow and methodical, and I think that suited Graf George's personality very well, since he was so eager to go. He had an engine that would never stop. That was something to get used to. In some of the warm-ups, he almost bucked me off. He shouldn't have been doing that at his age.

The dressage bronze medalists at the 2006 FEI World Equestrian Games in Aachen: Guenter Seidel, Debbie McDonald, Steffen Peters, and Leslie Morse with coach Klaus Balkenhol.

My teammate Robert Dover said, "You warm him up, and you think he's tired, but when you go around the ring and he hears the judge's bell, he will light up like a Christmas tree."

He was right. I had Graf George out for a good hour before one test in Los Angeles, the bell rang, and he pricked his ears. I went down the centerline and took my first turn for the extended trot, and he took off at a gallop. I learned what I had to do with him. I would ride 45 minutes in the morning on the day of a show and 45 minutes in the warm-up before the test. I felt bad riding him for so long in the warm-up, but I didn't practice any movements. I did a lot of trot/canter transitions—I wasn't torturing him with piaffe and passage. It was just that he had so much energy. He needed to be a little more settled. The timing of making this right is the key to your success with any horse. How much do you do to get the best performance out of your horse? You want him to have a spark, and you don't want him to be tired. But at the same time, you can't have him blow up in the ring. The right amount of warm-up is even more important with a horse that was as hot as Graf George.

When we got to the venue in Atlanta, he was quite fresh because I didn't work him much in quarantine. I was quite concerned. The stadium was huge, a little bit of an advantage for me because the stands were set so that spectators were far away. I warmed up for an hour in the morning. By the time we were ready to go, it was hot, but he certainly wasn't tired by any means. His temperament, combined with his ability to do all the collected movements, made him such a special horse. It was a great moment when I stood with my teammates on the podium as we received the bronze medal and listened to the crowd cheering for the home team.

Two years later, Graf George and I finished ninth individually at the World Equestrian Games in Rome, where we led the team to a fourth-place finish, just out of the medals. Graf George was U.S. Dressage Federation Grand Prix Horse of the

Year in 1998, when he also won the USDF Musical Freestyle Award and the Miller's/USET Grand Prix Championship.

As Graf George's career wound down, I needed another horse. This was Foltaire. When I got him, he was just doing a couple of single flying changes, so I needed time to bring him along. He was a bit of a handful, too, and pretty hot in his younger years, but never that explosive, and he suited my style of riding. I knew him for so many years, it became a really special partnership. I showed him at Prix St. Georges, Intermediate I for a couple of years, then he went as the reserve horse to Rome in 1998, after he was confirmed in Grand Prix.

When I rode Foltaire, I had to hike my stirrups up two or three holes so I could be in better proportion to his small size, since he was only 16.1½ hands. Luckily for me, he had a nice big neck and a beautiful front leg, which made him appear a little bigger.

Foltaire was my horse for the 2000 Olympics

Former show jumper Aragon had a special connection with Guenter Seidel: both were originally from Bavaria. They competed together on the bronze medal teams at the 2004 Olympics and 2006 FEI World Equestrian Games.

in Sydney. We got there a week and a half before the Games because of the quarantine issue. Two days before the jog, he colicked and had to be taken out of the Olympic venue to the clinic. I had decided to stay in the Olympic Village to soak up the atmosphere, and I was not close to the horses. I got a call in the middle of the night saying Foltaire had colicked. A driver picked me up and took me to the clinic.

Things were looking pretty bad when I got there. A team of doctors suggested they might have to do surgery and started shaving Foltaire's belly to prep him. Midge Leitch was our team vet at the time, and she was unbelievable. She talked to the doctors and pushed off the surgery, saying, "Let's not do it yet. Let's give it another half hour, another hour."

And in the morning, he finally did come around. Midge pretty much saved his life. Surgery would have meant he couldn't travel for a period of time and would have had to stay in Australia for who knows how long...and who knows how that would have come out? As it was, Foltaire only had to stay for another day in the hospital; then they told us we could take him back to the venue.

When we did, we had to unload him outside, and I walked him through the stable area on the way to his stall. I was overwhelmed at the way everyone there greeted us, with "Congrats," or "I'm glad he's back." It was an emotional moment, I have to say.

We had the horse inspection that day. I hadn't ridden him for three days, and the next day we had to compete. He was just a trouper. I'm sure he didn't feel that great, even though the vets said he was fine. When he colicked, he kicked a lot, and I think he got himself a little sore in his hind legs. I only did the Grand Prix and scratched the Special—it would have been too much for him, but he did contribute to getting the team bronze, which was just an amazing thing for him to do.

My next horse was Aragon. Klaus Balkenhol, who became the U.S. dressage coach and a mentor to me, saw him at a clinic in Bavaria. I come from Bavaria, so that was a nice coincidence. When I saw Aragon as a six-year-old, this horse that had been a jumper was really a lunatic. I went to try him, it was wintertime, and when you asked for a flying change, he would squeal like a pig and try to buck you off.

He was super-fresh and obnoxious. He'd come off the trailer and rear straight up. I needed to try him outside, since I didn't have an indoor, and he catapulted around. He was close to being dangerous. When he got nervous, though, he would piaffe for a 10. I ended up buying the horse—he wasn't terribly expensive because of all those temperament issues.

At the Rancho Riding Club, where I was based, there was no privacy and no quiet dressage ring. The first year I had Aragon, each day I wondered if I would survive. As I brought him up through the levels, he cleared the warm-up arena quite often, bucking and cantering around. He was out of control sometimes, but super-fun to ride when you had him. He was unbelievable, really light...a little similar to Graf George.

I had Nikolaus, who was my ride for the 2002 WEG silver medal team, at the same time I had Aragon. Both were going Grand Prix, but Aragon was only nine. In the selection trials for the 2004 Athens Olympics, Nikolaus was second, and Aragon, who I'd had for four years, was third. But since Nikolaus was more seasoned, we figured he would be the one for the Olympics. Aachen was the last qualifier. I had Nikolaus in the CDI five-star, while Aragon was doing the three-star Grand Prix. Aragon ended up winning that Grand Prix with a 74 percent, which at that point was a really nice score. He outscored Nikolaus by quite a bit. The selection committee decided Aragon would be the one to go to Athens.

Guenter Seidel waved to the crowd in his native Germany after finishing the Grand Prix Special on Aragon at the 2006 FEI World Equestrian Games. Guenter was 14th in that competition and 13th in the freestyle at Aachen in the country where he was born, calling it "a great end to my memorable 10-year run in the global championships."

He was young and inexperienced at that level, which showed up in his tests. But we did contribute to the bronze medal and even made it to the Freestyle. With a young horse, you have to be a little realistic. He wasn't going to be an individual medal horse at this point—he wasn't experienced enough—but to make the Freestyle was really great, and we ended up fourteenth.

Two years later, we were back at Aachen for the 2006 WEG, where we contributed to the team bronze medal. We also were fourteenth in the Special and thirteenth in the Freestyle at the world's most famous showgrounds in the country where I was born, a great end to my memorable 10-year run in the global championships.

MICHELLE GIBSON

Sending a Message for U.S. Dressage

The sensational Trakehner stallion Peron picked up where 1992 U.S. Olympic dressage hero Gifted (see p. 121) left off, delivering a record high score for an American horse in the discipline as he led the team to the bronze medal in the 1996 Atlanta Olympics under the guidance of 27-year-old Michelle Gibson. In the Grand Prix, she had a better score than every rider but Germany's intrepid Isabell Werth and the Netherlands' Freestyle star Anky van Grunsven. It was a watershed performance that served notice the United States was on the rise. "This is a turning point for us," Chef d'Equipe Jessica Ransehousen said at the time.

Michelle had been touted as a possibility for the first individual Olympic dressage medal won by an American since Captain Hiram Tuttle's bronze at the 1932 Games, and she would have earned bronze if Olympic dressage had run under its usual format. But 1996 was the first Games to offer the Freestyle following the Grand Prix Special, where Michelle had been standing third, and she wound up fifth in the individual standings.

After the Olympics, Peron's owners sold him and he went back to Europe, where the son of Mahogani stood at stud and resumed his competitive career. In 1999, he had an allergic reaction to an antibiotic shot and died. He and Michelle never reunited.

Michelle has continued riding, training, and teaching. She had two national champions at Small Tour, Lex Barker and Don Angelo. Based in Colorado during the summer, Michelle and her husband, Nicolas Hernandez, spend winters in Wellington, Florida.

With their elegant style and perfect harmony, Michelle Gibson and Peron led the U.S. team to bronze at the 1996 Olympics.

went to Germany in 1988 when I was 19, living with the family of an exchange student who had once stayed at our house in Georgia. I became a working student at the stable of noted trainer Willi Schultheis. Rudolf Zeilinger was his *bereiter* (apprentice) at the time and starting his own business. He needed help and asked if I'd be interested. That's how I ended up riding with him. I also cleaned stalls and tacked and untacked the horses, as most working students do.

I went home after two-and-a-half years and wasn't sure what would happen next. My father had a contact at the Atlanta Journal-Constitution, so they printed a half-page article about how I had been training in Germany, and that since the Olympics were coming to Atlanta, I needed a horse. Peron's owners, Russell Webster and Carole Meyer-Webster, saw the article and called me.

Peron at that point was living in a North Georgia pasture. They asked if I'd be interested, so I said I'd come and see him.

My dad and I drove up and I tried him. Honestly, at that time, I didn't know what I was looking for or looking at. I got on him in the middle of a field and rode him around. He tried to do everything I asked him to do, so we took him home. That was the beginning of Peron and me.

I paid all the expenses for him except shoeing and veterinary bills. About nine months after I got Peron, I took him to a clinic Rudolf was doing in New Jersey, and he offered to give me my job

The 1996 Olympic dressage bronze medal team *(left to right):* Robert Dover, Steffen Peters, Michelle Gibson, and Guenter Seidel.

again. I took it, and we did fundraisers where I was based at Applewood Farm in Alpharetta, Georgia, to get the money to ship Peron to Germany.

My dad always thought I'd ride in the Olympics, and it was a longstanding joke that by the time I got to the Olympics they would be in Atlanta, so it was karma when the city won the bid for the 1996 Games. In 1994 I was back at Rudolf's, still doing chores, including cleaning stalls, but I also was riding. We started showing and as each show was successful, we went on to the next. It kind of evolved. After you do well at a couple of the big shows, you think about the Olympics and say, "Maybe it could happen." In 1995, the year before the Olympics, I showed at Aachen, Germany's most famous show, where we were placed in the top six. The two most successful dressage riders in the world, Anky van Grunsven of the Netherlands and Isabell Werth of Germany, were there. I was all wide-eyed.

The U.S. Equestrian Team had been watching me, but it was kind of new territory for everyone with me living across the Atlantic. It was late winter or early spring 1996 before we started having conversations as we looked toward the Games. We agreed on the shows in Europe and the scores I'd need to qualify for the Olympic selection trials. So then it was: How do I get myself and the horse to USET headquarters in Gladstone, New Jersey, for the competition? Even though I was working nonstop, once going for six weeks without a day off as I rode 10 or 11 horses a day, I did not have the money to pay for our trip home. I had just enough money to live on, and that was about it. My parents didn't have the kind of funds that could cover travel for Peron and me, either.

Luckily, one of the German magazines did an article about how I had the scores to be able to go to the selection trials but didn't have a way to get there. That publicity prompted Guido Klatte International Horse Transport to step up, when even Peron's owners wouldn't do it, and sponsor the trip

The first time Michelle Gibson rode Peron was when she got on him in the middle of a field in Georgia. Her last ride on him took place at the 1996 Atlanta Olympics, where years of hard work put them in the spotlight.

to Gladstone for Peron and me. They're good people who did it because they ship horses for a living and I needed help.

I had never been to Gladstone, so it was very exciting and a whole new experience, including being introduced to potential team members I didn't know. I'd seen their pictures in magazines, but I had never really met them. I wasn't intimidated, though, because I was so driven. I had a lot of training and major horse shows behind me, so I was quite confident that I would do well. How could I not? I had put all of this time and energy and blood, sweat, and tears into this and had good results.

The first weekend of the selection trials, we won everything. The second weekend got difficult because something wasn't right with Peron, so I wasn't able to do the Freestyle on the last day. He became dehydrated in a heat wave. The New Jersey weather was so different from Europe, and he wasn't acclimated.

It was really a big deal as to whether they would be able to take me on the team if I didn't do the last day. Michael Barisone stood behind me and did what he could to support me during the stress of it all. I knew him from the days that I had been a working student at Michael Poulin's barn. In the end, they decided to take me. Peron was the only team candidate who had a total of more than 70 percent after the two weekends of trials.

Everybody on the team went to training camp at a farm west of Atlanta. It's hard when you take people who don't know each other and are competitive and put them all in a house together. It could have been a reality show! But we all did get along, and Guenter Seidel was fantastic: he was friendly and took me under his wing a little bit.

Rudolf came over two weeks before the Games so we could start training together again. It was important to me that he was there because of our longstanding working relationship. You have to believe in your trainer to be able to go in the ring confidently and do well.

There was a lot of pressure to get an individual medal, because we hadn't had one since 1932. I was the designated hitter for that. I had an unbelievable Grand Prix test, probably the best we had done in our career, and was marked at 75.20 percent. I was super-focused, super-driven; I felt, "We can do this." There's always this doubt and nervousness, "Oh my God, this is huge," but the drive and focus gives you impulsion.

Standing on the podium with my teammates, Guenter, Steffen Peters, and Robert Dover, felt unbelievable. At the same time, having the individual competition coming up, I had to focus on that. So it's like, "Hey, this is great, this is wonderful, but I still have this goal ahead of me." My whole family, my sisters, my mom and dad, they were all there. And it was really our hometown arena. So, no pressure!

I was always being asked, "Are you going to be the first American to get an individual medal since 1932?" My answer was, "I don't know." I was only 27; I just wanted to ride my horse. At the time, I don't think I realized how distracting everything was, including the fact that Peron's owners were getting ready to take the horse away. There were rumors he was going to be leaving me after the Games. It was tough for sure.

How do you know how to deal with all the politics when it's a situation you've never been in? We didn't have anyone helping us; Rudolf didn't step in. Maybe some of my story has helped make things easier for riders today—or maybe not. But if

so, it was worth all the heartache.

I'd had a great Grand Prix and a great Grand Prix Special, scored at 74.28 percent. I felt I had a chance for the individual medal. I was in third place before the Freestyle; I just had to get through it. And then life happened. We had a big mistake in the transition from the walk to the piaffe when Peron spun and turned around, and I knew that was the end of the individual medal. That was a behavior he came to me with. We worked through it and "fixed it," but when you have something like that, it's never completely gone.

Maybe I wasn't 100 percent on my game; it had been a long journey, he was tired, it was hot, there were a million things—like the perfect storm. Between everything, it just happened before I could catch it. It put me in fifth place immediately. That was a disappointment on everyone's behalf—the team and myself. When you're that close, it's a frustrating way to end years of work. There's no way around it.

The last time I saw Peron was the day after the Freestyle. He had a huge heart. He always tried, always—at least for me. We just clicked. I can't say why he worked so hard for me, other than the fact that I believed in him.

The sport is so different now than it was then—the horses, the riding, the judging, the expectations. It's like Dressage 4.0. But if I had the opportunity to go to the Olympics again, I would.

CHRISTINE TRAURIG
A Rush You Cannot Describe

Christine was involved in all aspects of horse care and training at her family's small breeding farm in Germany before going on to work at the Hanoverian elite sales. It was there that she met Bernie Traurig, the versatile U.S. rider who competed in dressage and eventing, as well as his specialty, show jumping. She came back to the United States with him in 1982 and embarked on a career as a professional horsewoman, eventually focusing on dressage.

Christine married Bernie, became an American citizen, and in 2000, she made the U.S. Equestrian Team's Olympic dressage squad. Riding Etienne as the anchor at the Sydney Olympics, she will always be remembered for a magical ride that clinched the team bronze medal for her adopted country. She also finished eleventh individually.

Christine, a California resident, is the mother of Natasha Traurig, a professional show jumper, and Lucas Traurig, a certified scuba instructor and photographer. She became the U.S. Equestrian Federation's Young Horse Coach in 2015.

When I think about it, competing at the Olympics probably was something I always dreamed of. But I also was pretty realistic about the fact that my chances for doing that as a German were very slim.

The number one reason was that I was born and raised as a barn girl in the country and my father was a breeder of Hanoverians. I was always more exposed to young horses that had to be marketed than to the opportunity to keep a horse for a longer period and train it up the levels.

Number two, the depth of quality riders going for the upper level with the goal to make a team was far more competitive at that time in Germany than here in the States. I owe this country, and I'm grateful for the opportunities that were given to me here. Of course, I also brought dedication, hard work, and passion to the table, but I was really rewarded by being in the United States.

At the age of 16, I had started working as a rider at the Hanoverian elite sales in Verden. When I was older, I did a full training cycle at the auction.

I learned so much there, during those years. It was wonderful, one of the best times of my life.

I came to the United States in October 1982. Warmbloods were just about to get really popular for the jumpers and hunters. Bernie Traurig came over to Verden that year and was looking at prospects. One of them was Amonasro, a horse I was riding. He ended up buying the horse and asked me if I would come to the States. If I liked it, he said, "Maybe you would like to work for me and train horses on the flat?" I had no idea what "on the flat" meant. It was embarrassing. I finally figured out it might mean the opposite of training over jumps!

When I moved to Wisconsin with Bernie, I didn't think I would survive the first winter there, it was so cold. Germany can get cold, but not *that* cold. I enjoyed working with the hunters and jumpers. Then Bernie started a sales business for dressage horses. We moved to California in 1986. At first, we were in San Marcos at Royal Oaks Farm. It was a wonderful time with Terry and Tracy Hodges, who had purchased the stallion Bernie competed in dressage and did the trials on for the 1998 World Equestrian Games. From there, we

cultivated other relationships, including the Saudi Equestrian Federation. Then we worked for Fahad Zahid, the founding sponsor of the Saudi equestrian team at Albert Court Ltd. I always had a few dressage horses to ride and compete. At that point, however, I did not pursue a career with dressage horses because we were busy with the jumpers.

I got my big break when Bob and Colleen Haas and their daughter, Elise, became clients. They were the ones who said, "We want to buy you a really, really nice dressage horse." That was Etienne. They were very generous in making that happen for me. They told me, "You do so much for us," which involved flatwork training for equitation horses, jumpers, and hunters. I would have never gotten the chance to have a horse like Etienne if I were not a rider who loved to train and solve problems.

Etienne came from Holland. Steffen Peters and his friend, dealer Norbert Gieling, found him for me. When Steffen was in Holland shopping, he called me and said, "I've got the perfect horse for you." I was a little biased, because I was born and raised in the Hanoverian area and my dad bred Hanoverians, so for my horse, it had to be a Hanoverian. For me, there were no other horses on the face of the planet. I told Steffen the horse he picked better be Hanoverian and dark brown. When he faxed me a copy of Etienne's papers, I was standing by the fax machine waiting to see the pedigree as it slowly scrolled in, the way fax machines worked during that era.

The first thing I saw on the papers was a W, which means Westfalen, an absolute no-no for me in those days. Then I looked at the bloodlines, and saw the horse had the Hanoverians Aktuell and Cardinal in his pedigree. I called Steffen and said, "We just saved this one, because there is Hanoverian blood in there."

Bernie and I went over and looked at the horse

Christine Traurig delivered a magnificent performance on Etienne during the crucial anchor ride for the U.S. team at the 2000 Sydney Olympics.

Overcome with joy and relief after clinching a bronze medal for the United States at the 2000 Sydney Olympics, anchor rider Christine Traurig hugged her mount, Etienne.

at a little farm out in the country. We walked into the stable and there's this horse—huge. I said to myself, "I sure hope it's not this one." But, of course, it was. They grabbed a halter and pulled him out of the stall, and there was this 18.1½-hand dark bay with a long face. I like long faces. We tried him, and in 24 hours, he was bought. It was really a match.

Etienne won the 1998 Intermediate I championships at Gladstone, and I was picked for a training grant to ride with Johann Hinnemann in Germany. That established a long-term mentor/student relationship. We were preparing for the 2000 Olympic trials, and I thought, "I'm never going to make this," because a lot of things have to become better, but in the process of making them better, you first feel things are undone and unglued. I was very doubtful, and my scores when I trained in Europe were not good at first. I told Jo, "I have to go home. I think I should start doing the trials at home and see how it goes."

At the trials in California, I got my confidence back a little. I had digested the information I got from riding with Jo and implemented it, which helped me get secure and confident. I made it onto the short list, and then there I was, back in Germany, doing the two final selection competitions, and I made it onto the team for the Sydney Games.

In Sydney, the atmosphere was wonderful. It was an amazing experience. I was the rookie on the team—Sue Blinks, Robert Dover, and Guenter Seidel were all more experienced. Jo was really great. He kept me at ease. I needed that. While we were training in Australia, it was made public that Etienne would be for sale after the Games, as per my contract with the Haas family. That, at first, shook me up a little bit.

Jo took me aside one day and addressed the

way I felt, that every time I schooled, people were watching, and the future sale of Etienne was on my mind. He told me, "You are here to ride for your country, your team, and yourself. We will worry about the rest later. I don't want you to think about it, and that's it. Be an adult. First things first."

I did as he suggested.

Jessica Ransehousen was our chef d'equipe; she went to the meetings and handled the draw for the order in which the teams would compete. We had discussed whether I should ride first or second for the team. Then after she went to the meeting about the team competition, she called me in my hotel, and said, "Oh, lovey, guess what? You are in the best spot: you get to go last. Everybody else will pave the way; you'll just do what you always do, look perfect and beautiful."

Being the anchor, however, turned out to be the key position in determining whether our team would get the bronze medal. When the race became close with the Danish team, Jo would not let anyone near me. I thought I was calm in the

Christine Traurig was the rookie of the 2000 Olympic dressage team; the other members of the squad had much more experience than she did. But as a perfect match with the 18.1-hand-plus Etienne, she was well-equipped for what would become a starring role in Sydney.

holding area before I went into the stadium as the last ride of the day, the last ride of the team competition. But then I saw the Danish team already was getting ready for the awards ceremony, expecting to claim the bronze medal.

Jo came up to me while I waited, as I felt Etienne's heart beating. We both were reacting to what was on the line. It was a nerve-wracking moment, but Jo slapped me on the thigh, getting my attention and breaking the tension. He said, as

he always did, "Well, what are we going to do? Up (in the poll), out (nose out), give it gas. That a girl."

I didn't know what score I had to get to secure the bronze medal. Jo wouldn't let anyone tell me anything. The fact is, though, when you ride for the team, you know within yourself you want to do your very best. Your commitment to the team is pressure enough, without thinking about the numbers.

As I look back on that crucial ride, I remember in the zigzag, which was so much harder than what we have to do today, thinking that was the best one I'd ever done. The piaffes were a little bit too forward. The extended trot was always where you felt with Etienne, "This is just incredible." Richard Davison, a dressage Olympian from Great Britain, was the commentator, and on the video he said, "Oh my God, look at that extended trot!" as Etienne flew along the diagonal.

Down the centerline to the final halt, in a situation like the one I was in, is a rush you cannot describe. I said to myself, "I can't believe it. I actually did this," and then I hugged my horse after the final salute. We had won the bronze with my score of 1,746, which gave us a total of 5,166 points to 5,144 for the Danes. So now *we* were the ones getting ready for the awards ceremony.

Being on the podium is an incredible feeling. Guenter and I are close friends professionally, and as we were standing there, I remember we held hands really tight, and I got emotional. I was hoping my father in Germany would see it on television, as he was ill and couldn't come to the Olympics. He died two weeks after the Games.

Other memories from that afternoon involve seeing my kids, Lucas and Natasha, in the stands, their faces painted with "Go Mom" and USA." They could see that all the sacrifices and travel and being away from them were worth it when we got the medal. In those days, it was tough to pursue those goals as a mother, especially when you definitely do not fall into that category of a "conventional mom" because you spend so much time focusing, concentrating, traveling. It's something I hope I was able to set as an example for my kids: when you're really passionate about something and committed, the kind of goals you can achieve.

After the Games, Etienne went to Europe to be sold, but he changed hands several times. At one point, a friend informed me, "Your horse is working his way back to you." That turned out to be right. I got a new sponsor and had a chance to compete

Etienne for another year and a half. It went so well I was named the alternate for the 2002 WEG in Jerez, Spain. We had lost a good seven months after he left me, but we got back together quickly. Even so, having that kind of a break takes a lot out of a horse. The brilliance of a performance has a lot to do with whether the horse and rider have a real bond, as Etienne and I did.

After our time together, he retired to a farm in Germany, where he got turned out with a bunch of broodmares in the pasture like a real horse, rolling in the mud. He would live another seven happy years after he stepped off the stage.

I love to train horses. I love to bring them from the ground up. That's how I grew up. They're like kids. It's the biggest thrill when they learn something, and they are confident and trusting, and you can develop their athletic ability. When the position as USEF young horse coach opened up, I immediately applied. My mission is that I develop a great depth in horseflesh that is trained here in America to field future teams. Actually, we are trying to develop beautifully trained horses that are made here in America for all aspects of the sport in our country. We still rely on the fact that people go to Europe and buy a horse that is already doing Prix St. Georges and up. That will always happen. But I'm hoping that we develop more depth in trainers who want to train the horses from the ground up. That is part of the culture in Germany, Holland, Denmark, and some other successful dressage countries.

I am passionate about the foundation. I believe by the time the horse is six, a foundation is laid for what we look for in the quality of a Grand Prix horse, as far as the horse being educated in the concept of collection. A younger professional who does not have a sponsor can start with a young one and maybe have a chance to develop a world-class horse. Buying a horse for millions of Euros must not be the only way.

SUE BLINKS

The Learning Never Stops

W hen Sue started the 1997 show season with Flim Flam, Robert Dover—who would become technical advisor of the U.S. dressage team after retiring from competition—predicted correctly, "Susan will go on to be a very big player."

At the 2000 Olympics and the 1998 and 2002 World Equestrian Games, Sue and Flim were indispensable members of the U.S. dressage squads. They contributed to the team bronze at the Sydney Olympics, where they were eighth individually, and stood on the podium as part of the history-making silver medal contingent at the 2002 WEG in Jerez, Spain, where they were seventh individually.

Sue went on to win international classes in California and Canada with her next horse, Robin Hood. She's had some very supportive sponsors over the years, including Louise and Doug Leatherdale and Fritz Kundrun.

Growing up in Rochester, Minnesota, Sue started riding dressage with Marianne Ludwig. She spent two years working with Walter Christensen in Germany. She also trained in Germany with Isabell Werth, who became the world's top dressage rider, and Dr. Uwe Schulten-Baumer. In addition, she worked with Klaus Balkenhol when he became U.S. technical advisor at the end of Flim's career. Even after decades in dressage, she still is on a quest to learn more.

After a sojourn in California, Sue moved back to Wellington, Florida, where she develops horses and trains riders.

The "flexible and uber-elastic" Flim Flam was a special partner for Sue Blinks as the two focused on representing the United States in international competition.

When I started riding the Grand Prix, it was so long ago that there was still one more zig and a zag on the centerline, the medium canter had a flying change at X, and there was also the back-and-forth rein-back movement. Dressage has come very far since then, with all the things that have happened involving the sport's rising standard, both nationally and in the world.

Remember what a star Alherich was at the 1984 Olympics in Los Angeles, where he and Reiner Klimke won double gold for Germany? Who can ever forget Dr. Klimke's impressive one-handed victory pass after the individual medal ceremony there?

But let's play Ahlerich and the quality of that horse and Dr. Klimke—who was a legend not only in his own time, but in forever time—against the standard of what's happening right now. It's just amazing how the sport has developed, the quality of the horses and their suitability. The level of sophistication where things have progressed in the twenty-first century is just astounding. At the same time, as was always the case, there absolutely has to be an incredible base and an incredible relationship with the horse, incredible timing, incredible concentration, and incredible physicality of the horse. It's hard to imagine how it all can keep getting better, but obviously it is.

When you think about some of the horses that were at the top of their game 20 years ago, nowadays they wouldn't get a share. Today's horses can be as obedient and hard working as the stars of two decades past, but they also have that physicality that's like, "Oh my goodness." I'm proud of my Olympic bronze and WEG silver medals. Those are things nobody can take away from you. And yet that would not have been the result for the same rides in today's rarified competitive situation. It's come so far—the quality of the horses, the quality of the riding, the standard. They're knocking it out of the park now. It's so impressive.

Even so, there's very little that can change the metrics of the interaction of two living beings. And what also hasn't changed is my belief in letting the horse keep his identity and progress in a way that is suitable for that particular animal, as opposed to some idealized version in the trainer's mind.

Isabell Werth has always been a total idol for me. I was lucky enough to spend some time training with her and her mentor, Dr. Uwe Schulten-baumer. Dr. Schulten-Baumer did not believe in training horses to a template. As he used to say, "When working with horses, you should keep in mind that the soul of the horse also has to contribute."

I've believed in emulating that approach, where the horse can hack, takes joy in his job, and is a well-rounded athlete, as much as possible. I think doing it this way affects how long horses can do their job, both mentally and physically.

Isabell, the most decorated dressage rider of all time, has the horses give their all, but they feel as if they're learning it as play. I was really impressed with that ability she has to let the horses be themselves and give them other things in their life as well as their job. That's always been a motivation for me, taken together with the time I spent working with Walter Christensen, giving me an old-fashioned German, classical, by-the-book base for my education, which resulted in these opportunities to go so many places with the team.

One of the incredible things about being on a team or in a situation of such happily sophisticated sport involves what you can learn. Traveling around was a real educational process, starting with the 1997 European tour when we went to Hickstead; Rome for the 1998 WEG; a tour that included Aachen in 1999; then Sydney, Australia, for the Olympics in 2000; the Jerez, Spain, WEG in 2002; as well as some Nations Cups in Europe after that. There is much you can glean from being with

U.S. bronze medal dressage team at the 2000 Olympics in Sydney *(left to right)*: Sue Blinks, Guenter Seidel, Robert Dover, and Christine Traurig, with Chef d'Equipe Jessica Ransehousen.

outstanding individuals in a closed circuit. That group includes your teammates and colleagues, but also, from one show to the next, the *crème de la crème* of the world that you can watch and try to emulate. You find out how many roads there are to Rome and how much you can pick up and assimilate from being in the midst of these people, the group with which you are lucky enough to travel. That's true whether you're already on a team or part of the tours that lead up to assembling the team.

It's all an incredible educational opportunity to be in this group of outstanding individuals with such achievement behind them. You decide what works for you and what doesn't, while solidifying your belief in what you're doing and traveling to these incredible events where you see the best

from other countries around you. You're in a vacuum with all these people, including the support team of the veterinarians, the farriers, and everyone else. It's an incredible evolution of your ability to be really good at what you do. The whole thing with these tours and the people you are around and immersed with is it's a big "soup" of learning where you can try this, try that. If you've got your eyes wide open, these opportunities are limitless when you travel with a team like that.

I learned a lot about horse care and management that supported my horses as I went through this learning curve. Some of it stemmed from watching other people fall into traps, as well as watching other people *not* fall into traps. The sun and the moon have to align how many times for a horse to be ready to go at a Games or a championship?

There are the training questions and the decisions you make on a daily basis about the physicality of what the horses do, when to call the vet, when to push through something. For me, certainly, it's not only the riding—the physical skills—but also the medical support, horse care, alternative therapies, and how they can bloom out to make a difference that is ultimately pivotal in success.

Flim Flam had his quirks, and as you must do to be successful, we learned to deal with them. He was a very sound horse, but if he had a hair out of place, he needed a day off.

It seemed as if there were no bones in Flim—as if he was attached with ligaments, he was so

At the 2000 Olympics and the 1998 and 2002 FEI World Equestrian Games, Sue Blinks and Flim Flam were indispensable members of the U.S. team.

flexible and uber-elastic. He required a lot of muscular support and needed acupuncture, but that wasn't something he would allow. So my veterinarian at the time, Dr. Carolyn Weinberg, managed him through the Olympics and World Championships by lasering the acupuncture points. In other words, it was a workaround—in effect giving him acupuncture treatment, but in a way he would tolerate. Flim actually loved undergoing the lasering. It got so when he heard the machine, he would go to a "happy place." The vet found the little missing piece for that horse, who was such a whiner and so unable to suck it up and get on with it! What Dr. Weinberg came up with is an example of finding something that helped keep him in such a place that physically, he could make it through all the stress of the Olympics and World Championships.

My belief is that if you do a really good job building the base, building the horse's confidence, and physically developing him, and do it all without pressure, it ends up where you want to be. If you look at where you want to be and you try to force it, that's not the best approach. If he's not straight, if he doesn't feel right in the hand, we need to look at the physicality of what's going on, we need to look at your position, your aids, your emotional state, the horse's emotional state. We need to think of what it takes to make things correct and logically build up to where we're going. It's easy for me to help people who think like that. Unfortunately, not everyone wants to look at it that way.

For my part, I've found the learning never ends. I love that. I'm working just as hard at learning now as I was in my days riding for the team. It's what floats my boat.

CAROL LAVELL

Gifted Was a Gift for U.S. Dressage

C arol Lavell and the statuesque Gifted made an inspired match, prompting the world to look at American dressage with a whole new respect when they made their mark on the international scene.

This combination served early notice of the potential in the partnership. Three years after Carol started working with the untrained Hanoverian, he was named U.S. Dressage Federation Horse of the Year at Fourth Level and Prix St. Georges. A year later, in 1988, Gifted was honored as the USDF Horse of the Year at Intermediate I. In 1989, Carol brought Gifted out at Grand Prix, and the pair made their debut on the European dressage circuit. Shortly after completing that tour, Gifted won an individual gold medal at the North American Dressage Championships in Canada. In 1990, Gifted placed eleventh at the World Championships, and in 1991, he was USDF Horse of the Year at Grand Prix. With Gifted, Carol was the first American to win the Grand Prix at the Hermes International Dressage Show in Goodwood, England. At the 1992 Volvo Dressage World Cup Final, Gifted finished fourth.

The highlight of Gifted's career came at the 1992 Barcelona Olympic Games, where Carol was sixth individually and led the United States to a bronze medal, the first Olympic medal in 16 years for the U.S. Dressage Team. They needed to score 1,524 points in the Grand Prix to bring the bronze home. Gifted's result was more than 100 points better than that, when he and Carol were marked at 1,629.

Named the 1990 and 1992 U.S. Olympic Committee Female Equestrian Athlete of the Year, Carol also received the U.S. Equestrian Team's Whitney Stone Cup in 1992, and was the 1992 American Horse Shows Association/Hertz Equestrian of the Year. At the 1994 World Equestrian Games in The Hague, Carol and Gifted finished ninth individually as the United States picked up another team bronze.

Carol, who graduated from Vassar College, worked in research with a biochemistry professor at Massachusetts Institute of Technology. She also taught lab research to students at MIT. The native of New England moved on from the classroom to turn her full attention to dressage, a discipline she has served as a judge, instructor, and guiding light, in addition to her outstanding riding career.

Carol, along with her friends and family, established the Carol Lavell Advanced Dressage Prize in remembrance of her mother, May Cadwgan, and in honor of her father, Gordon Cadwgan. Up to two $25,000 prizes are available annually from the Dressage Foundation to U.S. citizens in their quest to climb the "high performance mountain." No stranger to sacrifice in the name of her sport and turning down lucrative offers for Gifted in order to keep him going for the United States, Carol well understands what others go through on the road to their goals.

Carol and her supportive husband, Tom, who got married in 1968, were based for many years at a farm in Vermont before moving south and splitting their time between North Carolina and Florida.

When I went looking for a dressage prospect in 1984, I told a German horse dealer, "I want something special that stands out." He promised he would find it, and called three days later to say he had the horse. I told him, "I'm coming right away to see him. Don't sell him."

The bay marked with a big blaze and four white stockings looked very tall and hadn't been ridden, but he was the horse I had requested. This Hanoverian certainly stood out. I told the dealer, "You've got to get the tack on this horse, and I've got to be able to sit on him and look down, and see how the neck and shoulders fit into the saddle. You can lead me around."

He replied, "We'll have it done in three days."

And in three days, they hoisted me up there, led me around, and put me in a round pen in the indoor arena. This son of Garibaldi II knew absolutely nothing, but he was very cooperative and didn't do anything stupid.

The view from his back was quite impressive. He was turning four when I bought him, starting at what I thought would become a nice 17 hands and a little bit more. Then he grew into those withers, and the horse who was accurately named Gifted stood 17.3½ hands when he matured.

Although I had started out as an eventer, I never wanted to do Advanced Level combined training. I was afraid of the fences. I didn't like putting all my marbles in one bag and trusting the horse with everything. The fences were different in those days, and there were many rotational falls. It was a rough game when I was doing it. I liked it at the lower levels, but it was brutal at the upper levels, and I knew I couldn't continue.

"What are you going to do?" eventer Mike Plumb asked me when he took over the ride on my former horse, Better and Better (with whom he went on to win a team gold medal and an individual silver at the 1976 Olympics).

"I'm going to do dressage and I'm going to stay there," I told him.

I've had some good dressage horses—including Lilak, Much Ado, and In the Black—but Gifted was unique. His size, with his long stride and great presence, was an asset, but it also presented challenges. Everything had to be customized for him.

The U.S. bronze medal team on the podium at the 1992 Barcelona Olympics *(left to right):* Charlotte Bredahl, Robert Dover, Michael Poulin, and Carol Lavell.

We had pads made so the saddle would sit up far enough in the front but wouldn't run right over his shoulders. The saddle looked like a gondola, with a tall prow and a tall stern.

Rather than sloping, his withers dropped off into a very flat back, which then rose steeply for the hip. The base of his withers was constantly a sore place; it was difficult to keep the saddle where

it belonged. His saddle was always up against the neck. If I could have ridden with a crupper, the way kids do with their ponies, I would have. We had a special tree made for the saddle so it was wide enough to fit Gifted.

In 1992, everything was geared to the Barcelona Olympics, where the United States was hoping to win a dressage medal at the Games for the

Carol Lavell has played many roles in U.S. dressage, from ensuring the team bronze at the 1992 Olympics to judging, giving clinics, initiating a program to help up-and-coming riders, and being an inspiration to those who love the sport as she does.

first time since 1976. But with the Olympics, it's not just going there, riding a test, and coming home. It's a lot longer, harder, and more involved than anything you know. You're not just carrying a suitcase along with you.

For Barcelona, we were shipping horses below the 45th parallel, and it was hot. You had to cope with everything that goes with the Olympics, all the while giving the horses cool-water baths.

Then there's the pressure from other teams. You have to be pretty tough. You can't let people bother you. When Germany's Isabell Werth saw me with Gifted in Barcelona, she asked, "What's a nice little girl like you doing on a big horse like this?"

"Just lucky, I guess. Luckier than you…" I responded sweetly.

You have to have the pluck to stand up to them. They dish it out, but they can't always take it. You could be your own worst enemy if you let someone else get to you and unravel you. You have to be pretty tough and practice not letting other people bother you.

You can expect problems to crop up while you're on the road at the world's most important sporting event. It's not all fun and games at the Olympics. Two days before I was to compete in the Grand Prix, my bridle disappeared. That was very, very serious. There wasn't an off-the-rack bridle big enough to fit Gifted's huge head. We had one custom-made by Eiser's. Aside from that, we only had half of another bridle with extra-long cheek pieces.

After the bridle went missing, the coaches of all the teams got together and said, "This isn't going any further." The ground jury was horrified. Finally, somebody returned the bridle, but in the meantime, it was traumatizing.

Our team of Charlotte Bredahl, Robert Dover, and my coach, Michael Poulin, worked well together. We all knew none of us was in the running for an individual medal, so everything was geared to bringing home that team medal. The pressure was really on.

We had done a lot of work on polishing Gifted's piaffe while we were in Barcelona, so once we finished that segment of the Grand Prix test in my anchor ride, I felt I was home free. After my final salute, I punched the air in joy and relief, because I knew it was "mission accomplished."

I didn't cry on the podium, but I was overwhelmed, standing there and remembering how long it took to get to that spot, how hard it was, how much money it cost, and how long we'd been away from home to do this. It all comes to you when you're standing on this little podium, just for this thing that's hanging around your neck. I wouldn't do it again, but I'm glad I did it.

The Olympics is quite an experience, and I

The performance of Carol Lavell and Gifted at the 1992 Olympics lifted the United States to the bronze medal, the first time America had medaled in dressage at the Games since 1976.

took it all in. When you had an athlete's wristband, you could go anywhere you wanted. Going to the opening and closing ceremonies, watching the other teams when they're so good—I loved it and I went for the whole nine yards. It was meetings, demonstrations, not just hanging out on the beach. I even lived in the athletes' village. I wouldn't have missed it for the world.

A lot of people helped us, including the New England Dressage Association. My husband Tom, the man I call "Tom Terrific," assisted in so many ways. When my trainer, Michael Poulin, wasn't around to watch me when I was practicing in the run-up to the competition, for instance, Tom would stand in and tell me what he saw, using hand signals. If the horse wasn't round, he'd put his thumb and forefinger together. If his neck was too high, he'd put his forefinger in the air.

I flew home with Gifted, because he was so big that if he wanted to do something he could do it, and I needed to make sure he was safe. He was on a plane with llamas that were loose in pipe corrals. At first, Gifted was traumatized, then he was looking at them, wondering if they were going to stay in those corrals. Luckily, they did.

I like being around horses and I love teaching. I'm very proud of the $25,000 Carol Lavell Advanced Dressage Prize that is given through the Dressage Foundation. It hits the nail right on the head: You've got a good horse, you've got a good rider, you've got no money. That's no good! The grant is a big help. There are lots of horse and rider combinations, but when one finally hits the jackpot, that's it for our team—they're there.

EVENTING

THREE-DAY EVENTING (WHICH ACTUALLY IS RUN OVER FOUR days at most major competitions) was developed as a complete test of an all-around military horse. It is still called "the military" or *concours complet* in some quarters, but now generally just is known as "eventing."

The initial dressage phase tests obedience and the ability of a horse to respond promptly and efficiently to commands on the drill field.

The second segment involves not only endurance, but also a degree of speed, and the ability of the horse to clear what once were natural obstacles—such as tree trunks, walls, and ditches—but now have become more refined. The idea for the cavalry was to see how well a horse would handle the demands of getting his rider, carrying an important message, to the front lines. There are penalties for refusals and exceeding the optimum time, but a fall of horse or rider eliminates an entry.

On the final day, show jumping is geared to determining whether the horse is sound and fit to go on after the previous phases. Knockdowns, refusals, and exceeding the time allowed are penalized.

Women were not allowed to compete in Olympic eventing until 1964, when American Lana du Pont broke the ice and contributed to her team's silver medal.

Thoroughbreds once were the favored breed for this sport, but the increased importance of the dressage and show jumping phases, along with the shortening of the endurance segment, means that Warmbloods are now the horse of choice for many riders.

PHILLIP DUTTON

Doing It Right in Rio

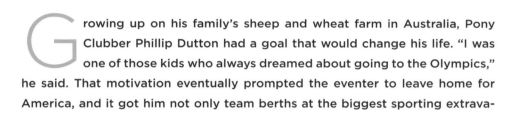

Growing up on his family's sheep and wheat farm in Australia, Pony Clubber Phillip Dutton had a goal that would change his life. "I was one of those kids who always dreamed about going to the Olympics," he said. That motivation eventually prompted the eventer to leave home for America, and it got him not only team berths at the biggest sporting extravaganza on earth, but also several medals.

Riding for the Australian squad, he earned team gold at both the 1996 Olympics in Atlanta and the 2000 Games in Sydney. In 2005, he was named the Number One FEI World Eventing Rider and was Number Two in that ranking in 2016. After becoming an American citizen in 2006, he earned team gold and individual silver at the 2007 Pan American Games in Rio de Janeiro, a location that nine years later would be the scene of his greatest personal triumph. Phillip received his first Olympic individual medal, a bronze, at the 2016 Rio Olympics. A U.S. Eventing Association Rider of the Year more than a dozen times, he lives at True Prospect Farm in Pennsylvania with his wife Evie, twins Olivia and Mary, and stepdaughter Lee Lee.

There are always plenty of hoops, trials, trot-ups, and final preparations you have to go through before you get to the Olympics. But when I made the Australian eventing team for the 1996 Atlanta Games, I remember being in the truck with the horses, driving into the Olympic Park at Conyers, Georgia, and thinking, "I've finally done it." This was one of those ultimate dreams come true.

When I left Australia for America in 1991 with one horse and only a few thousand dollars, my departure was not that popular with my family. They kind of felt as if I were abandoning ship. So I didn't have much choice but to succeed, because I wasn't going to go home and say, "I made a mistake and I'm coming back." I had to find a way to make it work. And it did, as it does a lot of times when you're motivated like that.

Phillip Dutton's early riding days were spent in true Aussie style with the Nyngan Pony Club in Australia. Here, he's second from the left next to Warrick Simpson *(far left)*. The other riders *(left to right from Phillip)* are Narelle Woodlock, Gary White, and Tom Ward.

It's interesting how much things have changed in eventing, just since my first Olympics. In Atlanta, there were two different competitions, one for the individual medals, the other for the team medals. You had to carry a minimum amount of weight, 165 pounds, a requirement that was eliminated when a campaign was started in 1997 by Carol Kozlowski (who became president of the U.S. Eventing Association two decades after that). The Atlanta event was long format, including roads and tracks and a steeplechase. Things began changing as the sport started evolving in the twenty-first century. But in Atlanta, there was no flying change in the dressage, a test that was simpler than it is today, and the show jumping was more basic.

After cross-country, our team was so far in the lead, I thought I would call my parents in Australia, even though it was one in the morning there. Not only was this before live streaming on cellphones, I had to go to a pay phone to get in touch with my folks. Despite the hour, my dad answered, saying, "Yes, I am the father of that boy." He'd had a lot of calls from reporters, you see, and it was a proud moment for him.

It resonated with me then how far-reaching the Games were. Up until you get to the Olympics, you're just in equestrian sport, and it's a pretty small sport compared to the rest of the world. But with the Olympics, the whole world watched.

When I got to Conyers, I had it in my mind

that the Olympics would be so different. But the technical delegate was the same, the judges were the same, the riders were the same ones I'd been competing against. After our team won the gold, though, everybody told me, "This will change your life." But nothing ever happens really quickly. I remember getting home and the phone wasn't ringing off the hook with people sending horses to me. It takes time. On the other hand, it certainly didn't hurt.

The next Games, Sydney, in 2000, were run in the long format, with a 13-minute cross-country course. In Atlanta, I was on my longtime partner, True Blue Girdwood. For Sydney, I was a fraction lucky to get picked, since I was on House Doctor, an eight-year-old who had completed only one three-star. Wayne Roycroft, who was running things for the Australian eventing team, had a lot of faith in me, and luckily, House Doctor went well.

Being in Australia in front of everybody I had ever known might sound like pressure. But it's kind of what you do—you just go out there and don't worry about that so much. Even so, it doesn't get much better than winning a gold medal for Australia with all my friends and family watching. Everybody thought it was one of the best Olympics ever. The Australian people really got behind it and welcomed everybody. It wasn't over-the-top expensive the way they did it.

Sydney had a tough cross-country track and some horses got hurt. So from then on, the FEI had quite an influence changing the difficulty of the cross-country and toning it down.

At Athens in 2004, the first short-format Olympics, the cross-country was more on the side of a two-star track than a four-star course. I realized then that things were changing as far as the Olympic Games and the way eventing was being run. I was not, however, a big supporter of the long format. It wasn't a bad thing to train and practice a little like that, but to me, the roads and tracks

and the steeplechase were not challenges that we needed in the sport. Dressage, cross-country, and show jumping are the three phases that are the proper test. I do believe the standard of the cross-country needs to be kept. Certainly, in Athens, it was a real step down. The FEI and International Olympic Committee want more nations to participate, but there has to be a way in course design to test out the best riders and horses and have the jump options involving time faults for less experienced riders so they can compete and stay safe. I felt show jumping played more of a role in Athens. The technicality of it all started to amp up a bit, and the dressage continued to improve.

By this time, the team and individual competitions were combined, with just a second show jumping round to decide the individual medalists. I rode Nova Top, an English-bred horse who hadn't been in the right hands for quite a while. It was not a great time for the Australian team, which finished sixth.

I changed my nationality after Athens, deciding that since I was based in the United States and my family was American, it was time for me to become an American, too. The biggest difference between riding for Australia and riding for the United States is the support crew and the enormity of what is behind the American team. In Australia, if I needed a veterinarian, I would have to find my own, and the same with a farrier. While so much is done for U.S. riders, I'm glad I grew up having to figure it all out myself. There's nobody there to tell you how much to gallop or how much flatwork to do. In Australia, the emphasis is back on the rider to get the results himself. Although we had access to the fitness people, nutritionists, and psychologists at the Australian Institute of Sport, I was a bit out of the loop, being in America.

The 2008 Games in Hong Kong, my first Olympics riding for the United States, involved very hot and humid conditions, even more so than Atlanta,

An individual bronze medal for Phillip Dutton at the 2016 Rio Olympics, where he rode Mighty Nice for the United States, was a special honor for the man who had been part of two Olympic team gold medal efforts for his native Australia.

Phillip Dutton was the only U.S. eventer to medal at the 2016 Rio Games. He was "ecstatic" to be on the podium with the individual bronze around his neck, calling it "a grand achievement and the most meaningful individual moment of my career thus far."

that fast. He gave it his all, yet was still getting time faults. He couldn't have done much better, but it wasn't a great time for the U.S. team. The shining exception was Gina Miles' individual silver on McKinlaigh, which showed you can train from America and still be world competitive, as she was.

For London in 2012, I had sort of a last-minute horse in Mystery Whisper. While Mystery was an exciting mount who could really move on the flat and was good on cross-country, we didn't have a great, great partnership, and it caught up with us in the show jumping. I will, however, remember London as really well done. British crowds are so knowledgeable. The cross-country course designed by Sue Benson was not overly big. She was quite limited by being in the park where they weren't allowed to have permanent jumps.

For the second time in a row, the team didn't medal. We hadn't been on a winning trajectory. In those days, everyone kept secret what they were doing. There was not enough back and forth among riders and staff, so it became more a competition about getting on the team than preparing well for the Games. Everyone was on eggshells for six weeks leading up to naming the team, because they were trying to prove their horses' soundness and how well they were going, rather than addressing some of the issues and problems that needed solutions.

London made me realize what an incredible first two Olympics I'd had. I took it for granted that it would keep going, and it didn't. It's tough even to complete the competition as a team. With 2014 World Equestrian Games course designer Pierre Michelet also laying out the cross-country in Rio,

where we had learned new techniques for cooling our horses. Luckily, the Hong Kong Jockey Club spared no expense for the horses, with air-conditioned stalls and air-conditioned vans. But training and competition had to be done either very early or very late, since from 10:00 a.m. on, you'd be dripping with sweat.

Earlier that year, Connaught had won the Kentucky four-star, and I was selected on him for Hong Kong. It was not an ideal place for him to be; he did not have a strong constitution and he wasn't we knew going in that things would be difficult, since we hadn't ridden that many of his courses, and the 2014 WEG route was a real cross-country battle, complicated by three inches of rain. It was a bit of a heads-up for what was coming at Rio, and there was a general feeling through the eventing community that Brazil wouldn't be quite as easy or as "soft" an Olympics as some of the more recent Games.

In hindsight, I think we could have prepared a little better with cross-country training. The horses were picked and the training was geared for the more conventional Olympic Games, rather than a cross-country that would be a little tougher than the last three Olympics. The thing that comes to mind with Pierre's courses is that the horse has to hold the line. If you have a forward-going horse, he learns to do it.

As I expected, the cross-country was by far the biggest influencer on the event. Once we walked it, everyone realized it was going to be a cross-country Olympics. We had four good cross-country riders. Boyd Martin rode smart and took some options. Clark Montgomery's horse had a bad day and didn't want to play, so he didn't finish. We were still in with a great shot until Lauren Kieffer and Veronica had a fall. That was pretty gutting, because then we were out of it as a team. As soon as Lauren fell, I changed my strategy, realizing the team and I had nothing to lose. I decided to go for it. If Lauren hadn't had that trouble, I might have had to go cautiously to make sure I had a clear round. But that was no longer the case, and I set out as quickly as I could on Mighty Nice. But Fence Six was a corner we hadn't seen before. It looked on the approach like a normal type of jump, but in the last stride, the angle of the jump went out in such a way that it kind of surprised the horses. Mighty Nice had a quick reaction. He saw the backside of it and tried to drift away from that. I held on for dear life and bless his heart, he stayed inside the flags. But then because of the awkwardness of our departure over Six, I had to take the slower option at the next fence. I knew I'd stayed inside the flag at Six with my body and his shoulder, but there's always still the question—what would the jump judge say?

I had to make up time, and then I heard whistles blowing in front of me. Oh no, I wondered, were they trying to stop me? Then I saw it was just crowd control. Mighty Nice continued to fly around the course and came up the scoreboard quite a long way. This was a little bit of full circle from Atlanta, where cross-country played a big role.

We went into the show jumping in fourth place, with one time penalty in the first round and a rail in the second. But Christopher Burton of Australia, the leader after cross-country, had two rails in the final round, which got me onto the podium with a bronze. It was a great moment for the horse. The late Bruce Duchossois, who owned him, would have been proud of him. I was ecstatic with third; it was a grand achievement and the most meaningful individual moment of my career thus far.

BOYD MARTIN

From Down Under, Up to the Podium

A native of Australia who moved to the United States in 2007, Boyd has created more than 20 different four-star horses and ridden in more than 40 four-star events. (Note: In 2019, the events formerly designated as four-stars, which had been the highest level until that time, became five-stars as all events were reclassified.) In Australia, he was long-listed for the 2000, 2004, and 2008 Olympic Games. Prior to that, he represented Australia at the Young Rider level against New Zealand at the Trans-Tasman Three-Day Event. The highlight of his competitive career in Australia was winning the last long-format four-star event in Adelaide in 2003 at the age of 23.

He spent his first two years in the United States working as assistant trainer to Olympic multi-medalist Phillip Dutton before striking out on his own. Boyd has been on every championship team since he started riding for America in 2010, with a shining moment being team gold at the 2015 Pan American Games. He enjoys the rare distinction of having competed in every four-star event in the world, including the Olympics and World Equestrian Games.

Boyd and his wife, Silva, a Grand Prix dressage rider and trainer, live at Windurra in Cochranville, Pennsylvania, with their sons, Nox and Leo, as well as several cats—Boyd's second-favorite animal.

Growing up in Australia molded me and lit my fire, especially with two parents who were Olympians. Needless to say, sport was very important to us.

My mother, Toy Dorgan, was an American speed skater in the 1968 Grenoble, France, Winter Olympics. She was a good mother whose mantra is "winning is fun," making sure we trained hard and gave our best when competing. My father, Ross, who represented Australia in cross-country skiing at the Grenoble Games, was a bit more of a humble sportsman. When my sister, Brook, and I were born, he took down his trophies and medals and put them in a box because he didn't want his kids

Boyd Martin won his first team medal at the Pan American Games in 2015 when he was on the gold medal squad riding Pancho Villa (right), with Marilyn Little, Phillip Dutton, and Lauren Kieffer.

feeling like they had to live up to something.

Horses were a huge part of our family life, but I was also encouraged to participate in other sports, including cricket, rugby, tennis, and sailing. We had three acres on the outskirts of Sydney, and I went to Pony Club every Sunday. It was a long day, because I had to ride an hour to get there and an hour to get home. We'd spend the whole morning riding on the flat and jumping. I'd tie the pony to a tree when I ate lunch, then we'd barrel race in the afternoon.

My first pony was Willy; his show name was Willy Do It. I must have been about 14 when I entered my first horse trials at the St. Ives

showground. I did a pretty ordinary dressage test, fell off twice in cross-country, and once more in show jumping. I think I finished on 380 penalties. While it wasn't the best start for my eventing career, obviously, I could only improve from there.

But first, I needed a horse, since I was outgrowing Willy. There was a 12-year-old chestnut Thoroughbred for sale. His name was Flying Doctor, and he had never evented. When I tried him out, he came to the jump, stopped, and I fell over the top of him. My parents didn't know that much about horses, but Dad said we should buy him, because unlike Willy, he didn't run away when I came off.

When I competed, I wore my high school's blue-and-white rugby jersey, and I still do today. My mum has to go to the high school I attended and buy another every time I need one.

At school, I was a little wild and out of control. Obviously, I wasn't going to be an accountant. Lucky for me, I loved sports. Not once did my parents say I should consider university. It's such a big deal in America, but it never crossed my mind to think about that. So when I finished high school at age 17, I packed my bags and moved into a bunkhouse at the New South Wales Equestrian Center with 14 other young riders, including Chris Burton, who went on to ride for Australia in the Olympics, and Jock Paget, who did the same for New Zealand. At the Center, where we worked seven days a week from 6:30 a.m. until midnight, I met a guy who really changed my life: Heath Ryan, an absolute lunatic, who I can remember screaming and yelling because he was so passionate about his sport and trying to get the best out of the riders. A dressage and eventing Olympian with two team gold medals to his credit, Heath was one of the

hardest-working blokes I ever met. When I groomed for him at the Werribee CCI three-star, he had three or four rails down in show jumping. After we got back from the event at three in the morning, following a 14-hour drive, he built a combination in the indoor like the one where he had the rails down and jumped every horse in the barn through it.

At 19, I did my first four-star on Flying Doctor. He was probably 19, too. We went down to Adelaide, 22 hours away. Heath refused to let anyone else drive, even though he was rolling the window down trying to keep himself awake. I didn't have a clue as to what I was doing when we went to Adelaide. I didn't even know about walking the distances between fences to try and figure out the striding. Ian Stark, the British Olympian was there, and I got a photo with him. We were all a bit star-struck.

I fell in love with riding in four-star events and finished fifth in that first one, a huge accomplishment that was a milestone for me. Finally, I was picked to ride for Australia and got lessons with Wayne Roycroft, Australia's national eventing coach. When I had my first sniff at a team, there were six in our training camp, and they had to select four of us. I always dreamed of representing Australia, and when I was left off the team, it was a heartbreaking moment for me. It wouldn't be the last one.

I needed to travel so I could learn more. I did three months in Germany at a dressage stable in

Hamburg, then went to Paul Schockemohle's to do show jumping. A year or two later, I got a job as a "horse breaker" in Japan. It was great money, but although I'd played around with young horses, I hadn't ever started one. Going over on the plane, I read Monty Roberts' book. When I went to the stables, they brought out this French Thoroughbred they'd just imported. People with video cameras came to see this master horse-breaker from Australia. I had no idea what I was doing, but I walked in the ring and started stroking the horse's neck, then got a saddlecloth and rubbed the horse with it. Finally, I got on the first of 40 horses I would break in there, and I was like, "Yes, I've done it!" So it went fine, but for three months in Japan, I couldn't talk to anyone, because they didn't speak English.

Back in Australia, the first guy who gave me a horse to ride had just gotten out of maximum-security prison for attempted murder. We always went to the farm via the police station because he had to sign in every day. But when you're starting out, you grab whatever horse comes your way.

I got the ride on a Prix St. Georges dressage horse that was barking mad. The owner wanted me to take the horse to a show that was a six- or seven-hour drive through the Outback, because she thought if we got a good result there, she would be able to sell him. It was raining, he put his head down and bucked, and the reins slipped through my hands. I fell off underneath him and broke my knee in nine places. It took an hour for the ambulance to get there. There were no doctors; there was no pain medication. They took me to a hospital where I was put in a room with a prisoner who was handcuffed to a bed.

In those days, I charged $20 a ride, so I told the horse's owner she owed me $620 for 31 rides. She didn't think I should charge for the dressage show, telling me, "You weren't really on him that long."

By 2003, I had ridden in several four-stars and made the top 10 a couple of times. But I always went around with 5 or 10 time penalties. At Adelaide that year, I told myself, "You've been an also-ran a few times, now you need to make a decision. If you're going to be any good, you're going to have to learn to have a crack at this."

I didn't have a coach or anyone to help. I realized that if you're going to be a winner, you have to risk it. I made a conscious decision to follow my own advice. I remember going as fast as I could to the first fence with True Blue Toozac. I wound up one second over the optimum time and had just one rail down in show jumping to keep me in the lead. I was 23 when I became what I think was the youngest person ever to win a four-star, and a proud moment was when I saw my dad in the crowd.

That was also the first time I met Erik Duvander who was over there coaching the New Zealand team. He eventually became the eventing performance director for the U.S. team. I was discussing going to America and riding in the Kentucky four-star. It was just before the 2004 Olympics, and I wanted to be on the Australian team. The Sydney CIC three-star was a selection requirement. I felt like a real contender until my horse tired badly halfway around the cross-country. He left a leg, tumbled over and bowed a tendon. Walking the horse all the way back to the stables, I was just crushed.

Looking back on it, I wasn't ready to go to the Athens Olympics. While I'd won a four-star, I was green. I don't think I would have been good at the Athens Games. It probably was just as well I didn't make the team. I wasn't trained and seasoned enough. I probably wasn't sufficiently focused, either.

Luckily for me, a nice-looking German woman came over about that time and cheered me up. You don't get too many Europeans in Australia. I gathered my courage and asked her to the races with a group of guys. It was a terrible idea. We took her to a restaurant and ordered wine, before realizing we didn't have any money. But she forgave me, and we got married. It's hard to find a life partner who understands our game. Silva's been incredible in her impact on my life, and she settled me down a bit.

By 2006, I'd done every three-star in Australia and New Zealand and felt there was something else out there for me. I boarded a cargo plane with a horse named Ying Yang Yo who was off the track, and headed for America. A friend of mine knew Phillip Dutton and arranged for me to go to his True Prospect Farm. Phillip wasn't there, but I met his wife, Evie, who was lovely, and Dr. Kevin Keane, who would become my vet.

I remember going to my first event in Southern Pines and not knowing one person. Then I met Phillip for the first time, and he offered to walk the course with me, making discreet suggestions about handling the fences and strategy.

After my parents and Heath, Phillip made the biggest change in my life. Training at Phillip's was the polar opposite of training with Heath, where he'd be yelling and you'd jump the same exercise 50 times. Ying Yang Yo wasn't a good show jumper and Phillip got him jumping great. When I got through the Kentucky Three-Day in eleventh place, I told Phillip I'd like to come back to America.

"Why don't you work for me?" he asked. Silva and I had a good business in Australia, but it was time for a move. I went back and told Heath I was moving to America. I think he was a bit crushed. He thought you could do it from Australia, but it was just too remote. Silva sold everything we had— the furniture, the horses. We had to start from scratch again.

Silva and I married just after Christmas, right before we were going to America. Then she got stopped at the airport because she had applied to be an American resident, and it turned out she had to stay in Australia until her application was approved. So she went to live with my mum, and I got on the plane.

Because my mother was American, I had dual citizenship, so I had no trouble getting into the country and hit the ground running. Phillip tweaked things for me, and I learned a lot watching him every day, such as how he selects horses and treats owners well. He's been a wonderful mentor for me and one of my best friends.

In 2009, I had to make a pretty tough decision about which country I would ride for. As a young kid in Australia, your idols were Australian event riders. I always had an American passport, so it wasn't like I was changing countries. But I was annoying the hell out of Phillip, riding around the indoor arena and always asking him, "What should I do?"

I made the right decision. I knew from the beginning America was the country I would live in for the rest of my life. My first real team experience came in 2010 with Neville Bardos, who was fourth at the Kentucky Three-Day. At the Georgia training camp for the team that would go to the Alltech FEI World Equestrian Games at the Kentucky Horse Park, Mike Huber, chairman of the selectors brought in all 12 riders who were team candidates. He told everyone how hard it was to make a decision about who should be on the squad.

Mike called out the four names, including mine. Inside, I was thinking, "I've done it!" but then I glanced over at friends who were just shattered at not making it. I hadn't forgotten my experience in Australia when I wasn't picked for the team. The WEG ended with me as the top-placing American rider, finishing tenth on Neville.

The following year, we had one of the most terrible things happen. I was renting a barn at Phillip's, where around eleven o'clock one night, a piece of electrical equipment caught on fire. As I was driving there, the massive orange glow was one of the most traumatic things I've ever seen. I was wearing only a T-shirt and shorts, with flip-flops. I remember trying to get into the burning

Australian-born Boyd Martin was excited to win the Fair Hill CCI three-star shortly after becoming a U.S. citizen, and rejoiced during the victory gallop on Australian import Neville Bardos.

barn when a fire marshal stopped me. I pushed past him and found Neville. I couldn't see, but I knew him by the cribbing strap he wore. From out of nowhere, Phillip appeared and got behind the horse to get him out. Neville was saved, but six horses died.

The horses we rescued had to go to the University of Pennsylvania's New Bolton Center for treatment. When it was all over, I was sitting on my porch at 5:30 a.m., as the sun was just coming up. I realized, "You can either call it quits and run away or not let it be a defining moment."

I didn't sleep that night; I had the painful task of calling all the owners. There was $3 million worth of damage. The fire was found to be no fault of Phillip's or mine; it was a faulty machine that caught fire. Neville had lung damage from the smoke, but he was tough, having originally been bound for the slaughterhouse before he was rescued from that fate. He recovered well, thanks to his treatment at New Bolton. That September, we went to Burghley, where he finished seventh. He also was named the U.S. Equestrian Federation's International Horse of the Year for 2011.

Luckily, there were plenty of good moments to balance the bad. In 2015, the team had a big task. We had to qualify for the 2016 Rio Olympics, and the only place we could do it was at the Pan

American Games in Toronto. The team pulled it off, winning gold, and I came close to an individual medal, finishing fourth on Pancho Villa.

At the Rio Olympics, I was so pleased Phillip got his individual bronze medal. No one deserved it more or worked harder for it. Over the years, what I've learned is that to succeed in this game, you need a good strong team around you—good coaches, good mentors, good farriers, good vets, and positive people. If you're in this sport long enough, it's probably going to have more lows than highs, and I've experienced plenty of both. To get from goals to achievements you need hard work and discipline; you need to make yourself do things you don't feel like doing. If you want to do this properly, you've got to be all-in.

DAVID O'CONNOR

Safety First

The multi-faceted David O'Connor has made numerous contributions to equestrian sport, both on and off the field. As an eventer, he is best known for winning the individual gold medal on Custom Made at the 2000 Sydney Olympics, where he also was on the bronze medal team riding Giltedge. David was part of nearly every U.S. eventing team from 1986 until his retirement in 2004. In 1995, he won both the Kentucky Three-Day Event and the Fair Hill CCI three-star. The following year, he rode Giltedge as a member of the silver medal-winning team at the 1996 Atlanta Olympic Games and was fifth individually aboard Custom Made. In 1997, he rode Custom Made to become only the second American to win the Badminton CCI four-star. David's performances at the Olympics and Badminton made him the U.S. Eventing Association's Rider of the Year in 1996 and 1997.

At the 1999 Pan American Games in Winnipeg, David and Giltedge were on the gold medal team and claimed the individual silver. David and Giltedge won the Kentucky Three-Day Event in 2001. The next year, they earned team gold at the World Equestrian Games in Jerez, Spain.

Changing gears, David served as the president of the United States Equestrian Federation from its inception in 2004 through 2012. He has coached the Canadian Eventing Team, which he led to silver medals at the 2007 Pan American Games and the 2010 World Equestrian Games. David also was the Technical Advisor for the U.S. team. He became Chairman of the Federation Equestre Internationale's (FEI) Safety Subcommittee, and in 2017, took over the chairmanship of the FEI Eventing Committee. David lives in Virginia and is married to his former teammate, Karen O'Connor.

David O'Connor in action aboard Tigger Too on cross-country at the Kentucky Three-Day in 2004.

Eventing is quite a different sport than it was when I started in the game. The emphasis on safety increased beginning in the late 1990s, but two decades into the twenty-first century, it came into even sharper focus.

When I did my first CCI (international event) in 1978, the fences were more substantial and upright. That era's version of "frangible technology" was a fence that broke. Upright bounces and upright gates were a part of the game. At Radnor in 1979, an upright gate halfway down the hill caused a lot of wrecks. It weeded out half the division, but I was able to jump it and because of that, I did well and got noticed.

Cross-country definitely was the big deal, the reason for eventing. Courses were not as technical as they are today; they were more straightforward and rewarded boldness, while the endurance side was a big factor, though that diminished after it was decided to drop the long format, which included roads and tracks and steeplechase.

Dressage in those days was rather simple and straightforward. At the same time, show jumping was more influential. When I began my career, it cost 10 penalties if you dropped a rail.

In those days, nearly everyone who evented also went fox hunting, or perhaps competed in point-to-points and galloped racehorses. It was much more about coming from that background than it was a few decades later. Pony Club, for instance, was very strong with eventing. As the years went by, fewer riders had that background, and their numbers will continue to decrease as more land is being developed. There is not as much opportunity anymore for future eventers to be involved in fox hunting or racing as easily as once was the case.

In the 1970s and '80s, the sport was smaller and the horses usually were Thoroughbreds who tended to be in their second careers: ex-racehorses or horses that were not fast enough or too careful for steeplechasing. By the turn of the twenty-first century, more and more horses were purpose-bred for eventing. While today's European Warmbloods would have had a hard time with the demands of the long format, dropping the speed and endurance phases suited their abilities, as a greater emphasis on dressage and the technical aspects of cross-country emerged.

In the 1960s, only two combinations were allowed on a cross-country course. Now there are 45 efforts in a CCI four-star (which became a five-star as the levels were adjusted in 2019) and no restriction on the number of combinations. It's a huge difference, because combinations are more intense and take more effort.

The effect of the changes means eventing is a

After becoming the U.S. Equestrian Federation's first president in 2004, David O'Connor started spending as much time in a business suit as he did in riding clothes, and went on to other posts in governance, including FEI eventing committee chairman.

different sport than it was when I started. I'm not a person who looks backward in a way of thinking that was better or worse. It's just different, and your job is to deal with it. That involves a skill set for riders, many of whom, as I said, lack experience riding at speed.

Doing the steeplechase was not great for the horses, and today they generally are sounder, which means in some ways, it's a little better for them. Cross-country now is the fastest thing you do, which was not the case when we were doing the steeplechase: after going 690 meters per minute, you'd head out on cross-country and go 570 meters per minute. I don't think Germany's Michael Jung—the former Olympic, World, and European Champion—has ever done a steeplechase in his life. Neither have Jonelle or Tim Price from New Zealand, but they're beautiful cross-country riders.

I don't get into the habit of comparing one generation to another. To compare a Bruce Davidson to Michael Jung is not relevant. Today's game isn't the one Bruce was playing when he won the World Championship for the United States in 1974 and 1978. If Bruce were in his thirties now, he would be one of the Michael Jungs of the world.

I don't think that kind of change is limited to just our sport, though. Think about concussion levels in football. Across society, there's a different look at many sports than there was 20, 30, or 40 years ago. That's just reality, and I think that's a societal thing.

When I was president of the U.S. Equestrian Federation, we held a safety summit in 2008 after seven international riders from around the world died during the 2006 and 2007 seasons. One of the questions that we asked was, "Are there things you can do about people getting killed?" We are trying to reduce horse falls, because if you do that, you reduce rider falls. At the safety summit, one of the first things we talked about was changing the culture, which takes a while in a sport like ours.

At the 2000 Sydney Olympics, riding Custom Made, David O'Connor became the first American in 24 years to win an individual Olympic gold medal in eventing.

Changing the culture is very important. Even from the time when I started, the winner sometimes was the last man standing. That's an exaggeration, but at that time, you were able to remount two or three times after a rider fall. Even after a horse fall, you were able to just get on and go on. The orientation of finishing at any cost, which started with the cavalry, does not fit with today's sensibilities, when it is no longer acceptable to put horses at risk in the rush to the finish line.

We are not going to stop horse falls altogether and get down to zero. The real barometer of success is: do we see that number coming down? At

Karen and David O'Connor with Giltedge and Custom Made during a 2003 retirement ceremony at Rolex Kentucky.

the summit, we asked how this could be turned around. The consensus was that one way involves riders' responsibility in terms of not entering competitions for which they and their horses are unprepared, and admitting it when they make a mistake. The principle involved is that responsibility equals accountability. We have to be willing to stand up and say, "That was my fault." That phrase should be used when appropriate not only by riders, but also course designers.

Now, with the change in the culture, you see people who've had two stops just walk off the course. I think that's all for the better. It's better for the horse and better for the rider. And yes, there has been a culture shift. Once you have that, people buy into a thought process. The dressage phase has gotten better, but not to the level where it has had an impact on the cross-country ride, unless some people overdo it. The quality of the riding in show jumping has gotten better.

It comes down to having the horses understand the questions and enjoy what they're doing.

That involves technique and communication from both members of the partnership. The horses of yesterday would have needed a completely different type of training if they were to return and attempt today's courses, with all the corners, which were fences we didn't jump a few decades back. If you took the course for the 2018 Tryon World Equestrian Games and threw it into 1968, no one would have gotten around it then because they didn't train for it.

With the change in the sport, you're seeing really good cross-country riding, really good show jumping riding, and really good dressage riding at the top levels. We're in a refining stage now, with angles and narrow panels cross-country. Looking at what the next change will be, there are a couple of different options. I don't believe dressage can go that much higher, though there's probably room for a few other exercises. I can see the horse trials show jumping being a little bit bigger. There might be a look at other ways to give penalties. How do you separate the excellent from the really good? That's a continuing process, but you can't make jumps any narrower.

For the 2020 Olympics in Tokyo, another big change in the way eventing is being run was mandated because the International Olympic Committee wanted to have "more flags," but the same number of horses. The only way we could get more countries competing was to have fewer riders on a team. So the Tokyo format is to be three on a team, instead of four, with a substitute rider available in case one team member is eliminated.

We want teams to finish, but we don't want to make the cross-country that much easier. So yes, you can substitute, but doing so, you can't win. The winner is going to be the team that goes all the way through with the same riders. It's quite different from the way eventing was conducted in other Olympic Games, but I 100-percent believe we need to stay in the Olympics—so this was what we came up with. I'm a believer in the Olympics. It has a big impact on the sport, a financial impact on the sport. And then there's the emotional drive for a child getting into the sport. It's had a huge impact on my life. I've been involved in the Olympic process since I was 18, so I'm a little biased. If we have to make some adjustments, well, so have a lot of other sports.

And this mandate is only for the Olympics. It will still be teams of four for the World Championships, the European Championships, the Pan American Games, and the Nations Cups. Looking ahead, I think eventing will survive, absolutely. The interest in the human/equine relationship is still very strong, and horses still make a difference in society. People look for games to play and people really enjoy this game. I do see the sport 30 years from now being here and riders around the world wanting to play it.

KAREN O'CONNOR
The Tall and the Short of It

———— 🇺🇸 ————

Karen O'Connor was a mainstay of the U.S eventing team for more than two decades and through five Olympics. Her first major international victory came at the Boekelo CCI three-star on The Optimist in 1984, followed two years later by her first team appearance on Lutin V at the World Championships in Gawler, Australia. She has won CCI three-stars at Punchestown, Foxhall, Kentucky, and the Fair Hill International, where she was victorious twice. With Prince Panache, she won the Kentucky CCI four-star in 1999. She was a member of the 1988 Olympic team, a team silver medalist at the 1996 Olympics aboard Biko, and a team bronze medalist at the 2000 Olympics. Karen rode on World Championship squads in 1994 and 1998, picking up a team bronze in 1998. She also rode Upstage as an individual at the 2006 WEG in Aachen. The next year, she earned team and individual gold medals in Rio de Janeiro, Brazil, at the 2007 Pan American Games with the phenomenal pony Theodore O'Connor. Another mount, Mandiba, had success as a five-year-old, winning the 2005 USEA American Eventing Championships. He was her mount at the 2008 Olympics. Karen was the highest-placed U.S. finisher at the 2012 London Olympics, coming in ninth on Mr. Medicott. After breaking her back in a fall that autumn, Karen ended her competitive eventing career and focused more on teaching and training. The Virginia resident married her former teammate, Olympic gold medalist David O'Connor, and has served as an active volunteer with the U.S. Equestrian Federation and the U.S. Eventing Association.

Biko, the eventing Horse of the Century, was a 17.3-hand Thoroughbred that anchored the U.S. team for a number of years and won team silver at the 1996 Atlanta Olympics with Karen O'Connor.

've been lucky to have had many great horses in my life, but two of the most special were Biko, the U.S. Eventing Association's Horse of the (twentieth) Century and the valiant little Theodore O'Connor (Teddy). They presented quite a contrast. Biko could be described as statuesque, while Teddy was a pony, standing just under 14.2 hands, the cut-off for that category.

We spotted Biko when I was on a buying trip in Northern Ireland with my mother and Vita Thompson, who with her husband, Dick, was a great supporter of our competitive efforts. William Micklem and Ronnie Duke owned Biko after William's brother, John, initially spotted him. As soon as Biko came out of the stall, Vita got really excited about him, because he had a big white blaze face and she loved another of our horses who had a white face, Nos Ecus. I told her she had to keep her enthusiasm under wraps or the price was going to go up.

Biko had just been started under saddle at the end of his four-year-old year, when he stood close to 17 hands. Even so, he was a very narrow horse, which meant I felt pretty comfortable on him during his tryout, though I wasn't able to jump him at that time. When Biko matured, he stood an imposing 17.3 hands, but because he kept growing, he didn't start his first event until he was seven.

He was quite feral as a young horse. It took me two years to be able to get on without somebody holding him. At the end of his career, he still wasn't a horse on whom you could take your coat off in a relaxed manner. I'll never forget being at Fair Hill on a hot day when I was relaxing on him for a moment, with one leg over the knee roll of my saddle. Vita brought me a very welcome iced tea, but when I shook the glass, the ice made a noise and Biko took off like a rocket toward a group of horses in the warm-up area.

Lo and behold, the one rider I was most terrified of in my young career was 1984 Olympic team gold medalist Torrance Watkins. Biko completely banged right into her horse. It was quite a scary moment for me. I wasn't sure if I was going to get hurt from Biko bucking and running off or from Torrance assaulting me. That was kind of a funny moment. Torrance was a fierce competitor, and I learned a lot from her. We are very good friends to this day.

Although he became calmer as he got older, Biko never was good at having a ribbon put on his bridle. Standing still in the prize-giving was always difficult for him. After all, he was a Thoroughbred whose full brother ran in the Grand National steeplechase. During the time he developed, the biggest asset for him was Kim Keppick, who worked for me. She took him on as a project. They went over all the properties where we could ride in Northern Virginia. She exposed him to a lot of different things, crossing rivers and jumping hay bales out in the field. That kept him grounded and in a frame of mind to want to be a partner and not terrified of his surroundings. Kim was a huge part of his success in the end, because she did so much foundation work in the beginning. I had been traveling quite a bit at that time doing clinics and teaching, trying to solidify my career as an instructor, so I didn't have the time to spend with him. But I went with Kim because she was consistent for him, and he really needed consistency.

Exposure continued to be key for him. At an event, I would do multiple rides before the dressage phase but wouldn't put pressure on him. I often just let him stand and watch and absorb the environment so he'd realize it wasn't there to "get him."

Having accumulated more than 1,000 points, he was the Horse of the Century without having won an international competition. But he anchored the U.S. team for a number of years. A highlight was the Olympic Games in Atlanta, where we won team silver. He did several Badmintons, with third place his best effort. He was clear at so many

The valiant 14.1-hand pony, Theodore O'Connor, was a super talent who inspired everyone with his bravery and made a magnificent partner for Karen O'Connor during his short career.

four-star events. We went to Pratoni del Vivaro in Italy for the 1998 World Equestrian Games, where he jumped a clear cross-country when there was truly a lot of trouble there. I remember after going down the slide and turning in a great gallop to the last fence, where he took off really long. A shaken Mark Phillips, our technical advisor, was at the finish, and warned me, "Don't ever jump the last fence like that again. It scared me. I'm just grateful he left the ground."

I replied, "Well, so am I, but I also made the time and that's what you asked me to do."

Biko was a horse that had "five legs" and really took care of himself, with incredible footwork. He was remarkable—very big but also able to be very "small" when he needed to be. Adjustability was a huge asset for him. I was impressed one week while I was reading *Horse & Hound*, that great British magazine, to learn that when perennial British team member Ian Stark was asked what horse in the world he would most like to ride, he said, "There's no question. I would have loved to have been Biko's rider."

I was very lucky to have had that honor. Biko had a very nice retirement, turned out in Virginia with some other famous horses—Prince Panache, Custom Made, and Giltedge—at Jacqueline Mars' beautiful property, living to the age of 31.

Teddy, a Thoroughbred (going back to Bold Ruler), Arabian, Shetland Pony cross, came to me through Christan Trainor, who called me and asked for dressage lessons since she wanted to go Advanced and was having trouble with the flying changes. She warned me he was a pony, and I suggested going Advanced might be a tall order. Then when I saw him, it wasn't that he couldn't do the flying changes—he didn't know how to canter properly. His hind end was so powerful that it was just running over his front end and scaring him. Teddy and Biko were very similar in their minds, always very stressed by picking up the mentality of a prey animal very quickly. You had to be very careful with both of them.

After that winter, Teddy's owner and breeder, Wynn Norman, called me to ask if I'd be interested in riding him, since she and Christan had gone their separate ways. It was remarkable how little Teddy was. I was five feet, six inches tall, and had to shorten my stirrups to ride him. He was so small I could put his wither in my armpit by leaning down. His jump was incredible, but he was afraid of a lot of things. He was always a little tenuous about your seat or your leg or where your weight was. He had to learn to relax into that and listen to what I was asking him to do. That took the better part of a year.

I got him up to qualifying for the three-star at Fair Hill. A lot of the riders said, "Are you really going to take him in a three-star?" I told them if it was too much for him, I'd pull up. But of course it wasn't too much for him. He galloped around like a big, grand glorious horse. The next year, 2007, I did two more three-stars, and started thinking about the Kentucky Three-Day Event. I had many horses going at the four-star level at that time. I wanted him to go first of my horses at Kentucky. I was thinking that in case we had a wet day, I felt Teddy should have the best ground possible. If his starting time was at the end of the day and it was a really wet Kentucky, he would have had to jump harder out of the mud.

The cross-country was very strong that year. I went to the first combination, a big corner to a vertical, and it was just crazy how he jumped it. Then he jumped the rails with the big ditch easily enough. By the time I got to the Head of the Lake, I was probably still 20 seconds down on the clock, because I was being a bit conservative with him. He jumped through the Head of the Lake so well, and after it, handled the massive angled open oxer with a big ditch under it so easily and so bravely. I landed on the other side, petted him, looked at my watch and said, "Alright, buddy, we're about 15 to 18 seconds down on the clock. Do you have

anything left in you?" I pushed him on and he went into high gear, about 700 meters a minute. I think I finished at six seconds over—and I had been between 20 and 30 seconds over at the halfway mark. Not only could he do a four-star, it turned out he did it as easily as any horse I've ever ridden.

When I came across the finish line, our stable manager, Max Corcoran, was there, and she was crying and my husband David was there, and he was crying. I got off, and I wasn't crying. I asked them, "What's the matter?" They answered, "Do you have any idea what you did?" I told them, "I'm sure I was riding the most talented horse in the field." It was a really cool moment. I had everything to lose that day and nothing to gain, I thought, but when he showed me how effortlessly he could do that strong a course, I did have a lot to gain. That little horse taught me so much about horsemanship, riding, and conditioning. He got the best-conditioned award that year, and finished third.

During the lap of honor, I had a chuckle, thinking about my exchange with British Olympic medalist Ian Stark earlier in the week when I was riding Teddy in the main arena as part of the familiarization process before dressage got under way.

"Hey, O'Connor, the Prince William Games are in the other arena," Ian called out, referring to the gymkhana for kids on their ponies.

I rose in my stirrups, turned and pointed at Teddy's hindquarters.

"Get a good look at this," I told him, "because that's what you'll be seeing going into the prize giving."

Sure enough, I finished third and he wound up eleventh.

Teddy had certainly proved himself and handled Kentucky well again the next year, finishing sixth.

It was a short span that Teddy and I got to know each other. I think we met at a very interesting time in both our lives. We each showed the other

Theodore O'Connor's appearance in the horse inspection for the 2007 edition of the Kentucky Three-Day had everyone wondering how the pony would fare in the Western Hemisphere's toughest eventing test. They shouldn't have worried. As rider Karen O'Connor noted, "Not only could he do a four-star, it turned out he did it as easily as any horse I've ever ridden."

what was possible. We went on to win the team and individual gold medals at the 2007 Pan American Games. The next year, Teddy was shortlisted for the Olympics, and we had just started putting him back into work when he had a fatal accident.

We were out hacking at the farm in Virginia. Max was on Teddy and I was riding Mandiba. We had been having trouble with black bears in the area—horses are terrified of bears—and there must have been one out in the field, because both horses went bonkers. Max had gotten off to lead Teddy, and he broke away from her. Galloping full-throttle back to the stable, he fell while turning and slid into the downspout of a drainage pipe, severing the tendons and ligaments on one hind leg. There was nothing that could be done to help him. Our adventure was over.

Throughout my career, I rode many different sizes of horses with lots of different temperaments.

You never can pass up a horse because it's too big or too small. You have to identify with the "look of eagles," and both Biko and Teddy maintained the look of eagles throughout their entire lives. The desire for them to be successful was their desire; I was just their custodian to show them the way. In turn, both of those horses showed me all the virtues that we as humans try to achieve throughout our lives. They were committed to excellence from the beginning. It was remarkable to be the person in the irons on both those horses, and I was humbled by that.

KIM SEVERSON

Success with a Horse Called Dan

The first horse to win the Kentucky four-star event three times, Plain Dealing Farm's Winsome Adante, is Kim Severson's most famous mount. Better known as Dan, the English import also was Kim's partner when she won team gold at the 2002 World Equestrian Games and the individual silver medal at the 2004 Olympics, where the four-time U.S. Eventing Association Leading Lady Rider of the Year was a member of the bronze medal team.

In 2004, Kim was ranked the number one international rider in the world. Kim and Dan were selected for the 2006 World Equestrian Games, competing in Aachen, Germany. Kim and Dan finished third at Badminton in 2007 before he was retired later that year.

In the fall of 2007, after 11 years at Plain Dealing Farm, Kim went out on her own in Charlottesville, Virginia, establishing Kim Severson Eventing LLC. She continues to produce equine stars, including Cooley Cross Border, winner of the 2017 Blenheim CCI three-star.

From a very young age, I always knew I was going to work with horses. Although we lived in Arizona, my mom, Jackie, grew up in New Jersey and rode English at boarding school in Maryland, so I didn't ride Western.

She was adamant about my equestrian education. I had to ride something like a third-level dressage test before she would let me go jumping. Regularly, however, I'd venture out in the desert and leap over the tumbleweeds and these sagebrush things we had out there. I don't think she knew that.

When the path I was heading down finally became obvious, however, she had me take jumping lessons in addition to my involvement with Pony Club.

There was a very popular trainer in Arizona with whom a lot of people took eventing lessons. But that wasn't the way my mother wanted me to go. I wasn't allowed to just go and do what the popular thing was. She was very smart about the safety aspect. There were clinicians who came down from Canada, and one of them was Dale Irwin. I took lessons with him from the time I was 10 until I

Kim Severson and Winsome Adante on cross-country at the 2004 Olympics where they were part of the bronze medal team and won individual silver.

Winsome Adante's owner, Linda Wachtmeister, left, joined Kim Severson and Kentucky Three-Day Executive Director Janie Atkinson for the retirement of the four-star event's three-time winner in 2008.

was 16, and we're still in touch. He even helps me with things if I need something. When I was 16, I moved on to Nathan Martin. He lived in Flagstaff, six hours north of Tucson. I ended up spending the summers and the first half of the school year there, living with a family. When I graduated high school, I rode Lippizans for a private owner. I trained them and the owner's daughter.

At the time, former U.S. Equestrian Team Eventing Coach Jack Le Goff was coming to Trojan Horse Ranch in Phoenix for training sessions. My horse got injured, so I catch-rode horses in the first session, and he asked me to stay on for the second session. He had a Galoubet mare named Sooner that I rode then, and at the end, he said I could keep the ride if I moved to Virginia. So even though I wasn't quite 18, I went off to Virginia with Sooner and my horse. But after Jack and I had a disagreement, I was on my own in Leesburg. I lost my mare to an aneurysm and wasn't sure what to do next.

I moved to Middleburg, where I managed Dominion Saddlery (now Dover Saddlery). It was there that I met Linda Wachtmeister and wound up basing myself at her Plain Dealing Farm. I was taking care of her horses, which were basically Fjords and a Thoroughbred. Linda became interested in my eventing goals and got more horses, while I started taking lessons with Olympic medalist Jimmy Wofford. He has a unique way of putting things that make you remember what he said, like telling me to leave the start box as if I were "on fire."

When I decided to move my horse, Jerry McGerry, up to Advanced at Pine Top in 1998, Jimmy advised me not to, but I did it anyway and won. It was the springboard for starting my success. After a nice show jumping trip at the North Georgia event, a man came up to me and said, "That was a really good round; well done." I thanked him, then quickly asked someone, "Who was that?" The answer was Mark Phillips, the U.S. chef d'equipe.

In the fall, I was named to the developing rider list. I remember at the training session having to do shoulder-in over and over again under the guidance of 1996 Olympic individual bronze medalist Kerry Millikin. It was something I didn't have a feel for. At that time, training was all you got out of being a developing rider, no grants or anything. But it was a big step.

How did I get there? From all the years my mother insisted I do dressage before I could jump, and all the instruction that she knew I needed, as well as the help I got from Nathan and Dale. I've been lucky to have some wonderful horses along the way, including Jerry McGerry, Surprise Deal, Over the Limit (with whom I won the 1999 Kentucky three-star), Royal Venture, and Cooley Cross Border, among others. But none of them had a record that could match Winsome Adante, whose barn name was Dan.

In 1999, I had spotted Dan at the Middleburg, Virginia, farm of Jan Byyny and Craig Thompson, who had been bringing horses over from Britain. Dan was a five-year-old who had done Novice Level in England. I said, "Oh, he's a cute horse, I like him well enough," but didn't think anything much beyond that.

In hindsight, though, it was surprising. He's not a specimen you would necessarily pick out of a field. He's nearly a hand shorter in front, he toes in like you wouldn't believe, he's got a big head, short neck, and long back. The truth is, it was his heart and our confidence in each other that made our partnership successful.

I don't remember ever having to teach him anything. I did have to spend a lot of time getting him strong, so he was able to lift his front end up for dressage. He was a workman, he did his thing, he was a "good egg" all the time. It's who he was. He was smart and quick. He wasn't a spectacular mover, but in dressage he didn't put a foot wrong, though we did have to work on the show jumping.

Kim Severson was a study in focus as she trotted-up Winsome Adante in 2005 at the first horse inspection for the Kentucky four-star event, which the duo won for the third and last time.

It was more of a strength issue than anything else.

Linda and I had a couple of horses together, but Dan was the first imported horse that Linda purchased. He was by Saunter, a steeplechaser who competed abroad, out of Juswith Genoa by Bohemond. I couldn't have known how successful he'd be. I don't think anyone would have ever bought this horse thinking that. Not in a million years. There was a reason he ended up in the United States; it wasn't as if people in England wanted him.

Dan came into prominence just as eventing was going from the long format, which included roads and tracks and steeplechase, to the short format, which dropped those segments. He was versatile enough to excel in both. We won England's Blenheim CCI three-star in 2001 and the Kentucky four-star in 2002. That got me a spot on the team for the 2002 World Equestrian Games in Spain, the last one run in the long format. Mark said if

The 2002 FEI World Equestrian Games gold medal team of David O'Connor, Kim Severson, Amy Tryon, and John Williams. It was the USA's first World Championships eventing team gold since 1974.

I hadn't won Kentucky, I wouldn't have made the squad for the World Championships as a first-time team member—but even so, I was the anchor rider!

My WEG dressage was late at night under the lights. They had just let out the big arena adjacent to ours, which meant there was plenty of noise, and Dan didn't do as well as he usually did. As a team, we drew the last place in the order, and I was the last rider to go. So for cross-country, New Zealand's Blyth Tait, twice world champion and an Olympic individual gold medalist, rode just before me. After he finished, everyone got up to leave because they figured the show was over. No one knew who I was. But Dan, being Dan, did his job and ended up with quite a quick trip, picking up just 2.4 time penalties. Even with three rails down

in the show jumping, we finished a respectable sixth and helped the team to the gold medal.

We had a difficult 2003. I didn't ride at Kentucky because I broke my leg. After recovering, I pointed toward the Burghley four-star in England. We'd never competed there. I had both Dan and Royal Venture in Britain, while Karen O'Connor brought Jacob Two Two. Sadly, all three horses wound up having colic surgery. It was awfully suspicious, that three American horses that would have been competitive wound up having colic surgery, but no evidence of anything untoward ever turned up.

In 2004, I had to qualify for the Olympics, so I went back to the Kentucky Three-Day. Dan finished cross-country in the morning before we had torrential rain, which caused a problem for many of the horses. We won the event, leading from start to finish as we ended up on our dressage score of 37 penalties, and we were set for the 2004 Athens Games, the first Olympics run in the short format.

Again, I was the anchor, which meant I could go to the opening ceremonies, since I did not ride until the second day of dressage. Those scheduled for the first day of dressage weren't able to attend, but I was lucky to enjoy a special memory, marching with all the athletes of Team USA. The flip side to that was our team missing a medal. I was fault-free cross-country after being second in dressage. For the team jumping, I had a rail, and one in the individual show jumping segment, which landed me in the bronze medal spot. At the end of the night, when I got my bronze medal, the only one who stayed with me was David O'Connor, the 2000 Olympic individual gold medalist who became president of the U.S. Equestrian Federation. It was incredibly nice of him to be there. Even so, it felt lonely because we were all depressed that the team didn't get a medal, and everyone else had gone back to the house where we were staying.

But that wasn't the end of the story. There was a very controversial finish to the eventing because Germany's Bettina Hoy had crossed the start line twice in the show jumping and was penalized 13 faults by the ground jury for exceeding the time allowed. The appeals committee overturned that decision and Bettina got the individual gold as her country took the team gold, while the United States finished fourth. Then the United States, France, and Britain all appealed to the Court of Arbitration for Sport, which said days later that the ground jury's ruling could not be overturned by the appeals panel. That meant we wound up getting the bronze, as Germany was moved down to fourth, and I was promoted to silver after Bettina was demoted to ninth while Britain's Leslie Law moved up to take the gold.

In 2005, Dan won the Kentucky Three-Day for the third and last time, finishing on his dressage score as he had in 2004 and winding up leagues ahead of the rest of the field. That was pretty cool. The next year, I didn't go to Kentucky because I got a bye as I pointed toward the 2006 World Equestrian Games. In hindsight, I learned that while you want a bye because you don't want your horse breaking before a championship, byes don't pay off because you have to be on your game at the level. The proof of that came when we had an uncharacteristic stop early on the WEG cross-country course.

We were back in it in 2007, finishing third at the Badminton CCI four-star. After that, Dan sustained an injury behind, and it turned out to be the end of his career. He made one more appearance at Kentucky, in 2008, for an emotional retirement ceremony, and has spent the rest of his life in the pasture at Plain Dealing.

I am so grateful to Linda, because without her, I wouldn't have had Dan. She was such an important part of our success. He was a once-in-a-lifetime horse. Even if I do have another one who's very successful, no one will take his place, because he made my career, and we had such a special relationship. It truly was an amazing time with him.

GINA MILES

Beating the Heat in Hong Kong

━━━━━━━━━━━━━━━━━ 🇺🇸 ━━━━━━━━━━━━━━━━━

Helping others achieve their goals is as fulfilling as her own riding for this Olympic individual silver medal eventer, who has been teaching since she was 15 years old. She coached several competitors to medals at the North American Young Rider Championships and excels at matching new horse and rider combinations. Gina enjoys teaching Pony Clubbers at the introductory levels and adult amateurs to be safe and confident, just as much as she likes working with ambitious riders to reach the top levels of the sport.

Gina's business, Gold Medal Equestrian, is located in the Bay Area of Northern California, where it offers training for all ages in eventing, show jumping, and dressage. She has served on the U.S. Equestrian Federation's Eventing Technical Committee and the USEF Hearing Committee, is a former chairman of the U.S. Eventing Association's Professional Horsemen's Council, and has been a Pony Club national examiner and Level IV USEA certified instructor.

Gina graduated cum laude in 1997 from Cal Poly Tech, San Luis Obispo, with a degree in crop science and agricultural business. She recently was inducted into the Davis Senior High School Hall of Fame. Gina has two children, a son, Austin, and a daughter, Taylor, who also likes to event.

There was a lot that was different about the 2008 Olympics. For one thing, all the sports but equestrian were held in Beijing, while we were in Hong Kong because China was unable to establish equine disease-free zones on the mainland. For another, it was only the second time Olympic eventing had been staged in the short format without the speed and endurance sections of roads and tracks and steeplechase. The 2004 Athens Games, the first in the short format, got a lot of criticism for being too "soft." And of course, it was my first time riding in the Olympics, which meant it was all new and exciting—especially in typhoon season, when we were going to be dealing with a lot of heat and humidity.

While the dressage and show jumping segments

"The amount of pressure was unbelievable" during the individual show jumping phase at the Olympics in Hong Kong, but Gina Miles and McKinlaigh handled it to win the individual silver.

were held at the Hong Kong Jockey Club's Sha Tin racetrack, the cross-country was an hour each way at the Beas River Country Club and part of the Hong Kong Golf Club in Fanling, so the time we took walking cross-country was pretty involved. Course designer Michael Etherington-Smith had a challenge building his route on a teeny piece of land. The whole team walked the course six times, figuring out exactly what we wanted our track to be. You had to be so precise and know every inch of every piece of ground.

It was hard to figure how horses would recover without having those long galloping stretches found on most cross-country courses. It ended up riding like a slalom course, and no one made the eight-minute optimum time, which was a record in terms of how short it was. But it was the same number of jumping efforts as we would have

Gina Miles grew up in Pony Club, "riding anything I could find," a work ethic that got her the opportunity to wear the U.S. Equestrian Team's scarlet coat and wind up on the medal podium at the Olympics.

had with a 10-minute optimum time. Since I was tenth after dressage, the pressure was really on for cross-country if I were going to improve my position. Being able to finish with no jumping penalties and only 16.8 time penalties moved me up to fifth, but it wasn't easy.

I wound up in a difficult position because our pathfinder, Amy Tryon, had an uncharacteristic fall early in the course and couldn't continue. Going second, that left me as the pathfinder, so I was a bit more conservative than I might have been had Amy been able to finish. With the need for accuracy and the angled questions on course, I took a little more time to get it done.

I was on McKinlaigh, a 14-year-old, Irish-bred horse by Highland King, who I owned with Thom Schulz and Laura Coats. He had a huge stride and was incredibly rideable. He could make his big self very small. McKinlaigh didn't look as if he was going fast, but his was one of the fastest times of the day. I had a great advantage because I never had to pull to set him up for a jump; you waste so much time when you're pulling on a horse. I always trained him using a heart rate monitor, so I knew he was very fit. The cool thing about eventing is that you spend so much time conditioning and training your horses that you know them inside and out.

The competition started at 8:00 a.m. to avoid the hottest and most humid weather. As it turned out, we were lucky, because it was one of the coolest days of the Hong Kong portion of the Olympics, with rain coming only after cross-country was finished. To cope with the weather, we took advantage of misting machines, which had first been used at the Atlanta Olympics.

At the racetrack, there were shade pens and fans by every arena, even the cross-country schooling arena. Because of the horse racing, the equestrian facilities were incredible. We were able to use the barns at the racetrack because there was no racing in August due to the weather. The stables were air-conditioned, so that was a big help too.

The horses were in nice, cool, comfortable conditions except when they left their stalls to work. Our cross-country schooling area featured misting fans, a great gallop track, and plenty of arenas. We had our own equestrian opening ceremonies because we couldn't get up to Beijing for the opening ceremonies for other sports. But after my competition was over, I took advantage of an opportunity to go to Beijing and stay in the Olympic village, being a part of Team USA. I also marched in the closing ceremonies. I had always planned to take full advantage of my Olympic experience. After all, it was a visit to the 1984 Olympics in Los Angeles when I was 10 years old that inspired me to take up eventing, after I watched our team take gold and saw Karen Stives earn the individual silver.

I had grown up in Pony Club, riding an Arabian and an Appaloosa I saved from the glue factory. I read lots of magazines and took lots of lessons. I kept working hard, riding anything I could find. They weren't always the nicest horses, but I learned how to get the very most out of what I had. So when I finally had a horse with talent, we just kept the same work ethic, and it got me to Hong Kong on McKinlaigh, who would be the 2008 U.S. Eventing Association Horse of the Year.

He had been poised to go to the 2004 Olympics after the 2002 World Equestrian Games, where I rode as an individual. But he had a breathing problem that cropped up in our final qualifier, the 2004 Kentucky four-star, so that took him out of the running for the Athens Olympics. By 2008, we had it under control, and I felt we had enough successful runs under our belt that we were ready.

When we went to the 2007 Pan American Games, I thought we had a good chance for a medal, maybe even a gold medal. I made the mistake of focusing on that and trying to make every

movement in the dressage a 10. He ended up getting really tense with the pressure and blowing his test. While we did wind up with a bronze medal, I learned about mental preparation and focusing on doing your own personal best performance, and not telling yourself, "I've got to go and win." Because you're dealing with a horse, you have to really listen, communicate, and work with that partner on the day. Instead of putting my focus on how I wanted to place, I put my focus on giving my own personal best performance at the 2008 Olympics. For me, that worked. It helped center me and give me the focus I needed for each phase. McKinlaigh had his personal best dressage test, one of the fastest cross-country rounds of the day, and then double-clear show jumping that put me on the podium.

My approach turned out to be the path that enabled me to handle the Olympic challenge. The amount of pressure was unbelievable for the show jumping phase, designed by Leopaldo Palacios and Steve Stephens. Going into the second round, the top 10 horses were all separated by fewer than 4 penalties, which is less than the cost of dropping a rail. Any mistake was going to change that top-10 placing around massively.

In the first round, the leader after cross-country, German dental surgeon Hinrich Romeike, pulled one pole with Marius and hit another so hard it was hanging out of the cup but didn't fall, prompting Steve Stephens to take a photo of it and show it around. If that rail had hit the ground instead of defying gravity, I would have won gold rather than silver.

We show jumped late to miss the worst heat of the day, though we were still sweating after the sun went down. The first round for team medals was at seven in the evening. By the time we got to the show jumping for the individual medals, it was 10:00 p.m. That schedule meant we had all day to contemplate what was coming up. It took so much mental control to not stress yourself out and get all worked up about it. I spent the day having to focus and not let my mind wander to what would happen if I pulled a rail, what would happen if I jumped clean; all those outcomes you can't predict. I just made myself think about riding my horse at his best and things I could control. I can't control what anybody else does, but I can control how I ride my horse. It was a long mental exercise that day—that was for sure.

The stands around the arena were filled and beyond them, you could see the glittering lights of the Hong Kong skyscrapers. It was a dramatic setting, so different from the way we usually compete in the final phase during the daytime. Early on in the training process, we had done some show jumping under lights to prepare and see how the horses would react to shadows. As it turned out, the lights were so bright that there was little in the way of shadows.

When I got on McKinlaigh to warm him up, he felt so good that I knew he was going to have a clean round. That's just what happened as I moved up to fourth place after the first round, but there was still the crucial second round to come. The two were very different. The first layout was a little more of a traditional course with related and bending lines. The second course was really a bunch of single fences, not a lot of related lines, although it was a little shorter than the first round.

As we finished, leaving all the rails in place, I had a feeling of unbelievable joy that I'd just put it together and nailed it. For me, going clean was the accomplishment. After I finished my trip, we were all celebrating when I heard a rail drop; the third-place rider had just moved down and I was on the podium. When it happened again with the second-place rider and I moved up to silver, it was definitely a bonus.

Being on the podium is very special. I was so proud to see the American flag go up. As part of the Olympic experience, you appreciate so much what everyone did to be a part of the team. I felt this for everybody, every single person who supported us along the way, who helped with the kids, who helped with the fundraisers, who helped get the horses places. It's such a big effort that goes into getting you there. It was incredibly, overwhelmingly emotional.

Going to the Olympics, particularly on the other side of the world, means you have to make a big adjustment. When you compete at a venue where you have been a hundred times, you know where everything is. In a new location, it can be a little chaotic. You can expect that they will change your warm-up ring or your warm-up time. If you're the kind of person who needs things to be a little more systematic, or if changes throw you off your game, you're out of luck. Interestingly, if you're competing and traveling with children, you learn to adapt. Actually, dealing with a two-and-a-half-year-old and a nine-year-old at the Games helped keep me grounded. I remember coming back to the hotel from the first trot-up and giving the kids a bath. That put everything in perspective. This is a very important sporting event, but the things that matter in life are your family and your friends. Whether you win or lose, you're going to go home on Monday. Life goes on.

An Olympic medal connects us as equestrians with the greater world outside of equestrianism. People might not understand anything about the horses, but they understand what an Olympic medal is. It opens the door for us to be able to share our sport, for other people to learn about our sport and respect it. Once you have the medal, you've checked that box and can find out what you love about the sport. My goal is to be a better rider and horseman five years from now. Having the medal allows you that luxury.

Despite the hot, humid weather in Hong Kong, McKinlaigh and Gina Miles had no problems answering the challenge of a cross-country course that demanded accuracy.

DEREK DI GRAZIA
Putting It All Together

The third American ever to design a cross-country course for the Olympics, Derek was announced in 2016 as the man who would design the cross-country courses for both the Tokyo 2020 Olympic Games and the 2018 FEI World Equestrian Games in Bromont, Quebec. Bromont eventually bowed out of the WEG, but it attests to Derek's stature in his profession that he was asked to design two championship courses in a row for the discipline's most important tests.

On an annual basis, Derek is best known as the designer for the Kentucky Three-Day Event CCI five-star, a competition held at the Kentucky Horse Park, which he won in 1985 on the Appaloosa/Thoroughbred cross Sasquatch, the horse who was his mount when he competed for the U.S. Equestrian Team the following year at the World Championships in Gawler, Australia. Derek also was the designer for the three- and four-star CCIs at the Fair Hill International in Maryland, where he was a winner in 1991 on Our Busby. He has continued training riders and riding himself at the three- and four-star level while designing courses, giving his work an extra dimension of insight. Derek serves on the U.S. Equestrian Federation's Eventing Sport Committee and prior to that was chairman of the USEF's High Performance Eventing Committee. In 2015, the U.S. Equestrian Team Foundation's Wofford Cup for service to the sport was presented to Derek and his wife, Bea. The two met when they worked for Olympic medalist Jimmy Wofford. The couple lives at their Stillwater Farm in Carmel Valley, California, and they have two children, Perkin and Ben.

My work in course designing has evolved over time and is still evolving. I originally started by helping build cross-country jumps for the horse trials at Huntington Farm in Vermont, the childhood home of my wife and her parents, Essie and Read Perkins. In 1984, we embarked on a new venture when an exciting opportunity became available in California.

Bea and I accepted the position as directors of the Pebble Beach Equestrian Center in Pebble Beach, California. This facility was a multi-faceted equestrian operation, which, among other things, hosted A-rated horse shows and dressage shows. Previously, many well-known combined training events had been held there. I did all the design for the show jumping classes at the horse shows, while Bea managed the dressage shows.

Over the years, we trained many event riders at this facility, as well as developing many horses for the sport of eventing. To help facilitate the training of horses and riders, I designed a cross-country schooling area that was built by Mick Costello, who eventually would become the head builder for the Kentucky Three-Day Event. Through my experience riding, as well as through my working with great trainers, I was starting to develop an understanding of what horses needed in their training to bring them through the levels. Many years of schooling horses and riders over many different types of jumps has enabled me to see how horses would deal with different situations, types of terrain, and combinations of jumps.

Being able to ride and train horses, or watch other riders over different lines of jumps, always proves to be educational, and certainly has helped

Sasquatch, a Thoroughbred/Appaloosa cross who got his name because of his big feet, was Derek di Grazia's most famous eventing mount.

me in my designing courses. Having the ability to continue competing in eventing has been an enormous benefit for me.

The first horse trials course I designed was a Preliminary track at Wild Horse Valley Ranch in the wine country of Napa, California. Mark Phillips, who went on to design the course for the 2018 FEI World Equestrian Games in Tryon, North Carolina, and the Burghley five-star CCI in England, was the designer for all the upper-level courses there. Mark was very helpful to me and served as an advisor for some of the courses I did. To this day, Mark has been available to advise when needed.

I went on to design a CCI one-star at what used to be the Ram Tap Horse Trials in California. My biggest break came in 1993 after word spread about what I was doing and I was asked to design the one- and two-star CCIs at the Essex Horse

From the courses he has designed at Fair Hill in Maryland to the Kentucky five-star to the 2020 Tokyo Olympics, Derek di Grazia's work always reflects the fact that he is a horseman, and the well-being of the horse is his first consideration.

Trials, based at the U.S. Equestrian Team headquarters, Hamilton Farm, in Gladstone, New Jersey. That job led to my getting other courses to design, which quickly started to occupy more and more of my time. Eventually, I was spending more time course designing and less riding, though my riding was still important to me.

I assisted Mike Etherington-Smith with the course for the 2010 Alltech FEI World Equestrian Games at the Kentucky Horse Park. That was very helpful for me in the transition to taking over designing the annual event's course at the Park.

I like to believe my courses are fair and educational for horse and rider. Obviously, the safety side is a huge part on which I really concentrate. The advent of the frangible pin and MIM Clip to help stop rotational falls is very important. I use quite a lot of them, and think it's great that we have these tools. The more we use them, the more we learn how to use them, and the locations where they work best. Everybody in our industry, as well as people outside it, is trying to come up with other devices to help make the sport safer.

Course designing is about trying to go out and do the best job you can every time you produce a course. You're always trying to educate and keep horses confident. Once you have horses that are backed off, it's often very hard to get that confidence back and to have the horses going the way you want them to go. You always must be very positive in what you try to do with horses and how you bring them along. You like to make sure that the horses see what they're doing. A lot of that goes back to the rider and the training. Horses should be trained to focus on the jumps they're jumping, pay attention to the situation that is upon them, and be able to assess the different questions in front of them.

When you come up to a jump and look at it, do you really see the front edge of that fence? If you don't see it, I'm not sure the horse is going to really see it, either. If you take a bare jump and start decorating it, you can change how the jump is perceived by the horse, as well as the difficulty of the jump. You want the horse to be able to see where the front and the back of the jump are, whether it's through how the jump is painted, the placement of flowers or bushes, or by using some form of ground line. You'll see spread fences that have flags on both the front and the back of the fence. Again, this should help the horses recognize the front and the back of the jump.

When you have jumps under trees and in areas where light and shadows might affect it, you try to minimize that issue as much as possible. If you have jumps where the light will change, you use brighter flowers or brighter ground lines, or make sure the shades of color on the fence are such that you'll be able to see them in a dark area.

When I first rode at Pebble Beach, I was able to attend the 1969 U.S. Open Three-Day Event, with riders from across the country, such as Jimmy Wofford and J. Michael Plumb. It's been interesting to follow the history of eventing over the years since then. You're almost talking about a different sport than what you had 35, 40, or 50 years ago, the cross-country has evolved so much. Taking away the endurance aspect (roads and tracks and steeplechase were dropped in the early twenty-first

century) really changed the game and changed the type of horses competitors ride. The riders also thought they needed a different type of horse because the level of the dressage and show jumping became more difficult. You still need a horse that's fast for the cross-country; however, the courses have become a lot more technical. The exercises are more difficult and ask more of the horses than even 10 or 15 years ago.

A big part of course design has to do with jump placement and the shape of the jumps. I like using terrain to develop different types of exercises on the cross-country. I also enjoy working with different pieces of ground to figure out how the jumps best fit into that space. The relationship of the jumps, one to another, has become more difficult over the years. That's not to say the questions are unfair, but what the riders can do has gotten so much better. The riders are quick to figure out what you're

In 1985, Derek di Grazia led from start to finish on Sasquatch as he won the Kentucky Three-Day Event, a competition for which he would become the course designer 26 years later.

asking and usually have access to cross-country schooling areas or even their own show jumping arenas where they can set up the various exercises to practice. Developing courses that ask new types of questions can be a big challenge.

Things changed in our sport when we went from the long format to the short format. At the time, you might have thought, "That's the end of eventing," and wondered what the reason was for the change. From what I understand, they were trying to keep eventing in the Olympics. It was quite logical, because putting on a full-phase competition with roads and tracks and steeplechase at the Olympic Games was difficult, particularly in today's world with limited space available. There wasn't any going back and obviously, we've stayed in the Games since then.

The long format made riders into better horsemen as they learned how to get horses fit to compete in this type of competition. There was a lot to be gained from knowing you had to have fit horses for these competitions. I think some of that initially was lost when we stopped doing the long format, because riders stopped conditioning their horses the way they used to. That caught up with them in the early stages of the evolution to short format.

Today, you'll find riders taking the conditioning a little more seriously than they used to. At the same time, I think we have ended up with a whole generation of riders who never learned how to get a horse fit, and that probably is more worrisome to me. They should understand conditioning and learn to do it correctly. It's getting better, but I can't say it's as good as it could be. I think one of the reasons many horses are sustaining injuries is because they're not properly conditioned.

In the bigger picture, Tokyo is the first time we're going to have teams of three at the Olympic Games, instead of four riders with the luxury of one drop score. To me, that's quite significant and something more to think about. It changes the dynamics quite a lot. Everybody on that team of three counts, and that's probably going to influence the strategy and certainly affect the selection of horses for the Olympic Games.

When you design for the Olympics, you try to build a course that's going to be fair, will create a good picture for the sport, and produce a good competition on the day. The pool of competitors will come from many countries, and while all must qualify to compete, some may not have the technical skills required to jump the course using all the faster options. So you're going to need alternatives at certain jumps in order to get as many finishers as possible. Everybody can have something come up that's a reversal of fortune—a horse takes a wrong step; a rider falls off.

As I focus on designing for the Olympics, I think about going out and producing the best course I can. After that, it's up to the riders and all involved to make sure they go out and do their job. The extra added factor about Tokyo is the potential for heat and humidity, which is another element that's going to come into play.

It's certainly a challenge, but it's also a great honor to design the Olympic cross-country course. Needless to say, I was really happy to get such a special assignment.

KERRY MILLIKIN

A Team Alternate Becomes an Olympic Medalist

Kerry always had a deep interest in nature and animals, particularly horses. She rode that passion from the U.S. Pony Club to the international level of three-day eventing, culminating in winning the individual bronze medal at the 1996 Olympics, as well as riding on medal-winning teams at the World Championships and Pan American Games.

Kerry earned a nursing degree, graduating magna cum laude and working in her very demanding profession while balancing it with training and riding. She also studied drawing and sculpting, but put her interest in art on hold as she pursued riding. When she stopped competing, Kerry, who lives in Massachusetts, began sculpting and painting full-time, using the knowledge of equine conformation and movement learned from the years she spent training horses. Her work makes her subjects come alive in all their glory, capturing the very essence of the creatures that she knows so well.

Perceiving her years of competition riding as an art form, Kerry is able to translate that into her artwork, displaying the elegance and grace of the equine athlete in a way unique to her understanding of the horse.

In June 1996, as I packed for the training camp leading up to the Atlanta Olympic Games, I asked myself, "Am I packing for two weeks, which meant I didn't make the final cut, or am I packing for six weeks, which meant I had made the final selection?"

With a firm belief in myself and my horse, Out and About (better known as Outie), I packed for six weeks, albeit with trepidation. If you're selected, you never know until it's announced. That's nerve-wracking.

At least there was one thing I didn't have to worry about: I had received the okay from the hospital where I worked for the time away from my nursing duties, and was glad I would have a job upon my return, Olympics or not.

After the last competitive outing, I was named as an alternate, which is not a horrible place to be—we could have been completely left off the roster. On the other hand, being an alternate is not exactly an enviable position. You are in the background while you watch the other riders come together as a team, part of all the press releases, fundraisers, and other activities, which were huge in 1996 because the Games were in America. Despite this, you must train with all your might, so you're ready to go if called upon. It's a lot of miles on your horse for possibly nothing, but hey, I signed up for it.

As the Games approached, we still had several weeks of tough training to go. We rode early in the morning because we were just getting used to the heat. This left us with plenty of idle time in the afternoons, so one day, I went to an air-conditioned bookstore and found *Seven Spiritual Laws of Success* by Deepak Chopra, a volume that was perfect for my situation.

The big message that popped out at me was that it's not what happens to us that matters but what we *do* with what happens to us. This we have control over, and it is our choice. *Ding,* the light went on. I decided that no matter the outcome, I would look on the positive side and make the situation work for me, not against me—a win-win no matter what.

With my new, more positive attitude, training was much more palatable, despite still feeling like an outsider. The energy getting closer to the Olympics was palpable; we were all champing at the bit. Our days were not as busy as when we are at home riding and training several horses, so our leaders had planned some activities with other nations that were also training in Atlanta, acclimating to the intense heat and humidity. Event riders often are referred to as competitive adrenaline junkies, an assessment that isn't far off. So the soccer games were quite active, to say the least, resulting in a few rider injuries—luckily none serious enough to keep anyone off the team. It did provide for some entertainment and great camaraderie with our friends from other nations.

When an alternate does move up to the team, it's because of another's bad luck, so you feel sympathy for that person. But such is the nature of sport. When a potential team horse did go lame, and Outie and I were named to the squad, I was the lucky one. However, before the 2000 Sydney Olympics, the tables were turned, and I was the unlucky one who got dropped because my horse had an injury. The lesson here is that when the pieces fall into place, make the most of it!

Once I was named to the team, we were quite close to the actual competition, so there was a lot of last-minute paperwork to be done, as well as trying to make arrangements for family to come, which wasn't easy.

The Olympic Games are like no other competition in which an equestrian participates. It's a *big* deal. None of our other championships have the broad international feel of so many nations and sports coming together at once for the same purpose. That tingling feeling of excitement overcomes you—you've made it!

Outie was very fit, sound, and training well, so we were ready to rock on, rising to the challenge with his usual unbridled enthusiasm.

Riding on the U.S. team is an honor that comes with a big responsibility. It's not enough to be named; the work has just begun. Our success, and/or failure, has broad-ranging consequences, such as funding for future development and teams, qualification to compete in the next Games, the perception of our sport, and as a role model and inspiration for others, to name a few—just to put on a little more pressure. But we were ready to show what we could do with a lifetime of dedication and hard work. Having studied other sports and top athletes, I had learned how to take my excited, nervous energy and channel it into performing at

Kerry Millikin on Out and About during the cross-country phase of the 1996 Olympics in Atlanta.

a peak level. At the top, the difference between the best and the rest is very small, so all details matter.

One of the details is our dressage test. In the weeks leading up to any team competition, tweaking your dressage is always tricky with a horse fit enough to run in the Grand National. There's a fine line between brilliance and disaster. This was especially true for Outie, who was a talented but fractious ex-racehorse. If you put too much pressure on him, a blow-up could result, which would take more time than we had to bounce back. Once he got nervous, the dressage test mandate to "halt with immobility" was a challenge.

Of course, our coach wanted us to be better and better, which means pressure, so it was a bit of a balancing act. Eventually, we did reach an agreement about when we were coming to that point of no return. Another piece of teamwork!

The last gallop before a championship is always stressful. Anything can happen in that last big workout, such as pulling a shoe. That can result in a bruise, which, in turn, becomes the dreaded abscess, or other strains that can result in a lame horse unable to compete. That would mean heartbreak after being so close. Luckily, we all came out in good shape, getting the thumbs up after the last trot-up in front of the vets and selectors. That was the point where the fun began, and we finally got to be on the field of play.

Moving to the Olympic venue meant saying goodbye to friends who were the reserve riders, leaving them a long, lonely drive home after much sweat and toil. They had to shift goals and plan to compete at Burghley or other autumn events. Although those events are worthy in themselves, they are not quite the same as the Olympics: so difficult to get to, coming only once every four years. International riders are fortunate to have one super horse in their career, yet trying to get that partnership to peak at the right time within an Olympic cycle remains elusive for most.

Feeling lucky to have made it this far, we got to the stabling, where you could feel the tension. Not only did the grooms have to deal with us, and our horses, they also had to deal with the other grooms and management, which had dynamics of its own. Getting on my horse and getting away from it all to do my job was my release; that's when I relaxed. I could finally do what I was there to do. It sounds funny, but for me, it was always about my horse and myself performing our best.

On our first venture into the main arena for "familiarization," we were struck by the enormity of the venue and the occasion. When you looked up, all you saw was a sea of seats waiting to be filled. I knew it would take all of my focusing skills for me not to be distracted, much less my horse. This time, just before the start of competition with all the other riders from other countries, is one of the best parts of international competition. We love seeing friends from overseas whom we know, as well as meeting new people.

During the U.S. Olympic accreditation process, athletes get their ID badges, which were pretty high-tech for the time. Everyone was sized for all the clothing, which was really cool. We got so much awesome stuff. There was also an information session on our responsibility as a member of the Olympic team. I found this so fascinating and different from competing on other U.S. teams at events that were strictly equestrian. Meanwhile, getting family and horse owners there was no easy chore. It created lots of stress. What I thought was brilliant was that they told us we were no longer competing for Team Kerry Millikin, but rather for Team USA. We were not responsible for any of our sponsors, family, or owners from that point on. Our job there was to compete to the best of our ability for the Team. This changed the whole outlook, actually taking the pressure off who got tickets where, and the worry about whether owners and sponsors were happy. At the same time, the pressure shifted from performing up to your own expectations to that of your whole country counting on you. Easy stuff...but it was a good sports psychology session. And there was the media session on guidelines for appropriate responses during interviews, pitfalls to avoid, and other good advice.

The three-day was the first of the equestrian events to compete in Atlanta, so we were on the grounds for the opening ceremonies. Participation was optional, but I wanted to go despite warnings of the long, hot, muggy night ahead.

Getting to the main stadium for the ceremonies was no easy task. The U.S. Equestrian Team's director of eventing, Jim Wolf, did an amazing job juggling all the many details he had to deal with throughout the whole experience. There were lots of challenging personalities involved. We had to take a bus to where most athletes were staying, in the Olympic village. Once there, I felt as if it were freshman year at college all over again. Some of the swimmers had to compete early the next morning so they couldn't come, but these young, strong guys were all hanging out on the balcony with American flags all over, chanting, "Go Team USA."

This was the start of the strong American spirit we felt throughout the Games, the excitement brewing. We all loaded up on the buses to the stadium, encountering huge traffic in the process, with lots of time spent sitting and waiting. But hey, I'd waited a lifetime for this, so what were a few more hours? Finally, we got to the baseball stadium where we would wait some more. It was next to the new Olympic Stadium. The nations were grouped in sections alphabetically, with the United States walking last, so the waiting began again, but we could watch the action on the big screen in our stadium.

During our wait, we got to see all these other famous athletes from other sports—very cool. I especially loved meeting the women's tennis coach

"When the pieces fall into place, make the most of it," is Kerry Millikin's advice, which she followed after being named to the 1996 Olympic team, starting out as an alternate and then winding up with the individual bronze medal.

Billie Jean King, someone I had always admired and respected as a great athlete and a trailblazer for women's sports.

As it got later and later, I was beginning to think I might have overrated this whole thing. But then it was our turn to get moving. As we walked in the dark, feeling herded like cattle going from one stadium to the other, the noise got louder and louder until we came to the breach where we entered. There we could see the whole stadium filled with masses of people. As we walked down the ramp, the roar of the crowd as the Americans entered the stadium rocked me to my core: this was *definitely* not overrated, an experience the likes of which I knew I'd never have again.

Kerry Millikin's knowledge of horses, gained throughout her riding career, is the basis for her accuracy in portraying conformation in action. This has created a demand for her sculptures. One of her most important works is presented to the top U.S. rider at the Kentucky Three-Day Event.

Walking our loop of the stadium, we met more athletes; the amazing basketball players were awesome to walk with. The place was a sea of people. I don't know how we stayed together and didn't get lost. I didn't even know what time it was when we got back to our room.

The next morning came pretty quickly, but there was so much energy it didn't matter. This day was the trot-up—the veterinary inspection for the horses. You never know what might happen, your horse could knock himself at the wrong time and not look right, so it's always a relief to hear the word, "Pass," as you go by the judging panel.

After that, there was plenty that kept us busy, especially walking the cross-country and steeplechase courses, figuring out our kilometer markers on roads and tracks, plus minute markers for all. There were no more fundraising dinners or other obligations. Now it was all about getting in the "zone," channeling your energy into the competition. The next day, the dressage phase began. Once the competition starts, it happens fast. Dressage, cross-country, and stadium jumping—everything I had been waiting for, just flew by.

The weeks, months, and years of preparation for Outie and myself all ended with a bronze medal around my neck and tears in my eyes, knowing it had been worth every minute of effort.

As I stood on the podium, many thoughts raced through my mind. Most of all, I was so grateful for having such a wonderful horse, and for all the people who had helped me along the way.

AMY TRYON

1970–2012

The Word Is Courage

Amy Tryon never had it easy. She balanced her riding with demanding work as a firefighter and emergency medical technician in Washington State, where lack of geographic proximity to events and training sessions added to the considerable effort she already exerted to stay competitive. Although her job was rigorous, it enabled her to work three 24-hour shifts each week and then have four days off to ride. She would switch shifts with co-workers to give her more time to go to competitions.

Her dedication and desire to succeed paid off with a former racehorse turned mountain packhorse named Poggio II. Starting with a fourth-place finish in the 1999 Pan American Games, she was a dependable pathfinder for the U.S. teams at major championships through 2008. Despite sustaining spinal fractures in a cross-country fall at the 2002 World Equestrian Games in Spain, Amy remounted and finished the course. The next day, after teammate David O'Connor jogged Poggio through the horse inspection because it was too painful for her to run, Amy made it around the stadium jumping route despite her injury. Shortly thereafter, she stood proudly on the podium as a member of the gold medal team.

She also was on the bronze medal squad at the 2004 Olympics, and earned individual bronze—an uncharacteristic honor for this team player—at the 2006 World Equestrian Games. That year, she turned professional and went into horses full-time. It was a dream she had since competing at the North American Young Riders Championships in the late 1980s, before having to sell her horse so she could pay for her education. Her husband and fellow firefighter, Greg Tryon, was always there for support and whatever needed to be done—for her or for the team.

A fall at the 2008 Olympics left Amy with an injury that plagued her, along with an infection she picked up there, and pain was her constant companion. Sadly, after an operation to fix a dislocated jaw in 2012, she died of an accidental overdose from a combination of painkillers, muscle relaxants, and antihistamine. It was an enormous loss; she earned great respect for her dedication, determination, and will to win. Here is how those who knew her best remember her.

"There are many adjectives to describe Amy, but if I could only pick one, it would be 'tough' in every sense of the word. Physically tough, mentally tough; she could be tough on herself sometimes. The one thing she was never tough on was her horses. She was a real horsewoman," said Jim Wolf, who worked with Amy when he was the USA's director of eventing and later its chef de mission at championships. "Amy was a fierce competitor, very focused, very loyal. No one had the 'git 'er done' mentality in this sport better than Amy Tryon. She was intense, very methodical. All those things that make successful people successful, she had. She really knew her mind and stood her ground very well. She would get in the start box and everything fell away, and she just did her job. She knew how to ride to orders better than anyone I ever knew. She 'made' her horses, even though doing it on the West Coast was a real challenge. At the time, it wasn't a hotbed for eventing."

Amy Tryon looking great on cross-country aboard Leyland at the 2009 Kentucky Three-Day Event, where she finished thirteenth.

"I think she was probably one of the toughest riders I've ever known," agreed Mark Phillips, who coached the U.S. team from 1993 through 2012.

But what she always displayed was courage. That was as much a part of Amy as the toughness.

"In Hong Kong, from walking in the water jump, she got an infection in her foot that came to rest in her leg. The pain she went through there would have killed most people," Mark stated. "The magic of Amy was she was super, super strong and super, super tough, but rode super light on her horses with a feel most people can only dream about. She was an unbelievably good team player. Her husband was level-headed and a fantastic supporter, not just for Amy, but for the whole team. She's one of the few people you're lucky to teach where you never gave her the same lesson twice. Two weeks later, you'd have another lesson and she'd gotten 80 percent of it from the last time and could go on to the next thing.

"None of her horses were million-dollar horses. Poggio was a packhorse. If it hadn't been for Amy's training, no one would have ever heard

Amy Tryon, always the dedicated team player, earned personal recognition with an individual bronze medal at the 2006 FEI World Equestrian Games, where it was presented by Princess Haya, then-president of the FEI.

of him. When I first saw him in a training session in California in the nineties, I said, 'Hmm, this one doesn't have a good enough trot.' But Amy got him well-enough trained that he trotted adequately. She'd change gears in the right places and be super-accurate and get a competitive team score. She performed a miracle with that horse. Despite her budget, she took unbelievably good care of the horses. She loved the horses and the horses loved her."

As her husband, Greg, noted, "She was intensely shy. But the world she loved was brought out by being around animals. Her dogs, her horses—they meant the world to her. She opened up when she was around humans who wanted to be around animals. She was gracious with her time. She was an amazing off-the-cuff speaker, both for the sport and for supporting those who just wanted an opportunity to try."

Ironically, she wasn't motivated by dreams of glory.

"She never had this desire to go to the Olympics. She was competitive as all get-out, but she wanted to go to Badminton, she wanted to test herself in what obviously was the granddaddy of the sport," Greg said.

She achieved her ambition and rode there in 2002, placing eleventh on My Beau as the only American to finish that year. Amy also competed multiple times in Britain's other four-star, Burghley.

"It wasn't about beating so and so, it was about whether she could compete at the level of the Mike Plumbs, the Jimmy Woffords," her husband explained. "This wasn't about fame and fortune. It took both of our salaries to get her to places. That genuine side of her would always win out, and people would see who she was. The reason she was a sought-after person on safety and rule committees was because she knew not only the arcane, but also the history and whys of how things came about.

"Amy was a complicated person. She struggled with the fact that people looked up to her. She didn't want to disappoint them. Amy was living for today; she never had these high expectations."

In the house she shared with Greg, there are no photos of Amy on the podium or competing. The pictures on the walls are of the horses and dogs. Her medals, her husband said, would only come out when she was doing a fundraiser. And she understood the importance of that.

"She was a super, super team person, so that

Greg Tryon was always there for his wife, Amy, supporting her eventing career while they shared the same profession as firefighters/emergency medical technicians in Washington State.

Amy Tryon at the 2008 Olympics on Poggio II, a former mountain pack horse who was as plucky as his rider.

helped the morale of the team. Amy really helped create a cohesive team spirit that would help people perform their personal best at that particular Games," Mark observed.

The 2006 World Equestrian Games in Aachen was not a good outing for the U.S. team, with the exception of Amy, who earned the individual bronze medal on Poggio II.

Typically, for Amy, it was about Poggi, not about her.

"I'm just really pleased with the horse. There isn't a day you get on him that he doesn't try. He came through for me," she said at the time.

"I'm glad Amy had her medal in Aachen," teammate Kim Severson recalled. "With that horse, she was always a team rider, never an individual rider. I'm so happy she had the opportunity to be that successful. She did it through a lot of pain and difficulty in her life; injuries she didn't ever resolve, but that never stopped her. At the WEG in Spain, she had a bad fall. She got back on and was in so much pain, but she finished. That's who Amy was through her whole career.

"I always think of her when I go out of the start box. I say, 'Come on, Amy, let's go for a ride.'"

DRIVING

COMBINED DRIVING WAS INVENTED BY GREAT BRITAIN'S PRINCE Phillip, who designed it along the lines of three-day eventing. It is contested by horses and ponies in single, pair, and four-in-hand combinations.

The first phase is dressage, in which horses perform a test at the walk and trot while following a set pattern around lettered placards in the arena for their tests. This phase demonstrates the obedience of the horses and ponies, as well as their way of moving.

The second phase is the marathon, where endurance is key. There are sections in which the horses walk and trot, but the focus is where the horses are timed as they wind their way through obstacles with tight turns, galloping to get the best readings on the clock. The drivers work with a navigator, who helps them remember the routes through the obstacles and proceed efficiently. Drivers wear helmets and informal garb, a contrast to the formal attire that is required for dressage and the final phase, cones.

In that last segment, horses are driven through pairs of cones topped with balls. Drivers are going against the clock, attempting to stay within a tight time-allowed, while trying to make sure the balls remain atop of the cones to avoid penalties.

CHESTER WEBER

You Need to Know the Mission

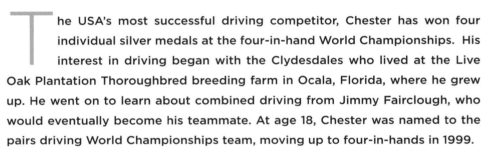

The USA's most successful driving competitor, Chester has won four individual silver medals at the four-in-hand World Championships. His interest in driving began with the Clydesdales who lived at the Live Oak Plantation Thoroughbred breeding farm in Ocala, Florida, where he grew up. He went on to learn about combined driving from Jimmy Fairclough, who would eventually become his teammate. At age 18, Chester was named to the pairs driving World Championships team, moving up to four-in-hands in 1999.

After Chester led the U.S. team to its first World Championships gold medal at the 2018 FEI World Equestrian Games, his sponsor, Jane Clark, was overjoyed. "There have been wonderful successes that speak to his commitment to horsemanship, to training, and to the sport, but none more fun and more rewarding than his team gold and individual silver in Tryon at WEG 2018. It was great to watch Chester and our horses realize a dream, a goal that we had since I began sponsoring him in 2010," she said.

Chester has been U.S. National Four-in-Hand Champion 16 times. He is a four-time winner of the U.S. Equestrian Federation's Becky Grand Hart Trophy, awarded to the outstanding competitor in international driving, endurance, reining, vaulting, or para-equestrian. A trustee of the U.S. Equestrian Team Foundation, he also is a member of the USEF's Driving Sport and Competition Management Committees.

Chester and his sister, Juliet W. Reid, are co-presidents of the Live Oak International jumping and driving show. He lives with his family in Ocala.

Chester Weber in the marathon at the 2014 FEI World Equestrian Games, where he won an individual silver medal.

f you're going to achieve excellence in horse sport, you need a depth of support behind you. I'm not talking about just winning a national championship or a Grand Prix. If you want to win 16 of them, or if you want to be on U.S. teams, you need a great deal of backing.

The USET Foundation certainly has become a hub for a lot of owners, and it offers a wonderful way to get involved in supporting the sport. But whether you use your family's resources or the resources of other individuals, you still have to manage the relationships with sponsors or owners.

Sometimes people think support in horse sport should be based on need. Actually, it should be based on merit, and then it's time to figure out how much support is needed by the person selected to receive it. What often happens in horse sport is that people say, "Let me support this person or

Chester Weber started out in his chosen discipline by driving the family's Clydesdales.

In 1993, before he graduated to four-in-hands, Chester Weber drove in the World Pairs Championship at Gladstone.

that person because the person doesn't have the resources." If one's goal is to win medals, then the support has to go to the athlete most likely to be able to do that.

One thing many competitive nations do in horse sport is really try to make sure there's support behind the best talent that's out there to produce medals. It's a pity that often the right people don't have enough backing. And if someone without a whole lot of talent finds a sponsor, I look at it as wasted resources for the U.S. medal effort. It's not going to help move the needle.

On the flip side, I don't think there's a great deal of education at the elite level of the sport on the best way to structure an owner- or sponsor-competitor relationship. There has to be a lot of transparency and communication.

What makes four-in-hand combined driving different from other equestrian disciplines, such as dressage or show jumping, is that while those disciplines may involve a barn full of horses with whom riders have to create bonds, they do it one-on-one. Drivers must work with four horses at one time. Even just stepping inside the arena involves dealing with sixteen legs, eight ears, eight sets of reins, and four hearts, all of which require top-flight care and attention for the horses to be the best athletes they can be. And all those numbers don't count the extra horses who can be rotated into the team or act as spares.

The sport has become so expensive that even people who are well-to-do can't do it on their own. I couldn't have been in the top five in the world rankings as consistently as I have been without the support of Jane Clark.

"Oh," people say, "you're from a family that can afford to do this."

Here's my answer: While I do spend a lot of my own resources, and I own a lot of horses, it would be impossible for me to compete at that level without sponsor support. Even though I work out of a 4,700-acre farm, it's not my farm—it's my mother's. She has her own interests and things she does. I live on funds generated by my own business endeavors. For instance, I own a piece of a funeral business in Ocala. Sometimes it's easier to invest in horses in a sport in which you're not seeking competitive excellence yourself. Show jumper Mario Deslauriers and I once were business partners. Because I'm not a show jumper, I could be more objective about the horses with which we were dealing. If you're seeking to be the best in the world, it's very hard to sell the most talented horses. The challenge with driving horses is the expense to keep them. Unlike the show jumpers, I don't go into any competition where I could win hundreds of thousands of dollars, because there's no prize money like that in the driving sport.

I do buy young horses and produce them and sell ones that don't fit in my program. That doesn't mean they wouldn't work well as a single or pair. Some of my colleagues teach a lot and see a lot of horses and are able to get some for themselves that are going to assist them in achieving their goals.

You have to define your goals. I always look at what my goals are, along with the mission and vision of what I'm doing. That helps me answer most questions. When I worked with Jane, we always had a strategic plan every year, with clear goals of how we would define success. Then we did our best in terms of horsemanship to allow the horses to be prepared for those goals. If your goals are competitive excellence, that's the critical aspect in having a successful relationship with a sponsor and getting everyone's interests aligned. If the sponsor's goals are different from the athlete's, you'll never arrive in Rome. If you don't understand what success looks like to the sponsor, it's hard to achieve something.

You have to interview different trainers. Talent's not all of it. You need to be able to fit with the people and their goals, which may not all

be competitive. Talk to the people who produce people.

Jane had six driving horses after the 2010 WEG. She asked if I would consider taking them. We put together a very competitive program that enabled us to amass a bunch of medals, including four individual silvers, attesting on a global scale to the success of what we were doing.

She and I ended our partnership after the 2018 WEG. We had achieved our ultimate goal of getting a team gold, and it was time for her to focus on other things. The years we worked together will always be an incredible testament of our shared passion for horses and for winning. We finished our partnership on top. Together, we elevated the competitiveness of U.S. driving, and I will continue to raise the bar with new partners. But I will always be grateful to Jane. Without her backing, I would not have achieved medals at so many championships and would not have been able to change four-in-hand driving history. She and I had a procedure that we followed during our partnership. Every year, we came up with a budget that Jane approved. We met once a year to discuss our plans and our budget. I try not to get in a situation where I'm nickel-and-diming somebody. I think that's just bad business.

There's no question that every owner wants success at some level. Certainly sportsmanship and horsemanship are the foundation of our program, but if I were not successful, Jane would have lost interest. It's important for a competitor to be respectful to owners and engage in a true partnership. But if a competitor is good company, yet doesn't deliver at the competition venues, eventually the owner gets tired of the situation.

I always keep in mind why I am doing this—I'm doing it to be successful and to win. The people who achieve competitive excellence are those who can make something happen with the opportunity. Usually, that involves a breakthrough horse with which someone gave them a chance.

The driving sport has changed a lot in the last 15 years. Most of the people in the Top 10 have a group of sponsors, a good depth of support behind them. There are five horses in carriage driving (four in a team and one spare), which means there are opportunities for multiple owners to become involved. When that happens, we want people who are like-minded and share similar goals and values. If you can put those things together, you can get some synergy.

I make sure every owner involved gets a monthly report that goes through subjective and objective information about what the horse does every day. It also includes the veterinary updates, body condition, the feeding program, and what the farrier is doing. You should educate owners and help them understand why this blacksmith and not that one, why this vet and not that one. The report also helps me make strategic decisions and understand where we are on the road to our goals. In the report, I describe our plan for the horse. The next month, I read the previous month's report to determine where we stand. Were we able to achieve what we wanted to do, or are we just kidding ourselves, thinking we're making progress? It's important to memorialize facts in those monthly reports.

For example, I weigh horses every month. It can be frustrating when an owner shows up and says, "Hey, this horse is skinny."

In response, I'll say, "Let's look at how much he weighs, how much he usually weighs, what his average weight was from the previous year." That's giving people objective data. I try having a clear agreement about what the goals are for that horse.

Jane had a huge amount of experience owning horses her whole life. That was a great resource. But she always said ultimately the coaching management team that includes me has to make the best decisions. The unique thing with driving is that while it's possible to have multiple owners, everyone's goals have to be aligned. Then you have

to know the mission—I print a mission statement at the top of my strategic plan to keep it in the forefront. It's important to understand what you are trying to do. That helps you make the right decisions.

Historically, combined driving is quite different now from the time it began. When Great Britain's Prince Phillip was developing the concept of combined driving, which he based on the template for three-day eventing, there were a lot of independently wealthy people who wanted to be involved in the sport. I've always tried to have commercial sponsors, and companies we already worked with that were happy to trade product for exposure.

The sport has become considerably more difficult. Most of the people now who compete are professionals. This is what they do every day. The dressage, marathon, and cones segments have become far more challenging than they were in the era when Prince Phillip was driving. The standard of the sport continues to reach new levels.

Consider what's expected from horses in the dressage test. The horses of 20 years ago weren't good enough movers to get a useful score today. My horses have a riding background that helps with the dressage. I have an eight-year-old with potential to be a ridden dressage horse. But I think that horse could be a huge asset to our program, so of course I want to keep him.

In the marathon, the hazards are much more technical and the speed expectation is much higher than in the past. The time allowed has changed drastically in cones, along with tolerances of wheel width.

There's a huge amount of combined driving around Ocala in the winter. I could go to a competition almost every week with a young horse without traveling more than 35 miles. This has become a real driving mecca, not unlike Wellington has become for show jumping. There just need to be more signature events. The driving sport should

The USA's first gold medal world championships four-in-hand driving team *(left to right)*: Chester Weber, Misdee Wrigley-Miller, and Jimmy Fairclough.

look at what show jumping has done successfully in bringing the sport to the people instead of bringing the people to the sport. People will come to traditional venues like the Live Oak International or Aachen, but the growth of show jumping comes from competitions such as the Global Champions Tour at a variety of high-profile sites in Europe, the United States, and Canada, or the New York Masters, because they bring the sport to a metropolitan area and the people. It's not impossible to do the same thing with driving. Our indoor sport has really grown. To be successful, driving has to find a way to have events in parks and cities. Most organizers of horse shows rely on the competitor to sustain the competition. The competitor is their customer, and that's how it happens with most driving shows

as well. At the Live Oak International, it's different because we get a crowd and the sponsors are our customers. We see the competitors as athletes.

So why would you sponsor someone in driving? If your driver is successful, that offers a chance to attend the "majors," such special fixtures as the Royal Windsor Horse Show, Aachen, or the World Championships. Like the French Open, the U.S. Open, and Wimbledon in tennis, they have a lot of appeal and offer a chance to mingle with like-minded people—or in the case of Windsor, an opportunity to be on the grounds with royalty.

I look for people who are interested in that, because with their help and resources, they could also be part of bigger accomplishments, such as perhaps winning an individual gold medal.

JIMMY FAIRCLOUGH

I Have Determination

The realization of a lifetime dream came 40 years after Jimmy started training for the inaugural world four-in-hand driving championship. As the United States claimed its first four-in-hand World Championships gold medal in 2018, he stood on the podium at the FEI World Equestrian Games with teammates Misdee Wrigley-Miller and Chester Weber, who had trained with him as a teen.

Jimmy's WEG marathon—where he had the disadvantage of being first on course—and cones scores both counted toward the team total. His propensity for coming through was illustrated in the cones segment, where he struggled with a control problem after one of his horse's nosebands broke. It had to be fixed with a zip tie when the teams were called back to the arena for the presentation.

No stranger to gold medals, Jimmy was on the 1991 winning pairs World Championships driving team. The victory gave the United States the right to host the 1993 World Pairs Championships in Gladstone, New Jersey, where it was deemed one of the most successful competitions of its kind ever held.

Jimmy has participated in more World Championships than any other U.S. driver. A national pairs and four-in-hand champion multiple times, he also has served both the USET and the U.S. Equestrian Federation in driving governance roles. Following the 2018 WEG, he decided to semi-retire and confine his competition to the United States. While he wasn't going to give up driving, he had no plans to pursue another World Championship abroad.

The president of his family's fuel company, Jimmy follows his equestrian interests at Top Brass Farm in Sussex County, New Jersey. He has two sons—Ryan, an arena construction specialist, and James II, a professional hunter/jumper trainer and rider.

Jimmy Fairclough was the pathfinder on the marathon course at the 2018 FEI World Equestrian Games.

As a kid, I rode ponies, jumpers, hunters, and also drove. My father was driving a four-in-hand, so even before I entered my teens, I started driving a four-in-hand with pleasure vehicles and a coach. I drove that coach around the Wanamaker Oval at the Devon Horse Show when I was 12 years old.

Combined driving made its appearance in the United States during the 1970s. In 1970, Phil Hofmann, a four-in-hand driver who was the father of show jumpers Carol Thompson and Judy Richter, put on the first U.S. FEI driving competition in Johnson Park, just outside the small city of New Brunswick, New Jersey.

My father won that competition. But afterward, he told me, "I'm not going to do this. It's too much work." He was running the family fuel business and despite his interest in driving, just didn't have the time to devote to it. In the autumn of 1978, I drove his horses at the Myopia event in Massachusetts and realized it was a lot more fun than riding a balky pony. One of the people against whom I competed at Myopia was German driver Emil Jung. I had beaten the other Americans at Myopia by a large margin, but Emil was ahead of me by 60 points.

In 1979, I started trying to qualify for the first world four-in-hand championships. Later that

In the cones segment at the 2018 WEG, Jimmy Fairclough had a tough time after the noseband on a horse's bridle broke, but he persisted and triumphed in his 40-year quest to earn a team gold medal for the United States.

A picture of elegance, Jimmy Fairclough drove his team in the dressage phase of the 2006 FEI World Equestrian Games in Germany.

year, Liz Whitney Tippett, who had been working with Emil, asked me to drive her horses. I went to Florida with them for the winter in 1980 and off to England after that, where we did some competitions before the World Championships, the first such competition to which America sent representatives.

The team was Deirdre Pirie, Clay Camp, and myself. The two alternates were my brother, John, and Jamie O'Rourke. I got eliminated in the cones phase for starting before the bell. It was a very expensive lesson, because I had done really well up to that point. I remember it like it was yesterday. I heard a buzzer and thought that was the signal to start, but actually they were using a bell for that purpose. I was clean until cone number 18, which was where they stopped me. We tried lodging an official protest, but that didn't work. It was a very valuable exercise in the end.

Emil was kind of the coach for the team in its early days because of his experience, though he didn't have the title. We had training sessions at the USET in Gladstone. Colonel D.W. Thackeray was running the program with Jack Fritz, executive director of the USET. Deidre and I were on the USET driving committee with Holly Pulsifer.

Things were so different at the time of the first World Championships. A majority of the carriages were wooden. In the 1980 championships, a Hungarian team came through the finish line of the marathon without a rear axle, only two wheels. Some of the stuff we had to do in the marathon

was just amazing. There was no room for finesse. It was survival. So many changes have been made since then. The quality of horses we've gotten into the sport has improved it tremendously. While the harness is pretty much the same, the carriages and the technology for training the horses are like night and day. A young person starting out today has all the training aids, carriages with delayed steering, brake systems and pulley systems. They don't have to be concerned about the horses rubbing against the pole anymore. It all has really improved the performances we have now.

Over the years, we've tried to make the sport more appealing to spectators and more mindful of the welfare of the horses. In the 1980s, sometimes the horses were nearly exhausted by the time they finished the marathon. Now they're flying through that last obstacle. It's not even half of what we used to have to do when the sport began. At the time

I started driving, the length of the marathon was 27 kilometers. Now the track may be only 14 kilometers. On the other hand, today the hazards are much more complicated. The carriages we drove in the beginning could never even make the turns that we do today. It was not physically possible.

Because of the number of horses and logistics involved, it was incredibly expensive to drive at world-class level. I was very fortunate to have sponsors who helped me, including Mrs. Tippett; Clay Camp, who gave me his team in 1982; Herbert Kohler; and then Jane Clark for 16 years. My former wife, Robin, a show jumper, also helped because we ran the farm together.

To stay competitive for 40 years, or even stay in the sport, is very difficult. It requires dedication every day, especially since I have a full-time family business. It's a lot of work to keep horses in that kind of training for that period of time. Five shoulder surgeries later and everything else—it's a lot.

The gold medal has made it all worthwhile, and I was pleased to be accepting it with Chester because of our long association. At one point in life, we kind of parted ways a little bit, but we always still worked on teams together, no matter what. Over time, it's worked out, which is great. He's worked very hard at our sport, so it's nice for us to have come full circle.

My thoughts on the podium during the medal ceremonies included influential people who worked hard to improve American driving but had passed away. A mentor for me was Ted Williams, who died in 1991 at the age of 105. He lived in the era in which our sport was established. His influence during my youth really helped a lot, and he helped me stay with it. Another person on my mind as they played the Star-Spangled Banner was Finn Caspersen, the former chairman of the USET, who brought the 1993 World Pair Championships to Gladstone and really put driving on the map in the United States. Finn would have been ecstatic about the gold medal. Ed Young, the four-in-hand Chef d'Equipe, who died in 2017, would have been overjoyed, too.

I have learned so much from my involvement with driving. It's why I have determination. It reinforced my work ethic and commitment, teaching me that if you wanted to succeed, you had to work at it continuously. It's commitment, dedication, perfection—all of that together. There was never a break, especially if I wanted to stay current with the sport, which progressed so quickly.

I cannot forget to mention the dedicated grooms and staff who have supported our medal quest. And, of course, this success would never have been possible without the wonderful and talented horses I've had the fortune to ride and drive. They all have taught me something. I would not be the person I am today without having been involved in driving.

SUZY STAFFORD

Pony Power Took Me to the Top

The first U.S. driver to win individual gold in a World Championship, Suzy Stafford collected three more World Championship medals after making her international debut in 2005. The list of accomplishments for the three-time U.S. Equestrian Federation National Single Pony Driving Champion also includes being named a USEF Equestrian of Honor in 2009, the same year she won the organization's Becky Grand Hart Trophy, awarded to the outstanding competitor in international driving, endurance, reining, vaulting, or para-equestrian.

In addition, she has taken honors in the Friesian ranks, where she earned the National Carriage Driving Championship in 2012 and the World Champion English Pleasure crown in 2013.

Certified in dressage and combined training by the American Riding Instructors Program, Suzy was a Pony Clubber who focused on eventing until an accident cut short her riding career. Turning to driving as an alternative, she began working with celebrated pairs driver Lisa Singer as assistant trainer. After graduating from driving ponies to horses, she teamed up with PVF Peace of Mind, better known as Hunny, the USEF's International Horse of the Year in 2015 and the number-one combined-driving horse in the country in 2016. She trained for years with Australia's Boyd Exell, ranked as the world's number-one driver.

Suzy runs Stafford Carriage Driving. She is based in Franklinville, New Jersey, with her husband, John Young, and spends winters in Ocala, Florida.

was 20 when I started my success in combined driving with ponies, after an accident in 1997 derailed my eventing career. While I was helping a student, her horse fell on me, and I broke my ankle. It didn't heal properly, and the cartilage in the joint died, which meant I had to have it fused. I could still ride, but riding competitively was really painful. I knew I couldn't be as good a rider as I wanted to be, so that's why I decided to change disciplines, to find something in which I was competitive enough that it would make me happy.

I met pairs driver Lisa Singer during the time I was riding because I was looking for something different to get my father, Bill Stafford, for Father's Day. I thought driving lessons would be fun for him. He bought an old Standardbred and took lessons from Lisa for a year or so. In the process, I got to know Lisa, and she asked me to help her at shows, even though I didn't know anything about driving. But I was a good groom. From my eventing

Suzy Stafford during her eventing days in the early 1990s, going cross-country with Barney.

background, I knew how to braid, clean leather, and prep a horse for the show ring.

After my injury, I sold my event horse and bought a pony, a cart, and a harness—sort of a "starter kit"—and took lessons once a week. At the time, I had a full lesson barn for riders and used to teach Pony Club. But I didn't feel I was doing a good enough job because I couldn't really school my students' horses that well, due to my injury. Then I just decided, "If I'm going to change gears, I'm going to change gears." So I shut down my barn and went to work for Lisa full-time as her assistant trainer.

I did quite well early on, though I may not have realized it at the time. I'm very competitive, I like to do a good job, and I'm probably my worst critic. It was a lot harder than I originally thought, however. When I was an event rider, I believed driving was a sport for old people, and figured, "When I'm old maybe I'll do this." At the time, I certainly didn't think I would be in the World Championships.

My first driving pony had an accident, and she moved on to another career. I bought a Morgan, Double M Eden's Quest, because that's what Lisa said I should buy. The mare taught me a lot, but I didn't think she was an international-quality animal. If I knew then what I know now, though, she might have been an international pony.

Then in 2003, Lisa's client, Beverly Lesher, came in with a 14.1-hand Morgan mare. That was Courage to Lead, who had been in the show ring. Her barn name was Katy. At some point, Beverly let me drive her. We just got along and I took her on as my training horse. I competed Katy a couple of times and did really well. Lisa and the owner talked and said, "Let's see where this goes." When we won the national championship, the question was, "Now what do you do?" There was an easy answer: "You try out for the team."

I did and was named to the team with Katy for the 2005 Pony World Championships at

Cefnoaks Bouncer was a "catch drive" who clicked with Suzy Stafford, so much that they wound up with a gold medal at the 2005 World Pony Driving Championships in England.

Sandringham in England. About a month before we were scheduled to leave, however, she was injured. I couldn't take her to the Championships; she wasn't fit to compete and had to stay home.

At the same time, however, Sybil Humphreys' Cefnoaks Bouncer, a 13.2-hand Welsh Cob, was already in England with his driver, Muffie Seaton, and they also had been named to the team. Then

Muffie and the owner parted ways. Bouncer was in the right place for the Championships, but without a driver. I was in the States and named to the team, but didn't have a pony. Someone suggested they should put me together with Bouncer. You can't do that now, because you have to be on the team with the pony you used in qualifying, but it was different in those days. The powers that be looked through all the logistics and I ended up flying to England three weeks before the Championships to meet Bouncer.

That was the first time I drove the pony. We decided I would show him as a little bit of a test run. We worked out some kinks and shipped to the Championships.

It was a catch drive that ended up with a gold medal, which was quite amazing. I still can't believe it. I went there with no expectations. I was in a much different mental state then than I am now, with a different type of pressure. I was just so happy to be there after I thought I wasn't going to be able to compete.

It took a while for what had happened to sink in. A competition is a competition, and I wanted to do well at every single competition. I didn't let the Championship put any more pressure on me than a local show, because I thought at the time, "It's just another ribbon," but obviously that wasn't the case. It was, I eventually realized, a much bigger deal than that.

In 2007, I qualified for the Championships again with Katy and made the team. This time, she was injured in a completely different circumstance a couple of months before the Championships. I called Sybil and told her, "It happened again." Then I asked, "What's Bouncer doing?" She gave permission to use him, but I had to rush around and get qualified, since they had changed the rules and you had to qualify with the horse you were taking to the Championships.

At the Championships in Denmark, I lost my navigator in one of the marathon obstacles. If that hadn't happened, we probably would have been in the individual medals. Luckily, my other two scores were good enough for the team, and we won bronze.

In 2008, I won the national championship with Katy. In 2009, Katy made it to the World Championships, four years after we were originally

Suzy Stafford shows off her silver medal from the 2011 Pony Driving World Championships in Slovenia.

supposed to go. We got the individual bronze, but after our long wait, it felt like a gold medal when it was put around my neck in Germany. Finally getting her there, and even the whole year prior, meant a lot to me.

Katy started my career and got me on the map. She had done a lot, and we retired from the international ranks after she won her third National Championship in September 2009.

In 2010 and 2011, I worked with Josephine, a Morgan/Arabian cross, and picked up individual silver at the 2011 Pony Championships in Slovenia.

After that, I thought, "I've done this and I've done well. Where do I go from here?" It was either horses or pony pairs as I moved on from the single pony ranks. The clients who were supportive were

Josephine, a Morgan/Arabian cross, went well for Suzy Stafford in the marathon at the 2011 Pony Driving World Championships.

pony people; their motto would be, "If it's 14.2 hands (or less) it's for us."

Yet I knew something needed to change. I had dominated the pony scene, and I needed to push myself a little further. The horse division is much more competitive. It's essentially the same competition in a different height class. So I looked for a horse and bought PVF Peace of Mind, who we call Hunny, as a three-year-old. I started competing her at the upper levels when she was six, coming seven. She is 15.2 hands and—of course—a Morgan.

Morgans have been good to me. Hunny was the USEF's International Horse of the Year in 2015, quite an honor for a driving horse up against stars of the Olympic disciplines, and she was the number one driving horse in the country in 2016. Her picture has been on the Triple Crown feed bag, and she had the honor of being named a Breyer® model horse.

Hunny gave me a nice transition to horses, but I will always be grateful to the ponies, who took me to undreamed-of heights in an exciting new career.

MIRANDA "RANDY" CADWELL

It Takes Two

The first American driver to win a marathon at a World Championship, Randy was the individual gold medalist for pairs in the 2007 FEI World Combined Pony Driving Championships while leading the way to the U.S. team bronze at the competition in Denmark. She was honored with the U.S. Equestrian Federation's Becky Grand Hart Trophy, awarded to the outstanding competitor in international driving, endurance, reining, vaulting, or para-equestrian.

Randy and her older sister, Keady, also a World Driving Championships veteran, have trained with Boyd Exell, a world champion in the four-in-hands. The sisters run a training business, based with their parents, Mason and Jennifer, at Tremont Farm in Southern Pines, North Carolina. Randy, who has volunteered as coach and Chef d'Equipe for the U.S. para-driving team, noted, "Our life is driving, and we all do it together in our family. We literally eat, sleep, and drive every day."

I started riding when I was five in Unionville, Pennsylvania, a very horse-oriented area. I competed at the Devon Horse Show in the junior jumpers, while my sister, Keady, evented through Preliminary level. Our father, Mason, drove our outgrown ponies. Then they became a pair of horses, and finally, a four-in hand.

He began in the pleasure ranks before moving on to combined driving events (CDEs) in 1976, when those competitions were in their infancy in this country. He kept busy, running the shows and getting involved in coaching runs with conservationist Frolic Weymouth. We would train my dad's horses at home; then he would drive them to all the functions.

When we were in college at Drexel University,

Cannon's Majestic Leyla, the 2015 reserve national champion, in the marathon at the 2017 World Pony Driving Championships with Randy Cadwell.

Keady and I stopped riding for the most part. We simply ran out of time for it between rowing crew and keeping the pleasure team going for our dad. We would only ride if one of the horses was misbehaving or we wanted to go out and hack with friends.

In 1990, Keady decided she wanted to do CDEs and took my father's pleasure four, with my father and myself grooming for her. It wasn't long before we decided we shouldn't be starting out in the combined driving game with a team of Hackney/Clydesdales that weren't suited for that particular challenge. We revamped.

We had started working with four-in-hand driver Bill Long after doing our first couple of CDEs. Keady was the driver; I would be in the background, training at home with her, helping her on the ground, and driving the horses occasionally.

Keady did the 1993 World Pairs Championships at Hamilton Farm in Gladstone, New Jersey, home of the USET Foundation. The horses we took to those Championships were four-in-hand driver Clay Camp's Dutch Warmbloods. It was the first time either of us had represented our country as a competitor. We did it with a lot of training and help from the many good people in our sport back then. I groomed for her. We still train together every single day.

There were 58 pairs of horses at Gladstone, coming from an amazing array of countries. It was definitely an experience to have the Europeans come. They won all the medals. When we saw in person how they drove, we said, "Wow." We'd watch other competitors warming up for dressage and wonder, "How did they make the horses do that?" We had never seen the Europeans, except for a video here and there. No one had YouTube back then.

It was a huge learning curve for us; we found out the sport could be much different than what we had been doing. Keady was just 22. We were too young and naive to be intimidated. She was thrilled when Great Britain's Prince Phillip gave her a ribbon for placing fourteenth in the marathon.

In the late 1990s, I owned the Potbelly Deli, a restaurant in very horsey Southern Pines, North Carolina, with Freddy Whaley, the brother of World Championships driver Katie Whaley. Keady and I would get up at 5:00 a.m, drive Keady's horses, then I'd run off to the restaurant to serve

The first American driver to win a marathon at a World Driving Championships, Randy Cadwell was the individual gold medalist for pairs in the 2007 FEI World Combined Pony Driving Championships with Toby and Taz.

breakfast. Keady would make cookies and all the desserts. My father and Linda Long, Bill Long's wife, would have soup wars. They would each make a soup and whoever sold the most that day would be the winner.

I had all the European VCRs and DVD players at the restaurant, so I would play sales videos of horses for customers while they ate lunch. This was still before YouTube, and not everybody had a cellphone. Different countries had their own video format, so you couldn't just play the European tapes on your home machine. People from Europe would call in to the deli and leave messages: "If Bill Long comes in today, can you tell him this?" I would have business cards lined up along the counter as to who had messages.

In 1998, Keady went to Germany, competing a four-in-hand of Welsh cobs. The breeder of the cobs sent one of them to America, but I didn't have a pony carriage. Four-in-hand driver Gary Stover is how I got into ponies. He bought me a pony carriage and told me I could pay him back by working off what it cost. I started competing a black stallion named Chinook in 2000, and I also competed his brother until he was injured. When the first combined pony World Championships were held in Austria in 2003, Kate Rivers said to me, "Why don't you take Red Robbo?"–her pony. Robbo started my love of ponies. Before that, I had just driven horses out of Keady's team. I never had the pony bug until I started driving Robbo, and then I was like, "Ponies are where it's at."

You train a pony to do something, sometimes he will perform it and sometimes he won't. Every day, it's something different and new. Horses are much more like, "Oh, you want me to do this? Okay."

The Championships helped educate me. I learned when you get an idea about something, even if you're at a World Championships, you follow your instincts. I didn't follow my instincts. I wanted to put Keady on my carriage for the

Randy drove Zahpier and Colby, half of her sister's four-in-hand team, at the Gladstone Driving Event in the mid-1990s.

marathon because it wasn't working out with the person who had come with me. I wasn't mature enough to say, "I'm following my gut and doing what I want to do." We wound up having problems on the marathon because my navigator wasn't listening to me and had his own ideas of what should be happening. I learned if I really think, "This isn't what I want," to open my mouth and say, "This isn't what I want."

I wound up fourteenth as part of the sixth-placed U.S team. I was so angry at myself, I knocked down two cones. As far as I was concerned, fourteenth wasn't good enough. I got another set of Welsh ponies and started driving a pair. Here's how that happened: Keady had looked at Toby and Topaz (Taz, as he was known) for herself but decided to stick with horses. I had begun working with United Kingdom-based Australian driver Boyd Exell at that time. I called Trevor Kimber, who owned Toby and Taz, and asked if I could buy them. The ponies had spent their lives together; that made them a natural pair. If one did something, the other followed and that was what worked so well.

Trevor had the ponies for 12 years, since they were three years old. Boyd negotiated an outrageously low price and told me, "You can't make these ponies single, they have to go together, they're brothers. You have to leave them as a pair."

So that's what I did. They were 14 hands; how bad could it be? They really weren't trained for CDEs; they just liked to go fast. The pair was known in England as "The Runaways."

We started over with their training. Boyd came to the United States from England five days a month to work with us. When he was here, the ponies would go as a pair and then go back to being driven single after he left. Aside from that, I never drove them as a pair until we got to the competitions, because they were so geared up when they were together.

Competing was expensive. We would always fundraise, and our father would help us out some. I went to England to work with Boyd in 2007 and 2009 for three months. We'd get enough money and then go. But there always remained, "How are we getting home?" "I'm not sure." We'd work off a lot of our training, once we got to Boyd's. We would take care of his barn and break horses for him in trade for our lessons and somewhere to live.

I always thought I could do well on marathons because I had spent a lot of time on the back of the carriage for Keady and Bill Long. I never thought I'd go to the World Championships and get a medal, let alone a gold medal. But that's what I did in the 2007 Combined Pony World Championships in Denmark with Toby and Taz.

It was pouring rain on cones day. The fellow who was to drive the cones after me, Lars Dau of Denmark, had beaten me at the same showgrounds in March. I thought, "Okay, he's a really good cones driver." I expected him to have a fault-free go after I had knocked down one ball.

I was sitting there in the rain with my ponies and thought, "I could get the silver, that's so great." Since I expected Lars would do well enough in the cones to win, I left the arena area and walked my ponies down to the USA camp, wanting to get out of the rain.

When I got back to my camp, there was an announcement about Lars' score, but I couldn't hear it. Neither could Tristan Aldrich, who was my navigator. They never announced all the penalties because Lars was from Denmark, the home side. The next thing I knew, though, everyone from the U.S. camp came buzzing down the hill, screaming that I got the gold medal.

I couldn't believe it. I thought, "You must be kidding me." It meant so much because both of my parents were there to see it. Later on, it occurred to us that I was the first U.S. driver ever to win a World Championships marathon. Subsequently, Jacob Arnold did it, but I had my moment.

You work so hard at something, and I had ponies people thought I was nuts to have bought. The second phone call I made after winning the gold was to Mr. Kimber, the 75-year-old man who sold me Toby and Taz. He was just in tears; he said no one would buy his ponies because everyone thought they were crazy. But they were his babies.

Taz was a very special pony. He was a needy child. He was sick at the World Championships, and we got permission to give him antibiotics. I was thinking I was not going to take him on the marathon. But when I drove him the day before, he was his usual crazy self. I used to drive him for an hour on marathon day before I set out on course, just to get him manageable.

After the Championships, the ponies went

Cannon's Majestic Leyla competing in the 2017 World Pony Driving Championships before the carriage tipped over. "You have to be willing to take the bad with the good," observed Randy.

home because I was going to help Keady with her horses while she was competing at the championships in Poland. My father called and said Taz seemed a little off. When he took Taz to the veterinary hospital at North Carolina State University, the vets said it seemed as if he wanted to colic. They did colic surgery and discovered the entire insides of his body were mush. They did a necropsy and still could not figure out what made him so sick, except that his liver enzymes were up. He probably was exposed to something years ago, and the stress of shipping around the world started something in his system. But he'd finished the Championships on heart.

Toby adjusted to the loss of Taz and was still competing at every FEI show for the season when he was 23. Taz never would have adjusted to the loss of Toby. Toby retired at age 27 in 2017. I kept on competing after getting my gold medal, driving in both the Pony Single Championships in

Germany and the Horse Pair Championships in Hungary in 2009.

In 2015, I had two types of breast cancer. After being reserve national champion with Cannon's Majestic Leyla in 2015, I had a double mastectomy. Then Keady got cancer. We took care of each other.

I went to the 2017 World Championships with Leyla, but I missed a turn, looked up, and hit a post. It was complete driver error. The carriage tipped over, and I left in an ambulance. Things like that happen, and you have to be willing to take the bad with the good, because there's often more of the former than the latter. Looking back, knowing what is needed to succeed puts an even brighter shine on a gold medal. The 2007 championships will always be very special to me. While it takes two ponies to make a winning pair, I had a fleet of people helping me and all the work came together at the same time. You couldn't have asked for a better outcome.

PARA-DRESSAGE

PARA-DRESSAGE IS THE ONLY EQUESTRIAN DISCIPLINE that is included in the Paralympic Games, where it has been a regular fixture since 1996. "Para" refers to being parallel to able-bodied sport. With the idea of creating opportunities for all people with impairments to compete and achieve their goals in equestrian sport, athletes are classified according to the degree of their disability.

Grade I is a walk-only test, while at Grade II, the test includes walk and trot work. Grade III is walk and trot, while Grade IV is walk, trot with lateral work, and canter. Grade V is walk, trot, and canter with lateral work.

In 2006, para sport joined the ranks of the other disciplines regulated by the FEI, with both national and international competitions.

VICKI GARNER-SWEIGART

The Para Pioneer

Vcki Garner-Sweigart brought home two gold medals for the United States at the first Paralympics to offer equestrian competition, the 1996 Games in Atlanta, which also was the first Paralympics to attract worldwide corporate sponsorship.

In contrast with today's highly sophisticated para-dressage scene, during the era when Vicki participated, the foundation for most Paralympians was therapeutic riding. At competitions, they rode horses they got through a draw. It would not be until the 2004 Paralympics that riders took part on mounts they owned or rode regularly.

Until an accident that left her paralyzed, Vicki was involved in showing jumpers, winning numerous awards throughout the 1970s and 1980s on her family's horse, Sarak, and her own First Investment. She helped break and train horses on the family farm. Despite her injury, she wanted to continue being a competitive equestrian so she got involved with driving as well as riding again on the route that would lead her to international achievement.

My father, Allen Garner, had shown jumpers and ran a business breaking young horses at our farm in Lancaster County, Pennsylvania, where my sisters and I followed his lead and competed in the jumpers. That ended when I had a life-changing fall in 1981. The horse I was breaking side-stepped when I was mounting. I went off the other side, sustaining a spinal cord injury at the level of T12–L1, while twisting in the air. After that, I wasn't able to move my legs and wound up in a wheelchair. But horses were part of our lives and the competitive spirit was still in me, so I just looked for avenues to keep that going for myself.

I competed at the Devon Horse Show's driving weekend in the 1980s. This was a new avenue for me and my former jumper, First Investment, a Quarter Horse. He was the first horse I purchased by myself. I fox hunted him and showed him in junior-amateur jumpers right before my accident. After my accident, we sent him out for training so I could drive him and maintain a relationship with him.

I started out along my new road by sitting on Pretty Boy, the reliable family Shetland pony we got when I was four years old. Then I became involved with the Thorncroft Equestrian Center for therapeutic riding in Malvern, where I got exposure to the fact that there were horse shows for the disabled. I showed Sarak at Thorncroft in the 1980s where they had equitation, trail classes, and some dressage. Things took off from that point. I realized if I wanted to do any of the more serious

Vicki Garner-Sweigart won two gold medals at the 1996 Paralympics, the first to include equestrian. She rode Miss Jane Marple, owned by Linda Fritsch.

competitions, I had to get into the dressage end.

While on the board of Graystone Manor Therapeutic Riding Center in Lancaster, I was introduced to Carol Henkel. She was head instructor for the program, rider, trainer, and an "r" AHSA dressage judge, who introduced me to dressage. One of Carol's students was planning to try out for the 1996 Paralympics, and I thought it was something I could try out for, too, even though I didn't know much about it. I had dabbled in wheelchair racing, so I knew about the Paralympics, but I didn't know equestrian was part of it (which actually didn't happen until 1996).

One of the first requirements for aspiring Paralympians who wanted to be considered for the team was a training camp at California Polytechnic State University in Pomona. It was there we were classified by our functional ability, giving competitors equal chances. That was a whole new experience. Just getting across the country to California was a particularly huge step. I wasn't much of a traveler. Flying was relatively new to me, and I couldn't have done it without the help of my sister, Heidi Ulrich.

I had never met any of the people coaching out there, and we were riding horses we didn't know. That was a growth experience for me. I was very challenged at the training camp, but at the same time, it was enlightening. I appreciated learning how other people managed their disabilities and the adaptive equipment they used to ride.

After the final selection trial in 1996, team members and coaches went to the Winslow Therapeutic Riding Center in Warwick, New York, for a final training session before going to Atlanta. The challenge was that you had to go alone. I was not allowed to take my support system. The idea was that we would get to know each other in the way we'd have to work together as a unit—without help from those outside the team. It was very scary for me. That was the time when cellphones weren't quite universal, so I felt a little disconnected. I was very comfortable and independent at home, but I wasn't really comfortable about leaving home and riding strange horses, especially on my own.

A big concern with the horses we rode was not only safety, but also suitability, to adjust to a horse chosen in a draw. My riding experience as a youngster helped considerably with my ability to adapt to different styles and types of horses.

We had a sports psychologist come in to talk to us during the session at Winslow, and we got to know our coaches. But there were other things to get used to. At home, my husband, Carl Sweigart, and my sister, Heidi, would lift me out of the chair and put me on the horse sideways. I would swing my leg over the front of the horse to finish the mounting process. Others on the team who were in wheelchairs were used to a ramp, where you'd do your own transfer onto the horse.

I felt we had good bonding and a good clinic in Warwick, but when we were leaving with Atlanta in our sights, I said, "Now I'm anxious." They told me not to be, and instead to channel that energy into being prepared.

All the U.S. athletes flew from Dulles Airport in Virginia to Atlanta on charter flights. I thought, "Why not drive down?" but I was learning how things are done when a team is involved.

We were all briefed on what was expected from us while representing our country. I hadn't realized when you're part of something international like that, there are rules and regulations you need to abide by. Whether it's wearing your uniform to be interviewed, the fact that there's drug testing, or lots of other little things, there was much I wasn't aware of.

When we got to the Georgia Horse Park in Conyers where the competition would be held, there was so much to take in. The stadium was big. Oh my goodness, I don't know if there would have been any place I could have ridden that would have prepared me for that. That stadium, the whole environment, and even the barn facility met up to my expectations for the Olympics. It was really, really awesome, the enormity of it. It lived up to all the publicity.

Just being in the Olympic Village with the teams from other countries—that whole experience was amazing. I was pretty comfortable in the barn and around the people there, but to be around all

Vicki Garner-Sweigart on her first pony, Pretty Boy. Riding was part of her life from the beginning, since her father showed jumpers and had a business breaking young horses.

Sarak, the Pennsylvania Horse Breeders Association Junior Jumper Champion in 1971, under the guidance of teenage Vicki Garner-Sweigart.

the athletes from different sports in the Village, that was quite something.

I was nervous, but not overly. I really did a lot of prep work at home as far as going to horse shows and working through things when they didn't go the way you wanted them to in the morning, or if your warm-up had some glitches. I felt I was well-prepared to go. We had substantial time down there to get to know our horses. Since someone else was caring for and feeding them, I could focus on the competition. Heidi had volunteered as a groom and was assigned to a rider from Great Britain, but it was very reassuring to have her close by in the barn. I was glad she was there and that the Games were on U.S. soil so my husband, friends, and whole family could come down in a half-dozen campers and share in the moment.

I had not done any international dressage competition before the Olympics, so I did not realize the level at which the Europeans were riding. The

overseas riders were looking for types of horses we didn't quite have yet, as far as their carriage and how they performed there.

I drew the best horse in Atlanta, Miss Jane Marple. I believe whoever rode her would have gotten a gold medal. Dottie Morkis, who rode on the 1976 Olympic bronze medal team, came to Atlanta and helped our coaches. I drew to go first. I can remember Dottie saying she didn't like that. I replied, "I don't have a problem going first; setting the time and they have to chase me." I was thinking of my days in the jumpers. "You just put in the best round you can and then it falls where it is because you know you did your best," I told her. It worked out all right.

I was classified as a Grade II, which was walk-trot. I got the gold in the team championship dressage test and the musical *Kur*, or Freestyle, to the music from *Oliver*, as well as winning the warm-up class. We didn't have a podium for the medal

Driving a 26-year-old family pony helped keep Vicki Garner-Sweigart involved with horses after a life-changing fall in 1981.

ceremonies, as they do nowadays. We were able to parade in on our horses while music was playing. Then the medals were put around our necks and we got flowers. The owner of Miss Marple, Linda Fritsch, got to lead her horse in. It was pretty emotional when they played the Star-Spangled Banner. Just to have the U.S. flag go up was quite something.

I tried out for the 2000 team and did not make it. While the costs weren't near what it takes to compete today, financially, it got a little hard to continue. And anyway, I had the ultimate moments for any Paralympian in Atlanta.

I was inspired by Hope Hand, founder of the U.S. Para Equestrian Association, who has done so much to promote our sport. She had a vision of where Para could go, and the work needed to be competitive against the European riders. I saw it reflected in the competition at the 2018 FEI World Equestrian Games, which I watched on the live stream. The steps they have taken to improve the competition are wonderful, and it's impressive seeing such talented horses, riders, and coaches take part. But it also was wonderful to be on the ground floor, at the first Paralympics to offer equestrian. I just wanted to enjoy the moment there, and I did. I had a great time.

LYNN SEIDEMANN

I Felt I Was Whole Again

Lynn became a paraplegic when a 1983 snow skiing accident left her with no feeling or function from the navel down. Starting her riding experience with two side-walkers and a leader, she became an independent rider by 1998. Lynn competed at the National Horse Show in St. Louis, Missouri, where she won the high point award for her division and earned the highest dressage score of the show. That was the impetus for the start of her international career.

The mother of two, Nick and Jena, Lynn has been very active in sports throughout her life, competing not only in dressage, but also in wheelchair basketball and wheelchair tennis doubles, winning silver at the 1992 Paralympic Games in Barcelona, Spain. After she switched sports, she won silver in the Grade I Individual Dressage Freestyle at the 2004 Paralympics in Athens. In the 2003 World Championships in Belgium, she took gold in the Championships test, and silver in the Freestyle.

The 2008 Paralympics in Hong Kong marked the fourth and final Games of Lynn's career and her third as an equestrian. She has served on the U.S. Equestrian Federation high performance and selection committees. Lynn, the USEF's 2007 Para-Equestrian National Champion, also was the vice president of the U.S. Para-Equestrian Association.

The Florida resident has trained a mini-horse to do therapeutic driving and hopes to focus more on that, or driving for the disabled, when she retires from her job as an information technology specialist.

The 2008 Paralympics in Hong Kong was the third and final equestrian Paralympics competition for Lynn Seidemann.

When you have an accident you're just thinking about how to survive. The first year or so is spent trying to find other people with the same issues and seeing how they are dealing with it.

It kind of threw me back into sports, which was my orientation from the days when I played soccer for the University of Cincinnati and dreamed of being a professional soccer player. Those I met after my accident would say, "Try this, try that." It helped me adjust to life in general by being around other people who were just trying to be athletes.

I knew I needed sports in my life and having been an athlete, I wondered, "How can I still do that?" I started off with basketball and then tennis. I went to the Paralympic Games in 1992 for wheelchair tennis and won team silver.

Tennis was a pretty huge strain on my body, however. So after '92, I thought I was retiring. But I loved being physical. I feel you need to be active and doing things, or you're not really living. I needed opportunities to keep me active. I couldn't just join a local basketball club or whatever.

I was looking for something that would give me strength in my stomach, sitting straight in my chair, help me keep continuing to work, and help me feel like I'm really a part of life. For me, it's mentally necessary to keep going and doing things. Then I heard about a therapeutic riding barn called Equest in Wylie, Texas, for disabled people. "They can't be putting people in wheelchairs on horses," I figured.

Through research, I found riding helps strengthen the abdominal muscles. When you're pushing in a wheelchair, you're always pushing forward, and it rounds your shoulders. Horseback riding involves always sitting straight, with your shoulders back. It encourages really good posture. So I thought I'd try it to see if it helped me keep active. I was not a horse person at all, and the first time I rode, I was stiff as a board afterward. I was

Lynn Seidemann on Phoenix at the 2003 World Championships. "The more I got into it, the more I liked it," she said of her experience with riding after becoming a paraplegic in a 1983 snow skiing accident.

like, "Oh, my gosh. This is the hardest thing I've ever done, and it can't be helping me out." Then it became a challenge. I saw another lady in a wheelchair who loved it and told me it relaxed her. Really? "Yes."

As soon as I did relax, it was so much easier. It started making me sit straighter and helped my stomach muscles. I loved being around the barn, the smell, taking care of animals. The more I got into it, the more I liked it.

When you compete, it gives you the goal to keep in better shape, to make the effort to be the best you can. I guess it's that challenge, "Can I do the next step? What's the limit of the capabilities I have right now?" This barn was promoting doing more. They started taking me to competitions. When I started with dressage, it was on a borrowed horse. I actually trained with one specific horse, a little Dutch Warmblood, Hershey, who was just right for me. I leased him from a therapeutic barn. Hershey wasn't too tall, I could keep my balance—he was perfect.

I borrowed a horse named Miss Jane Marple in 1999 to compete in the qualifiers for the 2000

Lynn Seidemann, who earned gold and silver medals with Phoenix at the 2003 Para-Dressage World Championships, also was a wheelchair tennis medalist.

Sydney Paralympics in Australia. She was the mare that Vicki Garner-Sweigart rode to two gold medals for the United States in the 1996 Paralympics, the first ever that included equestrian. I had not expected to be in the Paralympic Games again after my time in tennis. When you're an athlete, though, it really helps your mind and soul to use your body. Riding felt as if I were walking again. I had some great moments on horseback. They were doing a fundraiser trail ride at a therapy barn, and I was able to lope through a path with all these Monarch butterflies fluttering along the sides. Memorable.

I made the team for Sydney, and it was simply incredible. What a beautiful equestrian facility it was, and people there made for a really great experience. I was probably a little green when I went to Sydney. I just happened to get a good draw, but I didn't get a medal. It showed me where I needed to improve and that I needed to work on these skills to move up to the next level and be competitive.

There was so much more to the experience than that, though. It was really exciting how everybody came together, the whole atmosphere. That hooked me. We had a great team. We had races with the staff in the wheelchairs in the barn aisles.

I liked it when we changed to our own horses for the 2004 Paralympics. When you're catch-riding and you have a disability, each disability is slightly different. So horses drawn at random might not understand your cues. It wasn't fair to the horses to do it that way. It was very stressful trying to get matched up with horses. It's just so much better to have your own horse. You can really build a rapport with your horse, and that makes it a truer test of what you're able to do.

In 2002, I bought Mac, a Hanoverian who was fabulous. He taught me what it was to do dressage. Mac really knew his stuff, but unfortunately, he got hurt later that year after I qualified on him for the 2003 World Championships in Belgium. I had to borrow a Polish Warmblood, Phoenix, for those Games.

I was graded as 1B, which is walk-trot, and Lee Pearson of Great Britain was in that category as well. Lee went on to be a Para superstar, and was even knighted for his spectacular record. But in Belgium, I beat Lee. It was the only time I ever came close to him. I won gold in the Championships test. I also brought home silver in the Freestyle. And at the Athens Paralympics the following year, I earned silver again in the Freestyle, when Lee won. I incorporated lengthening, leg-yields, and serpentine into my walk to make my Freestyle more interesting.

All of these equestrian competitions have been a great experience. I love horse people; the passion for their animals and that partnership is really great. I felt like I was whole again when I rode. Any time I got on a horse, I could run, jump, and play once more. What bothered me was how much help I needed to do the horses. It takes a lot of extra people to enable me to do it. While I really wanted to be independent, when I did it, I told myself, "Take the help. They're willing to do it to give you this experience. You have to be a little more humble about it."

As an athlete, I want to be physically and mentally challenged. It's a great journey. I wouldn't change it. Going to the Games, talking to people, exchanging pins, and hearing a little bit of their stories is wonderful, as is the camaraderie among American athletes. And of course, getting the medals is really special. I think of how these opportunities have made me evolve as a better person.

It's so great that America provides this opportunity to represent the country. The U.S Equestrian Team Foundation and the U.S. Equestrian Federation play huge roles. There are so many people behind this to make it happen.

KATE SHOEMAKER AND ROXANNE "ROXIE" TRUNNELL

The Match Was Perfect

T he word "teammates" takes on new meaning when it refers to Kate Shoemaker and Roxie Trunnell, medal-winning members of the U.S. Para-Equestrian Dressage Team at the 2018 FEI World Equestrian Games in Tryon, North Carolina. Kate, an equine veterinarian, generously loaned her horse, Dolton, to Roxie for the WEG. Although Dolton was only six, the youngest age at which a horse is eligible for para competition, he and Roxie earned the bronze medal in the FEI Grade I Freestyle with a score of 75.487 percent. Meanwhile, Kate beat the odds with another of her horses, Solitaer 40, who had recovered from a broken coffin bone barely in time to qualify for the WEG, then clinched bronze in the Grade IV Freestyle there with a score of 73.230 percent.

The idea of having Roxie riding Dolton took root after Kate spoke with Laureen Johnson, the USEF's director of para-equestrian and Michel Assouline, the para team coach, about Dolton being a top prospect for the Tokyo 2020 Olympics as a Grade I horse. After several years of observing the top teams, Kate realized there was often a common theme: a top Grade I horse.

Kate, from Arizona, deals with motor-control dysfunction, muscle weakness, and spasms on the right side of her body. She compensates for the loss of three planes of motion control in her ankle with an ankle foot brace and uses special rein stops for added rein control. But nothing can stop her.

Kate Shoemaker and Solitaer 40 at the 2018 WEG, where they clinched a bronze Freestyle medal.

Roxie Trunnell thanks Dolton for a job well done at the 2018 WEG.

Roxie was a competitor in able-bodied dressage who aspired to be an Olympian. When she was a teenager, she created her own business to help purchase her first dressage horse, Nice Touch, known as Touché. She earned a U.S. Dressage Federation Bronze Medal and was close to obtaining her Silver Medal until contracting a virus in 2009 that caused swelling in her brain. She lapsed into a coma and suffered a stroke after a blood clot went to her brain. She now requires a wheelchair to get around for the most part.

Determined to ride Touché again, Roxie had the help of her family and friends to get her back in the saddle. After a long recovery, the native of Washington State slowly began to ride once more and completed her master's degree in psychology with a focus on equine-assisted psychotherapy. She is a veteran of the 2014 WEG and was tenth individually at the 2016 Paralympics. Her bronze at WEG in Tryon was her first medal in a global championship.

Kate Shoemaker and Roxie Trunnell with Dolton, the horse Kate loaned Roxie for the 2018 FEI World Equestrian Games.

KATE SHOEMAKER

When I first sat on Dolton as a three-year-old, I realized this horse was very special in terms of rideablity and temperament, and of course, we already knew the quality of his walk was very nice.

In the winter of his six-year-old year (the first year a horse is eligible for para competition), I hauled him to Wellington, Florida, from my home in Arizona, and Michel Assouline, the Para Team Coach, watched him go. Then he asked if Roxie could come and sit on him. When Roxie rode Dolton, the match was perfect.

That was when Michel said, "We need him for WEG." With Dolton only being six, I knew we had our work cut out for us to get him ready for an international-level qualifying competition in three months. The plan was to take it one step at a time to ensure he was not over-faced. Dolton went on to answer every question we asked of him.

Obviously, there was a big risk that by offering Roxie the ride on Dolton, I might keep myself off the team. However, my view was that the team needed Dolton, and the team I wanted to be a part of would include the best horses we had available. Therefore, I needed to make myself better if I wanted to earn a spot on the team. It pushed me to ride even better.

I feel immense pride when I see Roxie and Dolton being successful together. I find it a lot more stressful to watch Dolton go than what I feel when I'm riding. I just want so badly for them to be as successful as possible. When Roxie and Dolton won the bronze medal, it was huge validation for what we knew the horse was capable of. What's exciting is that it is just the tip of the iceberg of what is possible for Dolton.

I don't think anyone expected Soli and me to be capable of being in medal contention at WEG. On the international scene, we were virtual unknowns. Even one of the WEG commentators on Freestyle day said in the minutes after my ride that, in essence, the medal contenders were still to come. (What he actually said during the next ride was, "Now we start getting into the medal contenders.")

I'm experienced at being the long shot and perform very well in that capacity. In fact, it was a long shot that Soli would recover from his broken coffin bone in time to obtain qualifying scores; then we were the long shots for making the team, when we were seventh in the U.S. rankings, and after that, of course, we were long shots to medal.

After a rough start on the first day at the World Equestrian Games, when we ended in seventh place, we were lucky to qualify among the top eight from the individual competition for the Freestyle, but we gained form each day going from seventh to fifth to third.

I had many discussions with my trainer over the summer that I was going to be fifth at the WEG if all the riders put in their best tests. This meant I needed to do something special to move up into the medals. On the final day, I knew Soli felt different in the first minute of walking. He just felt good in his body. I realized through a lot of answered prayers that Soli and I were able to have the ride of which we were capable. And we did.

Ironically, for the first six months of our relationship, Soli really did not like me. He was always well-behaved, but I could tell how much he missed his "family" of people from Europe. In the years since, however, Soli and I have become extremely tight, and there is no doubt who his person is. He's a "highly connected" horse, and whenever I left town, I would get phone calls asking whether he doesn't eat much. As soon as I would get home, however, he would return to his normal self and appetite. I've never had a horse so bonded to me. He knows just how to "talk" to me to get me to stay with him as long as possible at the barn. I was actually quite worried at WEG due to the restrictions on the time that riders could be in the stables because

of logistics and other commitments, but thankfully, Soli also was quite attached to his groom, Alexus Sisley, who took care of him throughout the Games. I certainly owe her for how happy she kept Soli during the entire process.

My biggest ambition is to see the U.S. program become a powerhouse on the world stage of para-dressage. Ultimately, the team is more important than the individual. Even so, I still have big ambitions for my future. My personal goal is to someday win a gold medal at the Paralympics. I am working every day to become the best possible rider that I can be. I also hope to show what para riders can do outside of para competitions and I want to someday earn my U.S. Dressage Federation Gold Medal.

My schedule is 100 percent horse. I'm either working with patients or I'm working on my training. I eat, breathe, and sleep horse, as it is my true passion in life that fuels me. Being busy is what makes me happy and keeps me charging ahead. Para gives me the opportunity to strive to compete on a world stage at the highest levels. The chance to make a team and represent my country internationally allows me the opportunity to fulfill lifelong dreams. I am a very goal-oriented person and para-dressage gives me opportunities that I could otherwise only dream of. To say it is life-changing would be an understatement.

ROXIE TRUNNELL

It means a lot to medal, given that I am aware of all the work that has gone into getting the United States on the podium. There are so many who worked extremely hard to make the 2018 World Equestrian Games as successful as it was and I feel like there was a collective sigh of relief from everybody once the medals were achieved.

I've known Kate and her parents for several years through the para shows. I've always found her to be very positive, even when things are going wrong (she doesn't let the little things bother her). That's how I am too, especially at a show, since anything can happen during a test.

When I first was asked to try out a certain horse, I didn't know anything about him except that he was six years old and had an international walk. Later that evening, I received a text in which I learned that the horse was Kate's Dolton. I knew Dolton was very handsome and Kate had really worked on desensitizing him to "spooky" situations. So I felt comfortable getting on him, even though he was so young.

When I sat on Dolton, I was amazed at his quality, as well as how para-ready he was. While he will need more muscle development to be competitive as a Grade IV horse, the prospect that he will be a top horse for Kate is there.

I was surprised she allowed me to ride her horse, even if it meant that he could possibly outperform her current horse, Solitaer 40. For her to realize Dolton had the walk that a Grade 1 needs and then to trust him with another rider just shows how she believes in Dolton's potential to become a superstar. She fully understood that with Dolton as a Grade I horse, the United States would become a nation that could make it to the podium.

His personality is very goofy. You can tell he is a young horse by the way he acts on the ground, but when you get in the saddle, he is very much all business and acts far older than his years. Just being able to handle a huge championship like WEG is a testament to how smart and mature he is.

He helps me by not being reactive to things. Prior to Dolton, I rode a mare (NTEC Daytona Beach) who was always paying attention to what was going on around her to see if she needed to flee. When I'm in Dolton's saddle, you can tell by the direction in which his ears are pointed that he is listening only to my cues. That is very important when I'm riding, since my balance was affected by the stroke I suffered. If a horse makes any quick movement when I'm riding, I could become unbalanced and fall off.

Riding has mostly helped me mentally. Prior to becoming a para-equestrian, I would go to school or work and then go ride. This had been the norm for a good chunk of my life. When my friends would go to parties on weekends I would be going to horse shows. After I woke up from the coma, it was very important for me to go out to the barn as much as possible, even if I couldn't ride, just to feed carrots and cookies to the horses because that felt "normal" to me.

I have an incredibly special bond with my mare Touché. I have owned her since she was eight and rode all the way to Prix St. Georges on her. She is a very spirited redhead who has put me in the dirt more times than I can count. Everybody was nervous about having me get on her again because she can be rather difficult, but I was stubborn and wanted to ride her. When she saw me siting in my wheelchair, she bent her knees and leaned over to make it easier for me to get on her back. When I got off-balance in the saddle, she would slow down or do some kind of lateral work to help compensate and let me find my balance again. She recognized I was not the same rider I used to be, and she was going to make it her job to be sure I was safe. I ended up taking her to the 2014 WEG in Normandy, France, where she was the oldest horse there at age 18. But she showed the young horses how it was done by being the best horse on the U.S. para-dressage team.

I promised her there that I would never make her go down another centerline again if she just got me through my first big international show, and she did me so proud. I still ride Touché even though it's at a painfully slow walk or slow jog now (she's 24), but I will always keep her because she has done so much for me.

I smile when people say, "Oh, Touché is a nice calm para horse." She's a perfect para horse for me,

Roxie Trunnell on the podium at WEG 2018 with her bronze Freestyle medal.

but anyone else she'll have no problem putting in the dirt. That bond is something that has helped me mentally. I think, "Well, Touché has known me before I got sick and now knows me like this and can accept the changes, so then the rest of the world can just accept me as well."

That's not to say riding hasn't helped me physically, too. With my disability, I have an issue with my balance and coordination. My official diagnosis is *cerebellum ataxia*. Riding helps keep my core in good working order and having to do very small movements with the reins leads me to really concentrate on what I am doing with my body.

I also work out at a gym regularly, and while I'm in the wheelchair 90 percent of the time, I am able to walk with a walker, forearm crutches, or a cane. I focus on my walking several times a week to make sure my legs don't get weak.

It's very exciting being part of the highest-placing U.S. para-dressage team at a World Equestrian Games thus far. It was kind of like an underdog feeling in that the other nations haven't viewed the United States as a "podium threat," and then we walked out there and showed them that we were capable of getting the scores required to get there. I think that might have shocked some nations, while also giving others a hope that if the United States can up its game and put in the work to have success, then they could be capable of doing it as well.

Being part of the team has led me to focus not just on my ride but also on being available to help my teammates with their rides as well. At WEG, even when I had a bad ride on team test day, there were two other riders on the team that I could be there to help have stellar rides. That way, my "bad" ride wouldn't affect the team as much as it would have if I had just gotten angry and didn't support my teammates.

Being on a team has led me to ride not just for myself, but also to be more aware that a good or bad ride affects the other riders on my team. I realize it takes a contribution from every rider to get the U.S. team on the podium.

REBECCA "BECCA" HART

Touching the Podium

The 2018 FEI World Equestrian Games in Tryon, North Carolina, brought fruition to Becca's years of effort as a para-equestrian, when she won the silver medal with an impressive score of 73.240 in the Grade III Freestyle after earning a historic bronze—the first ever for a U.S. para rider at the WEG—earlier in the competition. A seven-time national champion, she has represented the United States in three WEGs and four Paralympics.

The Pennsylvania native got involved with the Paralympic movement in 1998 at a regional competition in Atlanta, where she decided she wanted to aim for international competition. Becca was born with a rare genetic disease, hereditary spastic paraplegia (HSP), a progressive impairment that causes muscle wasting and paralysis from the middle of the back down. The Pennsylvania State University graduate works with the Hereditary Spastic Paraplegia Foundation to increase awareness about HSP, and helps children who are dealing with the condition.

Becca lives in Wellington, Florida, where she trains with Melissa McLaren-Velix and works as a barista and manager for Starbucks.

The two most important rides of my life were in North Carolina.

The second was in Tryon at the 2018 FEI World Equestrian Games, where I won the USA's first ever para-equestrian WEG medal.

The first was decades earlier, when I was in the horse-crazy little girl stage, coming home from a vacation in that state, and saw a sign by the side of the road advertising pony rides. I screamed at my father to stop the car. Unfortunately for him, he stopped. They popped me on a pony and off I went in a little Western saddle. I was holding onto the saddle horn desperately because I was slightly terrified, but at the same time, ecstatically happy. I have a picture of that cute little fuzzy black pony, and I thank him every day. The rest of the car ride home

Becca on her way to a medal at the 2018 FEI WEG aboard El Corona Texel.

to Pittsburgh, I was like, "Dad, we have to do this at home. Can you find me someplace at home to ride?"

It took two years before we met Ray Harehold at Hobby Horse Farm in Fairview. He was a classic old horseman. I told him, "I walk funny, but I want to ride for real." He just kind of smiled and said, "Okay, we can work with that."

The first horse I ever rode for lessons was a mixed breed named Seaweed. I started out in the hunter and jumper ranks. I didn't realize para sport existed at that point. While many para riders began with therapeutic riding, I never went that route. Sport for disability wasn't really well-established until 20 years ago; it was much more on the therapeutic side.

I knew right from the beginning that even though riding is absolutely valuable physical therapy, as a 13-year-old kid, that wasn't what I was looking for. I wanted horses to be an equalizer and allow me to achieve things physically that I couldn't on my own. With horses, all of a sudden the disability was taken out. They became my legs, and I was able to ride just as well as my able-bodied counterparts, if not better. On that same plane, it evened the playing field. I did hunter paces;

Becca Hart took her first pony ride in North Carolina, where she would return as an adult to medal at the FEI World Equestrian Games.

I jumped and stayed on by sheer force of will. I was a little more able-bodied when I was 10 to 13 because my condition is progressive. I still had a little strength in my leg at that point. Now it's sheer balance and core keeping me on the horse, but I will still pop over a small rail here and there because I enjoy it.

While I'm a professional rider and athlete, unlike most able-bodied riders at the top level and some para riders, I do not have my own equestrian clients. I work for Starbucks in Wellington, Florida, basically managing the floor while I am head barista. Starbucks has been an amazing support to me. They were my first corporate sponsor, and I've been part of their elite athlete program since the Games in 2008. I'm financially backed by them. I can take six to eight weeks off to go on a European tour and still have a job when I come back. The ability to have my outside job and maintain my competitive career is huge. Starbucks has been incredibly flexible, where with other, more traditional jobs that is not always the case.

I have watched para-equestrian grow; it used to be like an intercollegiate-type sport, where there would be a pool of horses and you would draw a horse. You'd have about three hours to kind of figure each other out and then you would trot down centerline on the international stage and kind of hope for the best. The game totally changed when we could use our own horses, which started for the Paralympics at the 2004 Athens Games. It was the catalyst that grew para sport into what it is today. The quality of the horse, the riding, the training skyrocketed. The word "para" does not refer to being a paraplegic or a disabled person. It refers to being parallel to able-bodied sport. When we switched to our own horses, it truly grabbed that parallel, and we are held to the same standards and regulation as able-bodied sport. Having our own horses enabled us to truly embrace that.

A huge logistical strain for hosting para shows

used to be finding people who would donate a horse and let not only a strange rider, but a para rider, compete the horse. That made it challenging for management to find the number of horses needed to host an international competition. You can't use just any horse for para competition. Finding the one who doesn't take advantage and is willing to compensate used to be a little bit luck of the draw. If you got one of the better horses in the pool, you had a better chance. They judged it like a normal dressage test. You had to be fluid and accurate and harmonious and look the part. It was like any able-bodied rider having to take any Grand Prix horse and go down centerline and say, "Do your best test."

Now, when you use your own horse, it's taken a little bit of the pressure of the unknown away. At the same time, I have to say that I thrive in pressure situations. I enjoy that kind of competitive atmosphere. Having that little bit of extra positive tension and adrenaline helps put me into my bubble with my horse.

My parents, Sue Dobson and Terry Hart, mortgaged their house to buy my first international horse so I could continue competing when para had switched to a competition where you owned your horse. They sacrificed their dream for me. They had wanted to own their home outright and were only a couple of payments away when we were at the turning point in 2008. At that time, the quality of horses had skyrocketed and I didn't have access to that. I said, "I think this is my ending point," and they came back to me and said, "No, it's not." My parents are amazing.

We bought a Hanoverian, Norteassa (barn name Pippin). It was a breakthrough moment for me. When it's a horse you draw that you haven't ridden before, you need overall catch riding skills to get the job done. But you lose a little bit of the partnership, the harmony, and small detail of the communication between rider and horse. With Pippin,

Becca and Tex have a special form of communication that contributed to their success at the WEG.

I was able to finesse my skills. My body doesn't work the way an able-bodied rider's would, so I was able to say, "Okay, this shift means X,Y, and Z," and really smooth out the performance and harmony of the ride we were doing. I can just get a lot more detail and a lot more presence and power through communication that we established over the years, rather than just three hours. I have compensating aids I am allowed to use as a para rider that an able-bodied rider wouldn't be able to use. I do a combo of whip cues, vocal cues, and weight cues. In equestrian, there is the silent communication that is universal and standard classical, but within that, each horse kind of has its own dialect. That's what I was able to finesse, each horse's dialect.

"Pops" or "clucks" mean very specific things to individual horses. Pippin's vocal cues were different from the ones for Tex—El Corona Texel, the horse I rode in Tryon. Sometimes, a certain noise works for a horse in a certain way. I had to figure out which horse responded to which cluck, different ways that I was able to hold my body on the horse and shift with my shoulder. If I bring my shoulder forward and give a certain cluck, that means canter. It is a tiny, under-my-breath cluck.

A pop sound is a trot cue, a cluck is when I want a little more power within whatever gait I'm doing. A double-kiss is a walk. If I'm trotting and do a double kiss, it acts like a half-halt and the horse will come down.

Unlike able-bodied riders, I am allowed to use these voice cues, but I try not to. When you're in arena where other people are schooling or teaching, if someone says pick up the canter, it can muddy the waters a little bit.

WEG was my one-year anniversary with Tex, a nine-year-old Dutch gelding owned by Rowan O'Riley, my current sponsor, who has been fantastic not only for me, but also for growing the sport and sponsoring a lot of international para shows. It was time to do some horse-hunting after the 2016 retirement of Schroeter's Romani, my 2014 WEG and 2016 Paralympics mount I owned with Margaret Duprey of Cherry Knoll Farm, Barbara Summer, and William and Sandy Kimmel. I found Tex in Holland, where he was on a very professional able-bodied program. He has incredibly high-quality gaits and an amazing brain. He can be a little quirky, but he's the kindest horse I've ever met. He wants to do the right thing. I like to have a hotter horse because I would much rather contain the energy than create the energy, since I don't have the body strength to say, "Keep going, stay here."

When I first saw Tex, I knew I had to be very quiet and walk carefully. Horses can be a little reactive with how a para rider walks, since it's different. But my very graceful self tripped on a cobblestone, and I body-checked myself into this completely strange horse who had never seen a para rider before. He kind of stiffened. If he had moved away from me I would have fallen on my face, but he actually stepped into me and put me on my feet. Right there, I knew he was going to get it.

When I got on him, he didn't immediately understand my signals because he was used to classical communication via leg pressure. So he didn't always get the right answer. He always offered me something. To me, that was the mark of a horse who would make a good international mount.

In 2017, while I was showing Tex in Tryon two weeks after getting him, the Velcro tether on my lower leg that keeps it in place fell off. When Tex did a spin, I fell off. It was the first time, and hopefully the last, that I've fallen off in an international arena. There I was on the ground, and I couldn't get up by myself. The judge at C, Carlos Lopez of Portugal, came to my aid, picked me up and helped me walk out. When you fall it's a huge bash for your confidence. He eased the embarrassment of the moment by saying, "Your horse is phenomenal. You just need more time. Don't give up, you'll get there."

The pressure was at its ultimate during the 2018 WEG, because being in my home country, the people who normally couldn't come to international competitions, like my family, were there. It meant so much to be able to have them see me ride after 20 years of trying to touch that podium, because I have been close quite often. I felt like the eternal bridesmaid. I wondered, "Can I just step on that podium to finally have them experience it with me?"

It was quite an emotional time. I had ridden early in the individual test. There were seven rides left in that class before naming the medalists. I didn't know if my score was going to hold up. My sister, Katie, who's a year older than I am, sat there with me and squeezed my hand. She kept saying, "You've got this." But I wasn't sure. Then while we were waiting, Carlos Lopez came over. He put his hand on my shoulder and said, "I don't have to tell you it was good. You know it was good, you have the bronze."

And I did. When it was announced, I just burst into tears and Katie just burst into tears—and she's not an overly emotional person like that. It was such an amazing moment to share with her because she's been on this journey right from the beginning. To have my mom and dad and my very

Carlos Lopez, who encouraged Becca Hart when she was starting to ride El Corona Texel, congratulates her on medaling at the 2018 FEI World Equestrian Games. With them is Becca's sister, Katie.

first dressage riding instructor, Linda Fritsch, there was really special on our home turf. (Linda was the owner of Miss Jane Marple, the mare on which Vicki Garner-Sweigart won two gold medals at the 1996 Paralympics, the first to include equestrian.)

It was a culmination of years and years of work, not just on my part but on the part of everyone who had gotten me to that point. It was the first-ever medal for a U.S. para rider in the WEG since our discipline joined those Games in 2010. I thought back to being an adolescent with a disability, coming to terms with what my "normal" was going to be. All of those emotions were in that medal, and I cried.

Although my condition has the potential to someday make it impossible for me to ride, I am refusing to let it do that because I am too stubborn to get to that point. In hereditary spastic paraplegia, the nerve pathways from brain to muscle shut down, which is what causes the atrophy and spasticity, as well as the lack of coordination and control. Being in the para sport, you're constantly adapting to new and different things. It's an incredibly competitive atmosphere, but also supportive. If you tell the para community, "This is what I'm dealing with, does anyone have any suggestions for adaptive aids and cues?" you get lots of help. With that, I think I will be able to continue riding. I may have to modify it and maybe do it differently, but I'll still be able to do it. The 2020 Tokyo Paralympics is completely in my sights and ideally, I'll be standing up on that podium.

REINING

REINING ORIGINATED FROM THE MOVES THAT HORSES MAKE when herding cattle. It was recognized as a sport in 1949 by the American Quarter Horse Association. The managing organization of reining is the National Reining Horse Association (NRHA), formed in 1966.

Reining is designed to show the athletic ability of a ranch-type horse within a show arena; no cattle are involved. Reining patterns all include small slow circles, large fast circles, flying lead changes, rollbacks over the hocks, 360-degree spins done in place, and sliding stops that are the trademark of the discipline.

The NRHA rulebook states that the "best reined horse should be willingly guided or controlled with little or no apparent resistance..."

Reining, which first appeared in the 2002 FEI World Equestrian Games, is the only Western FEI discipline.

THE MCQUAYS AND THE MCCUTCHEONS

The First Family of Reining

Over three generations, members of the McQuay/McCutcheon family have been part of all the U.S. teams that dominated the gold medal history of reining in the FEI World Equestrian Games, ever since the discipline became a part of those championships in 2002. Tom McCutcheon was on the gold medal squads in 2002 (when his brother, Scott, was also part of the team), 2006, and 2010, winning individual silver on Conquistador Whiz in 2002, and individual gold with Gunners Special Nite in 2010. His father-in-law, Tim McQuay, took team gold and individual silver in 2006 with Mister Nicadual, and team gold at the 2010 WEG with Hollywoodtinseltown. In 2014, it was the turn of Mandy McCutcheon, who is Tom's wife and Tim's daughter, to win WEG team gold and individual bronze with Yellow Jersey. She was the first woman and the first non-professional to ride on a U.S. WEG reining team.

A third generation made its appearance at the 2018 WEG, where 18-year-old Cade McCutcheon, Mandy and Tom's son, earned team gold and individual bronze aboard Custom Made Gun. He'd already secured a page in National Reining Horse Association history earlier in his teens: At age 15, he became the youngest competitor to win the Level 4 NRHA Non-Pro Derby...but was too young to drive the trailer that he won.

The family also includes Colleen McQuay, Tim's wife and Mandy's mother. She has been involved with reining and the hunter/jumper end of McQuay Stables, which, after 30 years in Tioga, Texas, is now based out of Tom McCutcheon Reining Horses in Aubrey, Texas. Colleen was responsible for adding polish to reining shows, emphasizing hospitality and sponsorship along the lines of how it was done at hunter/jumper shows.

Three generations of reining royalty, photographed at the 2018 FEI World Equestrian Games *(left to right):* Tim and Colleen McQuay, Mandy McQuay McCutcheon, and Carlee, Cade, and Tom McCutcheon.

When Mandy McQuay McCutcheon was competing at the 2014 Alltech FEI World Equestrian Games in Normandy, France, her son, Cade, told her exactly what he planned to do at the 2018 WEG.

"He said, 'I'm going to the next one.' Cade was 14 years old, and he was dead set on doing that and already had started riding Custom Made Gun. He was convinced he and that horse were going to do that," Mandy recalled.

And Cade was right. He did more than simply compete at the next WEG in Tryon, North Carolina, however. Months after graduating from high school, he was on the gold medal team and earned an individual bronze, the third generation of his family to contribute to the USA's WEG medal count and be recognized individually there, as well.

It was almost perfect except that his father, who had been picked to ride on the team with him, couldn't compete because of a horse issue and wound up commentating for the FEI streaming coverage instead.

"Of course, Tom missed the opportunity of showing at those Games, but he's been there and done that. What was heartbreaking was not to be able to do it with Cade," Mandy said.

Sometimes it's more difficult to be on the sidelines than it is to be competing, as Tom experienced, watching his son ride.

"It started off, I was incredibly nervous," he acknowledged. "Then about the third or fourth maneuver into his run, when I could see he kind of locked his jaw, and I saw that confident look in his eye I could relate to, I knew he was locked in and his horse was locked in. So it went from being nervous to just enjoying the whole thing.

"I never expected any of this, even for myself. I thought it was for sure special being on all the teams I'd been on, winning the gold medals and whatnot, but we didn't put any pressure on our kids. Cade kind of jumped into it."

According to Tim McQuay, Cade's grandfather,

success was practically preordained for the third-generation reiner.

"Before he could ride, he would do the patterns on his stick horse," Tim recalled. "He would watch me train for hours."

Cade obviously picked up a lot there. One of his first memories is starting to ride at his grandfather's farm.

"I trotted for a long time. I remember everybody was happy when I loped the first time, and once I figured out to lope, I never stopped loping… and I never looked back," said Cade.

His only previous team experience was in 2017, when he went to Switzerland on the Young Riders' squad.

"It was a good way to get my feet wet to get

Cade McCutcheon, only 18 years old, became the third generation of his family to win an individual medal at the FEI World Equestrian Games in 2018 when he took the bronze on Custom Made Gun after riding on the gold medal team.

ready for the WEG. For the finals, I was nervous, but that's why you do this, for that nervous anticipation. I wanted to do well for us, for the United States," Cade said.

"I started riding the horse early in his four-year-old year. I did all the showing from then on and split the training with my grandfather. I've got a lot of idols, but he and my father are at the top of the list. It's a really good feeling to keep the family tradition going. It helps the whole business," continued Cade, who rides 15 horses a day, working for his father, with his mother keeping everything organized.

"It's a lot of work, but it's worth it."

Riding for the team was a watershed experience for Cade.

"It gave me the confidence to give up my non-pro card and go play with the Open Level big guys," he explained. "It was an experience I'll never forget; just being around the team the whole time."

A particularly special moment, he said, "was when I saw my score and then I saw my teammates were just as happy as I was."

The 2018 WEG medals were another entry on a continuing list of achievements for his family. In fact, the McQuays and McCutcheons have done so much for their discipline that Mandy says, "It's hard to pick what I'm most proud of. My parents changed the face of reining. They made it a higher-class sport and a much more respected sport; the horse shows are much more respected and much better run. They just brought everything to the next level, running horse shows, being on the NRHA board, through their breeding programs, through the way they ran their business that affected how other people ran their businesses, because they saw the difference it made. I think they stepped up the level of care for the horses in the Western (riding) world. Everyone wanted to do what the McQuays were doing because that was the best."

Tim McQuay won team gold and individual silver on Mister Nicadual at the 2006 FEI World Equestrian Games in Germany.

Mandy McCutcheon was in high spirits after earning individual bronze on Yellow Jersey at the 2014 FEI World Equestrian Games, where she also rode on the gold medal team.

From her perspective, she said, "Tom and I have tried to do the same thing. Tom has been on the USEF board, the NRHA executive board, donated his time and spent a lot of time on projects. He is one of those, along with my parents, who founded the National Reining Breeder's Classic. We've just dedicated our lives to improving the sport."

There's been no pressure within the family to continue the reining dynasty–besides Cade, daughter Carlee reins and rides hunt seat.

"We just want the kids to do whatever they're comfortable doing," said Mandy, while at the same time, she emphasized about Cade's commitment: "You couldn't be more excited, happy and proud of your kid to go on and do that."

Tom observed, "As a parent who understands the business, you just hope they have the talent that can match the desire, because not everybody does. I've seen a million guys who crave this, but couldn't get there. As Cade grew and developed, we felt more and more like he had the talent. He started winning more and doing it under pressure situations."

Nothing he had encountered to date was more pressure than the 2018 WEG.

"His first time on the world stage, and he was in a very pressure situation being the second guy out. It just didn't bother him at all, so that was really fun for us," said Tom. "Sure, he was nervous, but the difference between the ones who do and the ones who don't are the ones who can put it (nervousness) away when they walk through the gate."

Tom noted that being on the WEG team himself "would have been fantastic…it was a stroke of bad luck (not to), but I'll take Cade being on that team and being successful over me being on the team every day of the week."

Having reining as a part of WEG has been a plus. Reining was being done internationally before it was in the World Championships, but they gave it a boost.

"You get a different group of people to watch, some of whom have never seen a reining horse," Tim said. "It helped us grow. There are countries I never heard of that have put teams together."

The McQuays and the McCutcheons aren't ones to rest on their many laurels.

"I think if you're not trying to get better at everything you do, no matter what business you're in, you're going to fall behind. I think it is just a matter of keeping things going in the right direction and promoting our sport on a level where more people can see and learn about it," said Mandy.

"The hunters and jumpers are a sport that is looked on as 'the elite.' I think that is our next level, that's the next role–to step our game up to become what that world is." At the same time, she noted, "Reining is something everyone can do, from 'the elite' all the way down, there's a spot and a place for everyone."

"I would hope to say if we've done anything as a family, we've elevated the status of the sport with how we run our business and how we treat our horses, how we present out horses. I feel like we were a big part of that," said Tom. "My (gold medal) run in Kentucky (the 2010 WEG in Lexington) was a run you'd like to get out in front of people. Cade's 229 (in the first individual qualifier) in Tryon had 400,000 views on Facebook. It was the perfect run to promote reining. It was a fat, happy horse on a loose rein; everything was done correctly. Trying to present ourselves that way to the world, that's what we wanted to do most, and hopefully that's the thing we have done."

SHAWN FLARIDA

Solid Gold

After graduating from high school in 1988, Shawn went to work for his brother, Mike Flarida, a well-known reining trainer, then went out on his own six months later.

"I had eight clients. I barely eked out a living, but I never doubted it was what I was meant to do," he recalled. His talent and hard work paid off over the years as he went on to become the National Reining Horse Association's first-ever $6 million rider and its all-time leading money earner.

Shawn has won nothing but gold medals in the FEI World Equestrian Games. He began in 2002 in Jerez, Spain, when reining made its first appearance at the WEG. Shawn earned team and individual gold there with San Jo Freckles.

Eight years later, the Ohio-based reiner was on the gold medal team aboard RC Fancy Step during the first WEG in the United States at the Kentucky Horse Park in Lexington. In 2014, Shawn again traveled overseas to the World Championships, leading the team to gold and taking individual gold in Normandy, France, with a WEG scoring record on Spooks Gotta Whiz, the NRHA Open Futurity winner.

Domestically, he has six NRHA Open Futurity championships to his name and is an 11-time winner of the All-American Quarter Horse Congress futurity.

Shawn and his high school sweetheart Michele, who handles the administrative part of his business, have three children, Cody, Courtney, and Sam.

All I wanted to do was train horses, for as long as I can remember. I came home from school one day in second grade and decided that I had had enough. I didn't see any point to learning anything more when I could spend my time a lot better in the barn.

Horses have always been around my family. My father, Bill, worked as a welder, but he had horses since he was 10 years old. He bought his first horse for $15. He and my mother, Betty, were the Ohio Quarter Horse youth team guidance people for 30 years. Even though reining wasn't very popular during the 1960s and the early '70s, my father liked reining horses. He appreciated a horse

that was physical and could turn on its butt and was kind of quick.

Of course, I lived in Ohio, which is where reining originated, right there in Findlay. So it seemed fitting that I would be involved in reining, along with everyone else in the family. My brother Mike, a two-time NRHA Futurity winner, is a very successful reiner, and my other brother, Mark, is my farrier.

We have a 75-acre farm and about 50 to 60 head of horses. We have some broodmares, but it's primarily a training facility with a lot of young horses we are trying to train up and get going. My wife, Michele, takes care of the business and gets me where I'm supposed to be. I wouldn't trade jobs with her. She's also busy with the Buckeye Reiners, the Ohio Quarter Horse Association Congress, and several NRHA Committees. Then throw in several horse shows a month and a 40-stall training barn—it's hard to figure out how she manages it all. But she does.

My family is the most important thing in my life, and I know I wouldn't be where I am today if it weren't for the love and support of my wife as well. She's sacrificed a lot for me and my career.

Being able to compete in the World Equestrian Games was an important milestone. When I was on the first gold medal team in Jerez, Spain, in 2002, that was the first time I got to go out of the country and compete for the United States. I got to ride San Jo Freckles, a horse I had trained up since he was two.

It was an unbelievable feeling and an unbelievable experience to win two gold medals there. The opportunities that brought me were astronomical. On a personal level, as far as sponsors, it

Shawn Flarida's first double gold WEG experience in 2002 brought him "astronomical" opportunities that built to him repeating the feat at the 2014 WEG.

Shawn Flarida scored double gold at the 2014 FEI World Equestrian Games on Spook's Gotta Whiz, a follow-up to his two gold medals on San Jo Freckles in 2002 and his 2010 WEG team gold on RC Fancy Step.

A cowboy hat autographed by FEI World Equestrian Games multi-gold medalist Shawn Flarida is quite a keepsake.

kind of put me into the spotlight. It also helped as far as owners looking for a trainer and sending me horses and the opportunity to get more and better horses and go more places.

The NRHA always had some connections to Europe, but being able to compete in the WEG has given us a floor map, a way to communicate and the competition, which I think is really, really cool. It's nice when you have that special horse that can go compete at that level and those events are there. It sure makes you excited.

Now the European trainers come over here and purchase our horses. Some days, I talk to as many foreign trainers as I do American trainers.

At the farm, we have an Italian reiner, someone from Spain, a Brazilian, and a French boy coming. I always say the world is shrinking. I wish at times I did know another language so I could communicate better. But reiners do have a bond, and when I get around those guys, we're more similar than different. It's the love of the horse that brings us together. You'll be able to communicate through that horse, but maybe not be able to order dinner!

I've had a lot of great horses, but one that was very special to me was Wimpy's Little Step. He came along at the right time in my career and it was an important moment when we won the National Reining Futurity in 2002. He became a great producer whose offspring have won $6 million or $7 million.

I'm a very superstitious person who is known for wearing my trademark green shirt, and here's how that came about. At the time I was riding Wimpy, I had a favorite green shirt and favorite blue saddle pad. On the night of the Futurity, I used both of them. You can imagine they clashed violently and everyone started making fun of it. The blue pad had won a lot of money, so it got retired, but the green shirt stayed.

My younger son, Sam, is probably the one most likely to follow me into the family business. He started out as a winner when he was the co-champion of the first American Quarter Horse Congress short-stirrup reining class in 2013. He's only 15 now, but he's showing signs that training horses is something he wants to do. You can usually find him in the barn or studying videos looking for the next prospect. Sam showed for the first time in 2012 and quickly developed a reputation as a showman. He works very hard at it. I'm trying to teach him to be a horseman, and maybe be a horseman before he's a horse trainer. I want him to learn how to take care of the horse, learn what the horse is thinking, and learn what the horse *is*. And then, if you learn that part—and I think he has—it will take care of itself. Being a good horseman makes everything else fit in. I'd get him horses that maybe weren't perfect or easy to show and make him learn that part. The struggles you go through on a horse that's not the best or easiest—that's where you learn the most.

The sport is very humbling. You can be having a great run and one little bobble will go wrong and wreck the whole thing. You're only as good as your last run.

I cannot thank my horses enough, the horses that got me there and carried me and got me to those championships. The money changed me to a point, because it has enabled me to do a lot of things for my family, but I don't think it changed me for my horses. I still love to go ride; I look forward to the young stock. The old horses that have been successful for me, when they've been off at a breeding farm or the broodmares are turned out, I always go check on them and say, "Hi," to them. There's still the little kid in me that wants to go out there and pet the horse.

One of my favorite things to do when we're off on Sunday is to get up in the morning and sit in the barn and listen to the horses eat, just being around them. I really do love horses and money can't change that. You either do or you don't, and that's probably what allowed me to be as successful as I am. To say I do this for the money, that wouldn't be the case. I'd probably do it for free.

ANDREA FAPPANI

A Hobby That Became a Career

The youngest competitor ever to be a National Reining Horse Association million dollar rider, Andrea went on to earn more than $5 million in prize money. Born in Italy, he became an American citizen after starting a successful business in the United States, then represented his adopted country at the FEI World Equestrian Games in 2014. Andrea delivered for the United States, riding Custom Cash Advance to a team gold medal and an individual silver at the WEG in Normandy, France.

Andrea is based at Andrea Fappani Performance at Rancho Oso Rio in Scottsdale, Arizona, with his wife, Tish, an accomplished non-pro reiner herself. They have two sons: Luca, who is following his father into reining with great success, and Jeremy, who has been nationally ranked in motorcycle racing.

I started riding at age four when my dad put me on a horse. It all began with an English saddle on a pony at a local barn that specialized in starting young kids with jumping. It was a long process; the English way of doing it—you don't just jump on and go. We worked on a longe line for months and riding with no stirrups—all the basics of classical horsemanship. I would say my introduction to riding was definitely very different from the way most people begin in my sport.

I was raised in Bergamo, Italy, and the local stable was just down the road. My dad, Sergio, had a big dairy farm. My mother, Maddalisa, had ridden and owned horses, but she put them aside when

she got pregnant. A few years later, after my sister Elena and I were born, my parents wanted to bring the horses back, and they intended that I should be taught by a professional.

I still believe that approach has paid off. I tell people I think many of the compliments I get for my riding can be traced to my background in the English side of the sport. There's a big lack in the Western discipline, especially reining, to really teach young riders about horsemanship and the way you should sit on a horse before you teach the sport. It doesn't matter what style of riding you do. If you know where the balance center point is on a horse, where to sit, where to put your legs, then

Andrea Fappani started his reining career in his native Italy, but it was in the United States where he made it big and represented his new country internationally.

you can do anything you want. I think my background has paid off as far as the way I approach everything, from grooming a horse to reading a horse's mind to riding and performing. It's the basis of everything.

I moved up from a pony to a bigger horse when I was about eight or nine years old. My parents were all excited about my jumping. But I had a bad experience when I fell off while jumping. I was a little bit scared; those huge horses were intimidating.

A friend of ours had been taking reining lessons with a local trainer and told us about it. We didn't know anything about it. He convinced us to go watch him one day. I was amazed at how quiet these reining horses were. They were a lot smaller than some of the jumpers I had encountered, and their demeanor seemed a little bit nicer. I was kind of intrigued. I took a lesson and fell in love with it from the day I sat on a horse I could guide without needing to have contact on his face all the time.

He felt to me like he wanted to do the job on his own without me having to keep my legs on him all the time. That was a plus for me, because like any young kid, I was not very strong. Later on, I understood that I had to do a lot of other cues, but at the beginning, what attracted me was the fact that it was much easier for me to just sit on a horse with a loose rein. I liked it more than having a powerful animal underneath me that I had to contain.

When our friend first told us about Western horses, we kind of laughed at him and thought about John Wayne chasing cows. But the minute I understood what the sport of reining was and tried it myself, I found it was obviously another professional discipline, in some ways not very different from English riding. That's because very early on, I understood that horses are horses. It doesn't matter what breed they are or what they're doing. If you understand the horse, you understand the horse. The mindset might be a little bit different from horse to horse, but the way they approach things, the way you train them, they're all the same.

It took a few weeks to convince my dad that reining was what I wanted to pursue and to put the jumping aside for a little bit. Pretty soon, I was having three or four lessons a week and within six months, we bought our first reiner, and then I started showing the next year.

At that time, reining was just starting in Italy and was still very small. Because my dad always wanted to get the best animals

Jordan Larson, Mandy McCutcheon, Andrea Fappani, and Shawn Flarida *(left to right)* were on the 2014 WEG gold medal reining team under the direction of Chef d'Equipe Jeff Petska.

possible for what we were doing, we started going to the United States and Canada and entering some of the bigger shows. We began acquiring horses and bringing them to Italy. By the time I was 13 or 14, I was spending a month or so in the United States every summer with different trainers and doing internships. I was always interested in training, which was the big thing for me. The showing was fun, but I wanted to know how you got the horses to do all that! How do you train horses to do all these maneuvers? How do you train them well enough so they maintain that training all their lives? Early on, I showed a lot, but my main focus was always on training. Even if we were training my show horses at a pro barn, we always kept some horses at home for me to train and practice on. My dad loved the training part of it, too, so we used to do that together. That was my foundation, and it paid off at an early age by being able to come to the States and do well. By the time I was 20 and really started showing, I already had been training for quite a few years. Even if I had to learn new techniques, what I was really after was trying to get in a horse's mind and communicate to him what I was after. I think I was further ahead than many of the people my age. Most of the young people I met when I came here concentrated on showing and not a whole lot of training.

Reining was supposed to be just a hobby, but I turned it into a career. Both of my parents had a big passion for horses and animals in general. From the dairy farm to horses and cats and dogs—we were always surrounded by animals. I think early on, they wanted to teach me the responsibility of having to take care of an animal. The fact that I had to go feed them before I went to school and then take care of them when I got home, not only the riding but the other parts of it, that's maybe why I got started and it turned into something bigger. My parents taught me to think that the animal is something you respect and you don't train them

to do what you want. Instead, you ask them to give you the best of what they can do naturally.

I was a non-professional reiner in Italy when pro trainer Todd Bergen from Oregon came for a big show. He saw me riding when I was 17 and asked if I would be interested in coming to the States and working. I told him I never gave much thought to making reining a career. It was always something I would have on the side as a hobby while keeping the dairy farm going. But when he asked me that, it made me think, "Maybe I've got something he saw that means I should pursue reining and not just keep it as a hobby."

A few years later, I came to the States and worked for him, beginning on a trial basis and then becoming his assistant trainer. He was the first and last person I ever worked for. I stayed there for six years, the time I needed in order to understand his program. It takes a long time to really learn a program from beginning to end.

At the time I started with him, he was further ahead in the training than many others. I admired so much the way his horses looked, almost like dressage horses rather than the Western discipline. He knew how to put a horse in a body position that was collected, to where it was driving from behind with shoulders up. Maybe it was my background in English riding that attracted me to a horse that was more collected in a better body position, at least in my opinion, to do the maneuvers.

When I went to work for Todd, I had been showing for quite a few years in Italy. He realized I knew how to show, but what I lacked was the program for the first few months of training. Most of the horses we bought in Italy were already halfway through training. We'd finish them up and go show them and then try to maintain them. Todd explained I wouldn't show the first couple of years but would stay home instead and do the groundwork to get the horses started and make sure I did it the right way.

My first year with him was 1997. Until the end of 1998, I never even went to a horse show. I stayed at home and tried to learn the program. I struggled a little bit because it was something I wasn't really used to. Once I figured it out, everything came pretty easy and pretty fast.

The last two years that I worked for him, I won some big shows under his guidance. It really got me started in the right direction. When I went out on my own, I was able to adapt it to my personal style. It helped that I had a really good foundation. Todd is the trainer who influenced me the most because he taught me the basics of what I still do. Of course, things have changed here and there over the years, and I've adapted some of the techniques to a more modern style, but he gave me the background to become successful. He put me in the show pen beginning in 1999. At the end of the year, I won the Limited Open Futurity in Oklahoma City. It was kind of a big deal, although I wasn't at the top level, the Open, I was at the Limited Open, which was for younger riders. Even so, when I won, I said to myself that obviously, there's something here. I'm already competing with some pretty good trainers and I've been successful. That kind of gave me the reassurance that what I was doing had a purpose and that I had something to work toward because I was doing pretty well.

That's when I decided to stay in the States. The original plan was to come here and get as much help as I could to learn a little more and then go back to Europe. But I decided to stay a little bit longer just because things were going well. I told myself, "This is the top platform for this sport, and I'd be stupid to leave it if I have the potential to compete at this level." A few years before that, I started dating Tish, the woman who became my wife. She was a non-pro who showed all of her life, and she was at the barn when I first moved over here. Things became more serious with her, and by 2000, she moved to Oregon where I was working.

By that time, I had won some major shows and was thinking about going out on my own.

When Tish and I got married in 2001, I made the commitment to stay in the States. We always said that if I needed to, we could move back to Europe. But as long as things went well, the plan was to stay in the States. It took a few years to adapt to the whole new culture and really soak in the fact that this is where I wanted to be. The first few good horse shows, you're happy but still thinking your home is "over there." Then when the business was really successful, most of my clients were American, and I started a family here, the natural next step was to become a citizen. You see a lot of athletes from other countries become American citizens due to the ease of being able to compete at the Olympics on a strong team. I became an American citizen even before I thought about showing at the World Equestrian Games. It made sense because of the business and family and everything we do here.

The level of reining in Europe has stepped up hugely in the last 10 years. But even if the numbers aren't as big as they are here, the quality of trainers is really good and the top horses over there could compete here every day. As far as individuals, anyone can win at this point—there are good trainers everywhere. It surprised people in the United States when I first won the big open reining futurity in Oklahoma City in 2001, when I was 24. I was the first European, and still today the only European, to do it. If you're committed 100 percent, it doesn't really matter where you're from.

As far as a team being able to beat the United States, however…it's always going to be tougher just because the numbers are so much bigger, with so many more horses here. This is such an individual sport that we never are on teams, except for the World Equestrian Games. I really didn't know what to think about the WEG other than wanting to give it a try, because I saw (five-time gold medalist) Shawn Flarida and the other guys do it in the

Andrea Fappani won team gold and individual silver in his 2014 WEG debut on Custom Cash Advance.

years before and it always looked so cool to do it. I gave it a try, not even thinking I was probably going to make the team. Then when I did, it was pretty special. It gives a whole new meaning to everything you do. It's definitely not just another horse show. There's a lot more on the line, because it's not just for you and your owners. It's for everybody who's there.

My WEG was in France. It wasn't on American soil, so it seemed a big deal with an overseas trip. It's definitely pretty special. We win a lot of money at our horse shows in the States, but there, I didn't hardly win a dime with the team gold and individual silver medals…yet it was a lot more important than most of our other competitions.

I've had so many great horses, but the horse that really changed my career was RR Star, who won the reining futurity. The horse I showed at the WEG, Custom Cash Advance, also was a special horse. One of my best abilities is to find horses that really suit my riding style. There are a lot of guys out there who will ride anything and try anything. Now that I know what I get along with and what type of horse really clicks for me, I've been able to have a good eye on prospects that I feel are going to develop into horses I get along with. I try not to waste my time or other people's time riding horses I know won't be compatible with my personality. You can succeed at the top level only when the horse wants to do his job and feels comfortable doing it for you. A horse obviously has a mind of his own. So to really find qualities in a horse that are the type of qualities that help your program, I think, is the key. I've been lucky enough to be able to do that.

I know what it takes to be successful and it's not just me. You may see me in the limelight, but just as important are the people surrounding me and helping me through the years, from my parents to the trainers I've known, to the horse shoers, the veterinarians, and so many others. My wife takes care of everything other than training horses. It's a privilege not to have to deal with entry fees, scheduling, and everything a lot of other trainers have to do. She gives me the freedom to concentrate on riding and showing, which is what I love doing and what I'm good at.

I've got two kids. One trains and shows with me, the other does something different—on motorcycles. They're both competing and learning responsibility and what it takes to be successful. Those are important lessons, no matter what you want to do.

ENDURANCE

ENDURANCE RIDING TESTS COMPETITORS' ABILITY TO SAFELY manage the stamina and fitness of their horses along a track where they face challenges that include the distance, the climate, the terrain, and the clock. The rider who crosses the finish line first is not necessarily the winner, as the victory is not official unless the horse is judged "fit to continue."

Although there are many 50-mile competitions in the United States, for a senior international championship the test is a course of 160 kilometers (approximately 100 miles).

A veterinary panel supervises the condition of the horses, each of whom must pass a pre-ride examination in order to start the event. There are set hold times during the ride. They vary from a simple gate-and-go to one-hour rest holds. During these holds, the horse's physical and metabolic parameters are checked. The horse must pass the exam in order to move on to the next segment of the course. Each horse must also pass a post-ride exam in order to receive credit for completing the course before the awards are presented.

BECKY HART
Starting from Scratch

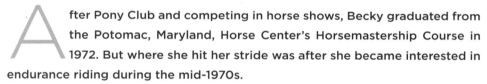

After Pony Club and competing in horse shows, Becky graduated from the Potomac, Maryland, Horse Center's Horsemastership Course in 1972. But where she hit her stride was after she became interested in endurance riding during the mid-1970s.

She is the only three-time World Champion endurance rider, performing the hat trick of titles in 1988, 1990, and 1992. Understandably, the 1990 American Horse Shows Association Equestrian of the Year is most closely identified with her mount for those victories, R.O. Grand Sultan, better known as Rio. Both Becky and Rio are in the American Endurance Ride Conference Hall of Fame.

The U.S. Equestrian Federation, successor to the AHSA, annually presents the Becky Grand Hart Trophy to the outstanding competitor in international driving, endurance, reining, vaulting, or para-equestrian.

A California resident, Becky is a Level Three Centered Riding instructor who also is in demand as a speaker.

Rio is the horse who really made my career. And he didn't cost a cent.

He was given to Courtney Hart (to whom I was married at the time) and me in 1983 after we called a man named Dick Rodriguez about another horse he had for sale. Courtney and I were interested in *that* horse, as he had done a few endurance rides. As we discussed the deal, Dick told us he had another horse he would give us.

He trotted out the free, 14.3-hand, bay gelding. We told Dick, "He's a nice little horse. We'll take him." When Courtney and I got in the truck to haul both the horses away, we looked at each other, and I said, "I think I like the free one better." He agreed.

We had thought the deal was that if we bought the one horse, he would give us the little bay. But in a conversation with Dick 20 years later, I learned belatedly that wasn't the case.

"I was going to give you that horse whether you took the other one or not," he told me. I eventually found out from his daughter that after a divorce,

Becky Hart canters across the finish line to win the endurance at the first FEI World Equestrian Games in 1990.

he kept his two best horses, but he was working in Southern California and the horses were up north, so he didn't have the time for them. Because they were such good horses, he felt they should go do something. And that's where we came in.

The gift horse, R.O. Grand Sultan, had only done one ride and finished last. That was understandable; he'd had just 30 days under saddle and was five years old. That was something else I found out 20 years later, and it explained a lot of things.

We didn't do much with the little horse the first year. At one point, I tried to sell him for $500, but there were no takers, so I leased him to a friend.

Meanwhile, Khameo, the horse we had bought from Dick, was a consistent Top 10 horse, but he'd always quit 5 or 10 miles from the finish. He wasn't tired, he'd always vet through. I suspect, knowing more now than I knew then, he might have had a sugar low. At the time, though, it was really annoying. Rio, as we called our "free" horse, did not have that issue—80 miles from the end of a 100-mile ride, he'd turn on the afterburners. It was amazing.

When my friend took Rio on an endurance ride, I crewed for her. She rode conservatively. Rio went out after the lunch stop. While it took most horses time to gear up after lunch, he was eager. "I get to go again. I must be the luckiest horse in the world," he was saying with his actions. He went out with that attitude and finished with that attitude. I thought to myself, "This is a nice little horse." His pulse was 36 at the vet check. I told my friend she could have gone a little faster. Better to be conservative than over-run the horse, but he had lots left in the tank.

Eventually, my friend said about Rio, "I'm getting too attached; I don't want to keep him anymore. He needs to be with you."

All I really knew about Rio when we got him was that he had finished a 50-mile ride, which implied a lot more training than he'd actually had. Turns out he'd only had arena time and two outings on the trail before he did his first ride. That explained why he reared up when I put the bit on him, why I couldn't put my legs on his side, and why he freaked out when we put a blanket on him.

So after the first endurance ride, we sent him to a trainer for six weeks to work on a few of those little things. I was way more ignorant then. We're just constantly learning and the sport keeps evolving. In those days, for instance, all we had to feed the horses was alfalfa and oat hay and oats and corn. There were no concentrated foods. Our choices were limited.

The first ride I took Rio on in 1984 was Mount Diablo, a 50-mile in the San Francisco Bay Area. He came into the first vet check in about sixty-fifth place, out of about 100 horses. He left the vet check in fifteenth place. Next was an eight-mile climb up a 3,000-foot-high mountain. This was where I started to get it and understand Rio's ability. He wanted to trot and canter. He wasn't going hard. Halfway up, there was a water trough. He stopped and took a big drink. Two horses came by and didn't stop. He followed them with his eyes but didn't stop drinking. We came into the lunch stop in fourth place. We recovered and then had a long downhill on a narrow trail. He was terrible— we fought all the way down because he wanted to go faster. He knocked a friend of mine and his horse off the trail. Then we had to climb up to the top of the mountain again. "Fine," I said. "You want to run, let's go now."

He cantered halfway up the hill into another vet check and recovered very quickly. When we got to the very top of the hill, Courtney met me and said the first-place horse, who had been five minutes ahead of us, hadn't recovered and wasn't back on the trail yet. Rio, meanwhile, recovered in three minutes, and we ended up winning the ride. That's when I realized he was a very special, amazing horse.

The horse I planned to ride for the rugged Western States Endurance Ride, known as the Tevis Cup, pulled a suspensory that year, so after Mount Diablo, I knew I would ride Rio for Tevis and thought we could Top-10 it. I decided this was a pretty special little guy, a product of good old Egyptian breeding. I just had a feeling about him all along and it turned out I was right. Tevis is very demanding, but Rio not only finished, he won on his first try!

Things have changed so much in endurance since then. Most of us didn't wear a helmet back in the '80s. I only wore one because I was riding this crazy horse. I rode in a bicycle helmet, because it allowed for some air circulation and was much cooler than the black velvet hunt caps worn for horse showing. I didn't wear a regulation riding helmet until I was required to for the 1990 World Championships.

In the old days, a lot of the Tevis riders rode in Western saddles, using big, heavy equipment. I rode in a Stübben Siegfried with padded knee rolls. Today, there's light BioThane tack and streamlined saddles designed especially for endurance.

There weren't World Championships for endurance until 1986. The first one was in Rome, and we were starting from scratch. We didn't know anything about taking horses to Europe because there had never been one. We didn't even know that we needed passports for our horses.

Before the World Championships, there was a North American Championship near Santa Cruz, California. Rio won that 100-mile ride. After that, we started to find out what we needed to do to make it to the World Championships.

The transition was rough for Rio. He didn't like the hay and he'd never been in a stall. That was my first trip to Europe, and it was a list of what *not* to do. I didn't know enough not to go see the sights of Rome, rather than stay there with the horse and take him out and let him graze. He eventually ate the hay and the Italians also found him some alfalfa, which they only feed to cows there.

We did finish the ride. They started 54 horses

Becky Hart and R.O. Grand Sultan, better known as Rio.

and 14 finished. We were fourteenth. The Italian press wrote me up as an "Amazona" who finished her ride in the dark. Other U.S. riders did better, with two veterinarians at the top of the podium. Dr. Sandy Schuler won on Rio's cousin, Shiko's Omar, Dr. Jeannie Waldron came in second, and the team won silver. That marked the start of the U.S. domination of the individual World Championship gold medals that would continue through 1998.

Rome was a big learning experience. For the next one, which was going to be in the United States at Front Royal, Virginia, in 1988, we flew the horses east from California, because hauling four days across the country would have been too hard on them.

The horses were pretty comfortable when they got there. It was mostly U.S. horses and European riders on leased U.S. horses. Lots of things went wrong. It had been 95 degrees and humid. The day of the ride, however, the tail end of Hurricane George dropped temperatures into the sixties. We had packed our crew bags for 95-degree weather, so we didn't have rain sheets. We came into one vet check with torn plastic bags to put over the horse. He ended up winning, which was great, with the U.S. team also taking gold, but we hadn't competed against the best horses in Europe or Australia, where Prince Aussie was winning everything.

The next time we traveled was to Sweden in 1990 for the first FEI World Equestrian Games, where Rio and Prince Aussie got to compete head to head. Rio and I won the Prince Phillip Cup and the World Championships gold medal there. It took us 10 hours, 33 minutes and 59 seconds to finish. Jane Donovan of Great Britain on Ibriz got the silver medal in 10 hours, 41 minutes and 14 seconds.

We always had to pay our own way until we went to Spain for the 1992 World Championships and started working with the U.S. Equestrian Team. I used to have a couple of people do fundraising for me, and we took out loans. For Spain, we had a per diem and our hotel was covered.

One issue at every international competition was making the 165-pound weight. I only weighed about 99 pounds, so there was a lot of dead weight on the saddle. By the time I went to Sweden, I was taking lessons, learning more about dressage and becoming a better rider. One of the things Rio had to be reminded about was how to carry all of that dead weight and use his hind end more. Because of the way he was built, it only took a few lessons before that was accomplished. When we got to Spain, we were still a little light on weight, so we used neoprene shims under the saddle to make up the difference. We didn't realize the neoprene created heat, which scalded his back. After we discovered his sore back at a vet check, we put ice on his back and took the shims out. By then, the saddle pad was soaking wet, so we made weight without any problems.

At the second-to-last vet check as Rio was ready to go out we noticed that he was missing a shoe. We had to put a boot on him, since his extra shoes were in a car a mile away. Benedicte Atger,

Becky Hart and R.O. Grand Sultan along the trail in the endurance competition at the 1990 FEI World Equestrian Games as they headed to victory.

the French rider who was in the lead on Sunday D'Aur, had been let out of the vet check early. I caught up to her cantering along. Suddenly, Rio took off as if he had been stung by a bee. I stopped him and saw the boot he was wearing had turned and was dangling around his pastern. Some of the men watching came over. One held Rio's head, the other cut the boot off with a knife. I had to dig through my pack to get out a spare boot from the bottom. After I put it on, I turned and saw one of the guys had redone my pack so I could get going.

I got Rio through the vet check while he was wearing the boot, and then the farrier came and put a shoe on that foot. The farrier looked at the other front shoe and noted it was worn thin from the lava rocks that abounded in the area. He asked if I wanted him to replace the other shoe. He told me it would take six minutes. Every minute was precious, but I told him to go ahead.

When the shoeing was finished, Rio shot out

at the gallop. The last six miles were up a lava rock hill. He cantered and cantered. If we come in second, I thought, there are thousands of people who would be thrilled to have won a silver medal.

"Well, not me," said Rio. I started to slow down to give Rio a breather then I saw the French rider, who was urging her horse forward with a crop. I let Rio drag behind her for a minute or so to catch his breath.

It looked to me as if she didn't have a lot of horse left. "Let's go do this," I told Rio. As we came to the top of the hill, we went out onto this polo field and there was a big track around it. No one saw me come into the field. I think it was because he was a bay horse and in a shadow. They were watching for the gray French horse.

A minute or two later, I heard a big cheer when she came on the track. They didn't know until I was almost at the finish line that I had caught the French gal. We beat her by 55 seconds, even with all the trouble we'd had.

A Spanish horse got the Best Condition Award. A couple of veterinarians felt the first-place horse should get it but they were outvoted. What mattered, though, was that we had won our third endurance World Championship individual gold medal in a row. Rio was 15 at the time.

An unfortunate souvenir from Spain was piroplasmosis. Rio had a positive test for the tick-borne disease, which the U.S. Department of Agriculture has fought hard to eradicate in the United States. The diagnosis meant Rio had to stay in quarantine for 60 days before coming home and receive chemotherapy-type treatment with his teammate.

We were shooting for our fourth World Championship at the 1994 WEG in The Hague in the Netherlands. But Rio fell and cut his knee to the bone, and later was pulled from the ride.

For the 1996 championship in Fort Riley, Kansas, I leased Rio to a Swedish friend after I didn't

make the U.S. team with him. Renowned animal behaviorist and founder of the Tellington Method Linda Tellington-Jones had a bronze sculpture created of Rio going over Cougar Rock on the Tevis Cup route that would go to the horse that won the Best Condition title at that championship. I said to her, "Wouldn't it be funny if Rio won it?" And he did. The woman who leased him finished fifth and got to keep her prizes, but I said since he was my horse, I was keeping the Best Condition Trophy.

Rio won his last race at 21 and had 10,305 miles in competition, making him a high-mileage horse. He was an AERC decade horse—he competed for at least 10 years, had 10 wins, 10,000 miles and 10 Best Condition Awards.

Rio got hurt in the pasture, and it took him a couple of years to recover. I used him as a school horse after that. He taught lots of people how to ride and was pretty patient with them. Then, in 2003, he was diagnosed with a fluid-filled tumor after we took him to the University of California at Davis, where it was drained. They put him on steroids and gave him two to three weeks to live. Of course, Rio being Rio, he stayed around for another three months. We held a celebration of Rio's recovery and all these people who knew him came. Afterward, we took his blanket off and he galloped away.

When it finally was time to put Rio down, my friend Nancy Elliott, a veterinarian, prepared a place to bury him at her farm. After he got off the trailer there, he took me for a walk. He had a great last day.

His career was one for the record books. Between 1985 and 1998 Rio started 151 times, finished 149 times, got Best Condition 46 times, won 68 times, was second 17 times and third eight, with a 78.8 placing percentage. He was the only horse to be an endurance World Champion three times.

And to think that we started from scratch with a free horse!

VALERIE KANAVY

Being in the Right Place at the Right Time

Atwo-time world endurance champion who has ridden more than 24,000 miles in competition, Valerie calls endurance "trail riding with an attitude." The 1994 (Pieraz) and 1998 (High Winds Jedi) champion, Val was second in the 1996 championship on TK Fire N Gold when her daughter, Danielle, won on Pieraz. Both horses made headlines once again after the championship. TK Fire N Gold was sold to Sheik Mohammed bin Rashid Al Maktoum and Pieraz was cloned in 2005.

Honors that have come to Val include the 1999 American Horse Shows Association Horseman of the Year, Virginia's 1999 Horsewoman of the Year, the U.S. Equestrian Team's Whitney Stone Award, and the Maggy Price Endurance Excellence Award.

In turn, Val has made a practice of giving back to her sport. She became an Arabian Horse Association delegate and then chair of the AHA Distance Riding Committee. A lifetime member of the USEF, she has served on its board of directors along with several other committees for years. She was a member of the FEI Athletes' Committee and the Athletes' Representative on the Endurance Committee from 2014 to 2018. Val also was a member of the FEI's temporary committee on endurance that in 2019 focused on the future of the sport.

In July 2018, Val won a two-star 120-kilometer ride with Amir El Arab AT, a week before celebrating her seventy-second birthday. She and her husband, Larry, have two boys, Trevon and Tim, in addition to their daughter Danielle, and live in Virginia.

Valerie Kanavy enjoyed her victory gallop on her $500 horse, Pieraz, at the 1994 FEI World Equestrian Games.

think I was born loving horses. It was a mystery to my non-horsey parents.

I used to beg them to take me to something called "Tiny Tot Land," near where we lived in Fresno, California, where I could ride the ponies. Rather than going in a circle on the pony, they had a little maze and you could ride the pony through it. I would pick the biggest pony, because surely, the biggest pony was the fastest. We'd go in the evening, and I remember trotting along and the lights looked like they were bouncing, because I didn't know how to post.

When I was going into second grade, we moved to Wichita, Kansas, where there were a lot of cow

ponies. I still was crazy about horses and dreamed of having one. I was the kid who asked for a horse every Christmas and galloped around the yard on a stick horse. I earned money by babysitting, pulling weeds, and scrubbing the kitchen floor.

When I was 11, I raided my piggy bank and bought a gray mare named Princess for $150. I paid $35 a month for her board. I was the oldest of six kids, and I think my parents were so busy with the others that they didn't figure out what I was doing. Looking back, I wonder, how did I do that when I was earning 35 cents an hour? As I went into high school, I sold Princess for $250, so you know I was a big entrepreneur.

I used that money to go to the stockyards auction and bought a Quarter Horse stallion, Clar Star. Fortunately, he was a nice stallion and ignorance is bliss.

When I was 16, I got a driver's license and a real job as a waitress, so I had a little more money. I would rent a horse trailer and go to some local 4-H shows and do a little bit of barrel racing and a little bit of Western pleasure. Every now and again, I'd win some ribbons. I loved Clar Star, but the question was, what to do with him? I was bored. Going to horse shows and doing walk, trot, and canter around the arena didn't light my fire. Eventually, I sold Clar Star and kind of got away from horses.

Then I met and married my husband, Larry. We moved back east near West Chester, Pennsylvania. A fellow who worked with Larry was married to Michelle Schofield, who owned horses and fox hunted. She invited me to go riding and took me over some jumps, something I had never experienced before. As a kid, I had ridden bareback much of the time, because Western saddles were heavy and a lot to lift onto a horse. Riding bareback had given me a decent seat.

"You actually can ride," my new friend marveled. So she started taking me fox hunting. I felt it was like, "Oh, wow, this is what horses were made for."

I always say that the day I met Michelle was the most financially disastrous day of my husband's life, because that's what pulled me back into horses.

As a young girl I was fascinated by Arabian horses. I read all of Walter Farley's *Black Stallion* books. There was an Arabian farm in Wichita, Kansas, Jameel Arabians, and the owner, Owen McEwen, would sometimes bring his Arabians to local shows. Even though I was living in Quarter Horse country, I thought the Arabians were to die for.

When I became serious about fox hunting, I returned to Wichita, and bought a Quarter Horse and a yearling Arabian filly from Jameel Arabians. I was fox hunting the Quarter Horse as the Arabian

was growing up. Eventually, I began fox hunting her. I didn't know it wasn't kosher to hunt on an Arabian. I didn't know they weren't supposed to jump. I didn't know anything. But at the end of the day out hunting, my little Arabian's tail was still in the air as she was jigging her way home, while the other horses were kind of crawling back to their trailers.

Larry and I found a farmhouse in Chester Springs to rent where I could also keep my horse. Robert (Bob) MacBurney was the neighbor over the hill. He was an old-time professional horseman who really knew his stuff. Prior to meeting Bob, my idea of horse training consisted of teaching horses their leads.

It was Bob who told me horses have to be physically fit to go out fox hunting all day. Finally, having a horse out my back door, I now had a legitimate excuse for riding almost daily. I didn't have any experience with making a horse fit but during that era, jogging and running were becoming popular. I started my own running and fitness program and transferred a lot of what I was doing with myself to the horse. Along the way, I read about the Tevis Cup, a 100-mile ride in California. I began to wonder just how "fit" my horse really was. Bob introduced me to a local rider, Davida Waters, who had some experience with distance sports. She had a horse trailer and took me to Bel Air, Maryland, in 1972 for a competitive trail ride. Davida rode the 50-mile division and I rode the 25, and we each won. That was the seed of my endurance career. You start out doing something and win right away—you're really hooked.

There wasn't much in the way of endurance competition on the East Coast back then. Competitive trail riding was the distance sport of choice. Horses were judged and placed on their physical condition. I was hunting in the fall and winter and doing competitive trail and the beginning of endurance in the spring and summer. I did so well, I just continued. I always say I was in the right

TK Fire N Gold was Valerie Kanavy's mount for the 1996 World Championships, where she finished second to her daughter, Danielle, who was aboard Val's 1994 WEG winner, Pieraz.

At the 1994 FEI World Equestrian Games in the Netherlands, Valerie Kanavy took the individual gold medal, edging Frenchman Denis Pesce, while Melissa Crane of the United States earned bronze.

place at the right time to get into my sport. I was a young mom with three young children on a limited budget. Riding was my relaxation and down time. I didn't have a trainer or a coach; it was all trial and error. And with error came learning.

The Tevis ride was always in the back of my mind. Veterinarian and endurance competitor Matthew Mackay-Smith and his wife, Winky, had ridden the course, and they encouraged Larry, who had begun to compete, and me to trailer west with them. The adventure of a lifetime, we thought.

It took five days of hard driving to get there. Pioneering horse trainer Linda Tellington-Jones' husband, Wentworth, met us when we arrived. His first question was, "What makes you guys think you can do the Tevis?" That wasn't the right thing to say to me at that point.

My husband replied, "Because we're tough, and we can cut it." I was practically in tears because I was exhausted and thinking, "What am I doing here?"

All we wanted to do was to finish and get "the Tevis buckle," the prize for completing the country's toughest ride on a sound horse. We weren't silly enough to think we could win. We definitely did not feel appreciated or welcomed. The Tevis motto, it seemed, was, "How can we help you—out of the ride?" Despite that, we all did manage to finish and earn those coveted buckles.

Endurance is mainly a recreational sport for most riders. But I was competitive and viewed those rides as a test of my training abilities. I've done over 100 hundred-mile events. I knew how to pace—competitive trail riding teaches you that—and my own running also gave me a feel for it.

Many people in our sport have a partnership relationship with a horse. But I found that when I made a top horse or a champion, I would lose interest. I needed the next challenge. I wanted to train another horse. Training each horse can teach you different lessons if you're paying attention.

In the summers, we would travel west, do an endurance ride, and then see some of the best of America. On one of our trips with the kids in 1988, we stopped in Colorado for breakfast, and I picked up the local "penny saver" newspaper. An ad in there caught my eye: "Arabian horse. Experienced rider only. $1,000."

I thought that might be worth a look. My

daughter, Danielle, went to see him and said, "I think he's your kind of horse." The people who owned Pieraz were in over their heads with him. He just had their number. That's one thing with a lot of Arabians. They can figure out who's in charge pretty quickly. I made a lowball offer of $500 in cash, and that's how Pieraz got the nickname Cash.

When I opened the trailer, he was so curious about the other horses inside that he walked on and I shut the door. The people were stunned that he got on the trailer. We drove from there to a campground outside Jackson Hole, Wyoming. We went for a ride on what I thought was a 12-mile circle, but it turned out to be 21 miles. He handled it fine. So I thought, this horse had some possibilities. Again, it was being in the right place at the right time.

Cash tweaked a suspensory early in his history,

A victory by Valerie Kanavy on High Winds Jedi in the 1998 World Championships in Abu Dhabi was the final U.S. endurance win in an unbroken streak that began with the first of these competitions in 1986.

and I had to turn him out to pasture for a year. After that, I made sure I rode the trail, rather than the clock, and Cash finished 100-mile competitions in the Top 10 during 1991. By the next year, he was Top 5 and by the third year, my husband was encouraging me to try for the U.S. team for the North American Championships.

Back then, the selectors picked horses and riders who had a history together. But my record was never a long history with the same horse, because of my fetish for riding different horses. That wasn't what the team was looking for. My husband told me to pick a horse and stick with him. When people from Italy came to the farm and wanted to buy an endurance horse, I let them pick between Cash and a little mare I had. They chose the mare. I said, "Okay, I guess Cash is my horse."

I rode for the Northeast Zone in the 1993 North American Championships in Alberta, Canada. We traveled out West early to acclimate Cash. It was a really chilly, rainy summer, and Cash caught a cold. I couldn't medicate him the way I wanted to because of the drug rules.

My goal was to finish this championship in sixth place or better to have a chance to be chosen for the U.S. Endurance Team at the 1994 FEI World Equestrian Games. I started the race with the front-runners. When I arrived at the first vet exam, it took Cash 15 to 20 minutes to recover. I knew we were in trouble.

I thought I should pull back, calm down, and pace, something I knew well how to do. Amazingly, I crossed the finish line sixth. I was elated, but my happiness was short-lived. In the cold north wind, waiting for the final vet exam, Cash developed a cramp and trotted out dead lame. I was devastated. Eliminated at the finish! I said, "This game is too hard. I'm not playing anymore."

My husband, always supportive, said, "I'll devote the whole next year, take you anywhere, so you can make the team, but you have got to start winning." I was too depressed to say that would be great or even think of the possibilities.

Then we went to a race in Kentucky: Land Between the Lakes. Cash finished fifth, but he won the Best Condition Award, and that made me think, "Maybe we can." The next race at the end of 1993 was in South Carolina. I said to Cash, "Today you will win or hit the wall." Every time a horse came near us, I closed my leg. Cash understood, he got it, and he won.

One of the most memorable races that year was the Longleaf in Mississippi. The last loop was 16 miles of perfect footing, sand road. One of the competitors was American Endurance Ride Conference Hall of Fame rider Nina Warren and the other was Melissa Crain, both formidable competitors. They knew the course, and about four miles from the finish line, they both fired their horses, racetrack style. Cash followed, and I thought, "Okay, today I will be third."

But then, as the road curved, Cash fired and passed them. I was shocked. Nina and Melissa fired their horses again, but Cash just went faster. It was an eye-opening glimpse into my horse's capabilities.

Cash was really intelligent; he knew the game. He could be a pain in the neck to ride for the first 80 miles. But when he hit the 80-mile point, he wanted to be first back to the barn and would take off. From November 1993 until the following November, Cash and I did eight 100-mile races and won all but one, setting several course records.

In preparation for the 1994 FEI World Equestrian Games in The Hague, Larry and I traveled to the Netherlands to inspect the course. I knew there would be a lot of sand, as a good portion of the course was along the beach. So Cash and I went to the racetrack in Middleburg, Virginia, and did a lot of training in the sand.

There was such a strong group of U.S. riders going to the Netherlands in 1994 for the WEG,

I was surprised to find myself in the lead in The Hague. By my calculation, the best I could do was fourth. Again, ignorance is bliss. Foolishly, I didn't think any Europeans were even in contention.

Near the end of the race, Cash and I were alone until the French rider, Denis Pesce, and his horse, Melfenik, caught us. Cash being his relaxed self, didn't even acknowledge Denis and his horse. I thought he had lost interest in the race. But then when he arrived at the last vet check fully recovered, I realized he wasn't even working.

The last loop was historic, with Denis and his horse nearly catching us. When I saw Denis, I asked Cash to go. I knew my horse's potential from the Longleaf race. I didn't believe anyone would dare to run that fast on pavement let alone know a horse was capable of doing so. I was right. Denis got silver; I got gold.

Winning the gold was an unforgettable and amazing experience, but the day after was anticlimactic. When you've worked so long and hard for something, it's like, "Now what do I do?" I shouldn't have worried. There was a lot more to come.

At the 1996 World Championships in Fort Riley, Kansas, Danielle rode Cash and I rode TK Fire N Gold. We were the first mother-daughter team to represent their country in a World Championship. Since Cash already had a gold medal, we decided that Fire should win if we were together as we headed for the finish line. But when Fire spooked at the crowds and banners lining that final stretch of the course, Cash took advantage and poured on the speed to finish ahead of his stablemate.

Two years later, I found myself at the top of the podium again, continuing the USA's unbeaten streak in the individual World Championships that began with the first such event in 1986. I got one more gold medal at that 1998 World Championship, which was held separately from the WEG, in the UAE, and High Winds Jedi came through for me. We were in the right place at the right time.

MARGARET "MAGGY" PRICE

1932–2007

True Grit

When Maggy Price set out to do something, it got done. She was a transformative president of the American Endurance Ride Conference from 1990 to 1992, one of those larger-than-life people who make a difference in their sport. She fought for what she believed was right. Totally devoted to the discipline of endurance, Maggy worked to ensure it got the kind of worldwide recognition and inclusion she firmly believed it deserved.

A 1992 FEI World Endurance Championship team silver medalist (Ramegwa Kanavyann) who also took the individual bronze, Maggy was instrumental in the development of international endurance in the United States.

Maggy, who was inducted into the AERC Hall of Fame in 1994, is honored with The Maggy Price Endurance Excellence Award, presented annually during the U.S. Equestrian Federation convention to the top senior rider. The award is sponsored by Gold Medal Farm and Larry and Valerie Kanavy, in memory of Maggy.

(Left to right): Deborah La Berge, Maggy Price, Becky Hart, and Suzanne Hayes at the World Championships in 1992 in Barcelona, Spain.

"Maggy was class, without a question," said Mike Tomlinson, a former AERC president, citing "her ethics and her character." Maggy also had a unique style and never let down her standards of appearance.

"She's the only one who kept a southern drawl, even though she had left the South when she was a little child," he remembered with a chuckle. "She would stop right before she got to the finish line of a 100-mile ride to put on lipstick and do her hair. She always looked perfect." More important, he said, "She cared about the horses, the people, and the sport. It is because of her almost single-handedly that we (endurance) are in the FEI."

Originally, he said, the United States was not going to be involved with FEI endurance, because AERC did not want to be part of the international scene and said "No" when the FEI asked to use its rules. The FEI then decided it would use the European Long Distance Riding organization's rules.

"Maggy said no, the United States must lead. She got us involved. She was amazing."

One of her goals was to get the U.S. Equestrian Team to accept endurance among its disciplines. She achieved that, and it made things so much better for team riders.

"In 1992, riders paid their own way to the World Championships," remembered another former AERC president, Stagg Newman. "In 1994, that was the first year USET paid our expenses, due to her efforts. Her proposal to USET was, 'You bring us the money, we'll bring you the medals.' In the first six endurance World Championships, the individual gold belonged to Americans," he noted, and at the 1994 FEI World Equestrian Games, the only U.S. gold medal was in endurance.

The USET leadership in the early 1990s was formidable and imposing, not easily swayed. But former USET Executive Director Bob Standish recalled, "Maggy stood up to all of them and was supportive of her discipline when they were

Maggy Price was so proud of her team silver medal from the 1992 World Championships that she liked to wear a T-shirt proclaiming the achievement.

allocating dollars. She fought for every penny she did get for that discipline. She was totally dedicated to her sport and very well-respected."

At the same time, "Maggy was a total character, warm and friendly, not afraid to get her nails dirty as long as she had her lipstick on," reminisced three-time endurance world champion, Becky Hart. "She was so proud of the team silver medal she won in Spain. She had a sweatshirt made that said, 'Ask me about my grandchildren,' but 'grandchildren' was crossed out and instead, it said 'silver medal!'"

Valerie Kanavy, the 1994 and 1998 endurance world champion, called Maggy, "a real lady. She was a southern belle, a thinker, and a doer. She got things done and she didn't put up with any stuff from anybody.

"She started off in competitive trail riding and ended up going into endurance," said Val, noting Maggy had done some horse showing before

Maggy Price was never without her lipstick and her hair was neatly coiffed. She always made an impression with her appearance, as seen in this 2007 photo.

Maggy Price at the 1993 North American Endurance Championships in Canada on her homebred Ramegwa Kanavyann, the horse on which she won team silver and individual bronze at the 1992 World Championships. She is riding with Stagg Newman on another horse she bred, Ramegwa Drubin, and to the right is Judith Ogus on R.O. Grand Sultan, the three-time World Champion horse who won the competition, while Stagg and Maggy finished third and fourth.

going into trail and endurance and organizing some competitive rides.

"She bred good horses," said Becky. The horses' names all carried her Ramegwa prefix, comprised from the names of her children, Ray, Meg, and Walter.

Stagg, who was a close friend of Maggy's, called her "a good listener," but in turn, he learned a great deal by listening to the woman he called his mentor after he brought a horse from her.

"One reason her horses did so well is she had two pastures, a 60-acre and an 80-acre. She would go out there in winter and scatter the piles of hay so the horses had to run around to find the hay. Maggy's horses were pre-conditioned; they were pasture-bred, not hothouse-bred. Maggy raised her horses tough, although she was very concerned with horse welfare.

"One of the most important things she did for the sport, together with Kerry Ridgeway, was to lead the fight for the 'Fit to Continue' standard. Until the mid-eighties, it used to be when you crossed the finish line, you got your completion award without a vet check first," he noted. "Fit to Continue is the worldwide standard today, from the FEI down to local rides, but it was quite a long battle to get there. It was a fight, and feisty is the word to describe Maggy. She presided over AERC during its fastest growth. She started the Each One Get One campaign, where each member was asked to bring in another member." Those who did that got a bumper sticker for their trouble.

"She taught me so many things," Stagg said, noting she emphasized how important it was to, "Carefully understand your objectives and what your horses can and cannot do." She believed in long slow work and emphasized the importance of rest after a major competition, giving them time to just be horses.

VAULTING

EQUESTRIAN VAULTING IS A COMBINATION OF GYMNASTICS and artistic dance, performed on the back of a moving horse by both teams and individuals. As in figure skating, competitions consist of compulsory movements and a Freestyle to music. That segment offers eye-catching costumes and an opportunity to indulge in awesome creativity.

While at one time the sport was dominated by the Germans and other Europeans, the United States has since made its mark with both team and individual gold medals. Vaulting is not an Olympic discipline, but World Championships are contested every two years.

It is not unusual for individual athletes and teams from different countries to share a horse on which they compete. That makes vaulting unique and is especially advantageous for the smaller countries in the sport so they can take their place on the world stage. Vaulting is the most accessible of equestrian sports, since no one has to own a horse to compete.

MEGAN BENJAMIN GUIMARIN

The Gold Medal Came Early

M egan was the 2006 FEI World Equestrian Games Individual Vault-ing Champion with the horse Leonardo and Lasse Kristensen on the longe. She became the first American (and actually the first non-German) to earn that title. At the same Games, she was also a member of the silver medal U.S. squad, along with the horse Grand Gaudino and longeur Silke Bartel. That made Megan the first vaulter to win two medals in a single World Championships.

She went on to earn a team bronze medal at the 2008 World Champion-ships in Brno, Czech Republic, again with Leonardo and Lasse Kristensen. With partner Blake Dahlgren, she earned a pas de deux bronze medal with Jarl and Lasse Kristensen at the 2012 World Championships in Le Mans, France. She was the first vaulter to win a medal in all three vaulting events.

Megan was editor-in-chief of *Equestrian Vaulting Magazine* from 2010 to 2016. She served on the American Vaulting Association board of directors during the same period, as well as the U.S. Equestrian Federation technical committee, and was on the FEI Athletes' Council as well.

Since retiring from vaulting, Megan lives in San Francisco with her husband, Michael, and her two daughters, Alice (born in 2016) and Cora (born in 2018). She is the founder of Also Mom, a product recommendations site and podcast for women who live full lives and are also moms.

The story rarely unfolds the way we expect it to. Sometimes the story doesn't even unfold *when* we expect it to.

In the summer of 2006, I was crowned Individual Women's Vaulting Champion at the World Equestrian Games in Aachen, Germany. How and when I became World Champion was nothing like the scenario I'd imagined. Not even close, actually.

Let's start with a little context and a quick timeline of the important events that preceded the summer of 2006.

1996: I first was exposed to vaulting and knew I just *had* to try it. I did, and I fell in love with the sport.

1997: I was singled out by world-renowned coach Emma Seely (who became my lifelong coach) and pulled onto our club's elite team, where I became the "little one who stood atop shoulders." At the ripe old age of nine, I knew very little, but I did know we were vying to represent Team USA at the World Equestrian Games in Rome the following summer. The seed was planted and in the privacy of my childhood bedroom, I placed a participation medal around my neck, squinted my eyes, and pretended I was atop the highest podium, feeling for the first time what it might be like to be crowned a champion.

2001: I became one of the youngest Americans at the time to reach the highest level of individual competition (gold level), but I was still too young to compete internationally. I started to see a future where a World Championships medal was a distinct possibility.

2002: My family purchased a humble Danish Warmblood for a bargain price in partnership with Lasse Kristensen, the man who would go on to transform that horse into the best vaulting horse in the world. The stars started to align.

2004: I started to realize my potential, winning my first National Championship title at the gold level and qualifying for my first World

Megan Benjamin on Leonardo at the 2006 World Equestrian Games, where she won the individual gold medal.

Championship team as an individual. I placed ninth, which was better than I'd expected.

And then 2006 rolled around.

By that time there were high expectations for me within the U.S. contingent. It was more or less assumed that if I did my job, I would qualify for the 2006 FEI World Equestrian Games, both as a member of the squad and as an individual. It was also more or less assumed that if our squad did its job, not only would we qualify to represent our country, but we might very well earn a World Championship medal, possibly even a gold.

Focused entirely on our squad's mission to stand atop the podium, I spent most of the summer that year training with my squad in Pfaffenhofen, Germany, where our borrowed German

Devon Maitozo, Rosey Ross, and Megan Benjamin (on the neck) atop Grand Gaudino at the 2006 FEI World Equestrian Games, where the U.S. team won silver.

horse, Grand Gaudino, resided with his longeur and owner, Silke Bartel. Although Silke's club was "nothing special" by German standards, the veritable cornucopia of reliable Warmbloods she had in her stable left me gaping. In the United States at the time, you'd be lucky to have one prized horse at your club. Silke had more than a dozen, most of whom were being vaulted on by the youngest, least experienced vaulters at her club. I had never seen anything like it.

Among her herd, Silke had a little gray named Centuro, who, at first look, seemed like nothing special at all. He was tiny by vaulting standards, standing less than 17 hands tall, and—a typical gray—he was almost always stained brown and green from his romps around the fields. Regardless of stature, I knew better than to let appearances deceive.

To me, Centuro was royalty. Nicola Stroh, one of my vaulting idols then and still, had become World Champion atop his back just two years prior. He had made her look even more powerful, even more graceful than I already knew she was. A great horse can do that.

I was dying for a chance to hop on and feel his canter, but instead of asking—like any good horse girl—I wooed Centuro himself. I offered to walk him, to help groom him, and gave him pats and kisses. Then one day, as I sat watching Silke's vaulters train with Centuro while I rested between squad training sessions, I was invited to vault along with them.

It was instant harmony—his stride and size and shape all seemingly designed just for me. Silke encouraged me to do my entire Freestyle routine, and I did it without a single mistake on my first try—a rare feat for a new pairing. Centuro carried himself differently with me on his back. His confidence triggered my own confidence, and I vaulted without hesitation or qualms.

My coaches noticed, and Silke did, too. A light went off for all of them as I danced atop the World Champion's back. 2006 might be *my* year.

Silke invited me to vault with her and Centuro at CVI Munich later that month, where all the heavy hitters would be out to play before the WEG later that summer. We knew the competition would be important for our squad, where we were trying to establish ourselves as the team to beat, but I had no idea Munich would turn out to be so important for me individually, too.

It was early YouTube days, so very few people had seen what we were capable of until the first day of training sessions.

"Have you seen the American team?" the crowd gossiped. "Who is that American girl vaulting on Nicola Stroh's horse?"

And with all eyes on me, "the American girl," Centuro and I delivered the best routines of my life to date. Our squad won first place, ahead of the Germans, the Austrians, the Swiss, and all the other nations I had forever considered unbeatable. I also placed second individually, ahead of half a dozen of my vaulting idols. I couldn't believe it.

I suppose this is when expectations started to mount for me. As the world began thinking of me as a "contender" individually and as a member of the squad, I continued to feel no pressure at all on my individual performance. I was focused on training with my squad, and anything that happened individually was a bonus.

So when Centuro pulled up lame a couple of weeks before the WEG, I was sad—mostly for him, because I don't like to see horses hurting—but I don't remember feeling devastated. My back-up horse for Aachen was my own horse, Leonardo (Leo), who lived in Denmark with my trainer, Lasse Kristensen.

I had only trained with Leo in Denmark for two weekends that summer—four vaulting sessions total—since my squad was stationed in southern Germany, but this didn't worry me. I knew Leo and Lasse well (I had competed with them for every European competition I had attended for the past

four years) and was fairly confident we could pull off a good partnership if push came to shove and Centuro wasn't ready in time.

What I didn't understand was that quietly, in the background, Lasse had been transforming Leo into a superstar. He had been working with elite dressage trainers to perfect Leo's canter, optimizing Leo's diet, giving him confidence to perform under pressure, and timing everything so that Leo would peak just in time for WEG. The result was a horse that was primed to receive the best vaulting horse scores the world had ever seen—a critical component of the overall score in elite competition.

Long story short, Centuro healed in time to travel to Aachen, but he had been on stall rest for a few weeks and was neither sufficiently fit physically nor mentally to endure the multi-day competition. After a rocky training session on Centuro and a rock solid training session on Leo, I made my choice. I would compete with Leo and Lasse, both of whom I considered family, and we would do our best. The real goal, after all, was four years away at the 2010 WEG in Kentucky.

A German fan found me after my training session with Leo and handed me a small stuffed horse. "A good luck charm," she said, "for the future World Champion."

I was humbled, and thinking of Kentucky, I slipped the horse into my jacket pocket.

In vaulting, the very first event of the competition is the most technical and—at least for me—least fun: the compulsory round. Seven exercises must be done as close to textbook perfection as possible, counting for 25 percent of your overall score. Compulsories always had been my weakest link, and I knew if I had any chance of standing on the podium that year, I'd have to do my best, hope for generous scores, and then climb my way up the standings with the best Freestyle and technical test performances of my life. It was a strategy I had seen work before.

Megan Benjamin on Lanson in 2009 at the Young Riders demo in Kentucky.

After the first round of compulsories, I found myself in first place. Leo's epic horse scores had helped tremendously, and my vaulting hadn't been too shabby either. I had beaten my German idols, my Austrian idols, my Swiss idols. All of them.

And suddenly it became real. If I didn't mess up...I could win.

After the first Freestyle test, I was still in first place. I tried not to think about it too much, focusing my energy on my squad's performances, but my stomach turned all day and all night. I started shaking any time I was sitting still. I took to skipping and throwing aerial (no-handed) cartwheels to keep my mind and body busy. With each aerial, my mind

quieted for a few seconds and gave me some peace.

At the time, vaulters competed in reverse placement order in the second round, so I would be the last to compete in the final two rounds of competition—the technical test and the second round Freestyle test, and the women's event was the final event of the championship. I was going to have to survive with these panicked butterflies in my stomach for the duration.

After the technical test, I was still in first place.

"I could really win this," I thought.

"Stop it. Stop it. Stop it," I said aloud like a crazy person. Cutting myself off was the only way to stay grounded in reality.

I tried to redirect my mounting anxiety, focusing on the squad competition. The pressure was high there, and it was nerve-wracking, but at least I had six teammates with whom to share the pressure.

The final day of competition, our squad vaulted our hearts out, had a couple of mistakes, and earned the silver medal instead of the gold by a sliver of a point. I remember feeling relief that it was over, which lasted about 10 minutes before the dread set in that I still had to perform my final individual Freestyle. The World Championship title was mine to win or mine to lose, and everyone knew it.

That day, the only thing I managed to eat was a single German bread roll, torn into pieces and dipped into a jar of Nutella before I willed the morsels into my mouth. I couldn't stop shaking.

As I warmed up for my final Freestyle, I continued to shake uncontrollably. I fell off in my simplest move, a forward standing lunge. Dusting myself off and willing myself to focus, the rest of my warm-up wasn't much better. I bumbled and doubted myself and fell off half a dozen times. And then the clock ran out. It was go time.

As I walked through the bridge to the stadium, my friend and mentor, Kerith Lemon, applied a final coat of red lipstick to my lips and told a stupid joke to make me laugh. The ground rocked with the enthusiasm of the 7,000 spectators packed into the stadium. Most of them were waving German flags, eager for another German champion. I decided then to keep things simple, to take out my riskiest moves and play things safe. I didn't need the difficulty to win anyway. All I needed was a clean performance.

When my name was announced, Lasse, Leo, and I ran into the arena. I remember the crowd quieting for Leo's trot circle—the obligatory pre-competition formality to verify the horse's fitness to compete. Leo pulled a little maneuver then, squealing and bucking a bit as if to get his own nervous energy out. "Please be good," I probably muttered aloud.

And then I don't remember much else. In fact, I don't remember a single thing until after I landed my aerial dismount, at which point, amidst the deafening roar of the stadium, I quietly said aloud, "I think I just won the World Championships."

And I had.

There are certain expectations of champions.

Expectation: The tears of relief and of ecstasy upon hearing the scores.

Reality: Smiling and bouncing and hugging my coaches self-consciously, not knowing what else to do with the eyes of thousands upon me.

Expectation: Pure joy standing atop the podium and another tear or two as the "Star-Spangled Banner" plays.

Reality: Joy, certainly, but no tears, and with a hand upon my heart, standing next to my Danish longeur, I questioned whether I really knew the words to our national anthem after all and mouthed them subtly, rather than singing them proudly.

Expectation: The gracious and gregarious post-competition interviews.

Reality: I was literally quoted as saying, "I've never done this well before." That was the best sound bite I had to offer.

Expectation: After-party antics.

Reality: In bed by 10:00 p.m., relieved and exhausted from feeling body-wracking nerves for a solid week.

Victory has a bit of a script, and I didn't follow any of it. I had accomplished my biggest goal—becoming World Champion—four years early. I hadn't been prepared for it all to come together. I hadn't been prepared for it all to end.

"Now what?" My mind looped.

From the time I was eight until age 18 when I won the gold, I ate, slept, breathed, and dreamed vaulting. Nothing else. It's what allowed me to become champion, sure, but it also handicapped my identity. I was a vaulter, an athlete, and a horsewoman, but what else? What would I work toward now that I had reached the top of my sport?

Sharing a wagon in the closing ceremonies parade, I asked Kai Vorberg, the 2006 Individual Men's World Champion, how it felt to have earned his title.

"The sun still rises and the sun still sets," he said coolly in his German-accented English.

I nodded, but I only started to understand what he meant by that years later. I learned that winning the WEG was absolutely one of my life's greatest moments. It was also just one moment, one day bookended by a sunrise and a sunset. There would be other great days, and while this may have been the pinnacle of my vaulting career, it didn't have to be the pinnacle of my life.

I've been lucky enough to experience a similar euphoria many times since—once when I married my husband, Michael, once when I gave birth to our daughter, Alice, again when I gave birth to our second daughter, Cora, and honestly, most days these days. My life is full of little girls, laundry, and love—mundanities compared to that August day I was crowned World Champion. And yet, I've never been happier.

The sun still rises and the sun still sets. What a great day that was. What a great day today is, too.

KERITH LEMON

Paving the Way with Silver

———————— 🇺🇸 ————————

A nine-time national vaulting champion and three-time individual silver medalist at the World Championships, Kerith was instrumental in gaining new worldwide respect for American vaulting with her achievements.

She has a degree in mass communications from the University of California at Berkeley and works as a commercial and film director. The artistry that was her trademark during her vaulting career has been a good fit with her directing efforts.

Kerith, who runs her own production company and has provided color commentary at international vaulting events, also has served as a trustee of the USET Foundation.

She does a lot of traveling for work, "not unlike my life when I was in vaulting," she observed, but home is Washington D.C., where Kerith lives with her husband, Mike Gugat, and their son.

By the time I was seven, I had tried all the different sports available to kids my age, yet nothing caught my attention. Gymnastics, for instance, moved too slowly for me.

I really loved ponies, but we lived in Santa Cruz, California, which wasn't horse country. Besides, having my own horse was never an option financially. But my mother had a friend whose kids did vaulting with Nancy Stevens-Brown at the Timberline Club. When we checked out the classes, my mom gave me the option of vaulting or Girl Scouts.

It was an easy choice: I didn't want to wear the green Girl Scouts' outfit and look like everybody else. That foreshadowed my future. I made all of the road-less-traveled choices along my path and vaulting was probably the biggest one for me.

We got to Timberline just as one of the older canter teams was bringing the horse down from the arena. They ran right up to us and somebody took me over to a barrel. Within minutes, I had already learned some of the compulsory moves. Because the learning curve was so high and offered a challenge, it grabbed me right away. For my first actual lesson, I immediately was able to stand on the horse.

The next day, I ran around my school telling everybody I was doing vaulting, this thing no one else knew about or nobody else was doing. It was nice to be distinguished from my friends who were doing traditional sports. I liked that about it. That goes with my name, Kerith, being pretty unique. And I was always up for adventure and discovery.

I was an athletic kid, putting on dance performances in the living room or teaching myself cartwheels in the backyard. I was always on the move. The thing we all loved about vaulting was that it was so family-oriented. My whole family would go when we went to competitions. After I started training in Europe, my brother and sister would come along and live with German families while I was over there.

What's so special about the vaulting community beyond the club you're with is that you interact with everyone else. There was a larger camaraderie in the sport than I'd experienced in others. We were borrowing horses for competitions, and you would often see vaulters from two countries using the same horse. Vaulting always felt like an even playing field to me, and having an equine partner gave the sport an element of the unknown; everyone had the same chance of the horse spooking or taking a misstep.

I rose quickly through the ranks after spending only one year working at the trot. I moved up to the B team at the canter because I was little and could be a flyer on the other vaulters' shoulders. The next year, I was on the A team. We hosted some of the German vaulters when I was nine, so I understood the idea of competing at a higher level. Germany dominated the sport.

My interest was piqued by meeting new people and getting to travel. When the first team went to Europe in 1986 to train for the World

Even as a small child, Kerith Lemon was showing gymnastic prowess.

In 1983, little Kerith Lemon already was comfortable in the basic seat for vaulting on Narah.

Championships, I wanted to be on that squad and wear the USA uniform. I associated it with the Olympics (even though vaulting is not in the Olympics), because I loved to watch the Games on TV.

When my opportunity came for a spot on the U.S. team in 1990 at the first FEI World Equestrian Games in Stockholm, vaulting already was my life. I was in middle school, but I was bypassing birthday parties and extracurricular activities to go to vaulting practice. Vaulting definitely was the most important thing to me and I knew I wanted to compete at the highest level possible.

Our 1990 team won the bronze medal at the first WEG, held in Stockholm. We were the only U.S. discipline at that WEG to medal as a team. When I watched all the Germans standing on the medal podium for the women's individual competition, I saw my goal. I remember turning to a teammate

At the 1994 FEI World Equestrian Games in the Netherlands, Kerith Lemon won her first individual silver medal on Maxwell 8.

and telling her I wanted to stand on the podium someday. She told me, "You'd better get a German passport." I replied that I was going to do it my way, the American way. And I did, going on to win four individual medals.

It surprised me that it happened so fast, because I had imagined it being quite a long journey. For the 1992 World Championships, the Mount Eden team had one member out with an injury, so I filled in. Working with eight other people in a team environment, I also competed as the reserve individual. I finished fourth in the competition for the

reserve vaulters and understood where I needed to improve.

When I got back to the States, I really focused my efforts on being an individual competitor and made some changes in terms of my coaching and my club. I went to Emma Seely who was more of an individual coach, while Nancy Stevens-Brown concentrated on teams.

The first time I represented the United States as an individual was at the 1994 FEI World Equestrian Games in the Netherlands. That's a pretty big first international stage. Before the competition, we would set goals in stepping stones. The first goal was to make the first pass (the Top 12), then the Top 6, then the Top 3. After the first round, I was in fourth place. I had a really strong second round. I made the podium, just as I had envisioned two years previously.

I had borrowed a horse for that competition from a German club that sent two individuals. I was on a different horse but had the same longeur. One of the two German girls was touted to win individual gold. We had spent the whole summer training together and were dear friends by the time we got to WEG. In the compulsory test, my horse was uneven in his canter, and I made a bit of a bobble in my stand. German longeur Gabrielle Ibendahl was disappointed in herself and felt it wasn't fair to me that the horse didn't go his absolute best. She went to the organizers and pointed out the situation. The organizers put in a rake break to fluff the ground in between my horse and that of the leading Germans, so I could have some moments with my longeur and the horse could be at his absolute best.

I knew the other girls' routines and could hear the crowd while I waited. It was mentally unsettling, but I had to remain focused. Everyone was doing everything they could to make sure I had the best possible go. The longeur did some extra training moments to make sure the horse was listening to her.

Kerith Lemon on Pasio I at the 1998 FEI World Equestrian Games, where she won individual silver.

By the time I went into that arena it was electric. The crowd had to wait because of the raking and they were quite loud, doing the wave.

I wore bright pink with swirls of purple and yellow. You could not miss me on Maxwell, the black horse I used, who had all black tack. I went in and knew I would do it. I performed a pretty close-to-perfect routine. I did a unique back walk-over dismount, which involved a backbend on the horse, kicking up into the air with a backward handstand, and then landing on the outside of the horse in front of the spectators.

When I landed, I knew I had done the best I could do. That was where Emma and I always focused, being on the journey, rather than on the destination. I could not have been more pleased and proud of my performance; it was exactly what I trained for. My Freestyle scores were very high, putting me up just enough to take the individual silver medal.

I always looked back to see where I needed to improve, but I was very realistic about the politics of our sport. I never would have won the gold, no matter how perfectly I vaulted. That was the case throughout my career. It just was, and that was accepted.

In the video footage of me after the awards, I looked like a zombie. I was in a daze and so stunned I had won silver that I almost couldn't answer questions. It changed the trajectory of my life. I was supposed to go to a four-year college the next year, but instead went to a community college because that gave me more time for vaulting and to figure out what I wanted to do further down the road.

I never won the gold, sadly, but continued to compete for three more World Championships after that and took an individual medal every time: In 1996 in Kapsovar, Hungary, and 1998 at the WEG in Rome, I got silver; in 2000 in Mannheim, Germany, my medal was bronze.

I do feel I paved the way for Megan Benjamin, the first American individual gold medalist at the WEG in 2006. There were a lot of political hurdles to knock down, and I feel as if I helped to do that. The sport was very rooted in Germany; the Germans were the best for a very long time. I was only the second American individual to win a medal—Jeannette Boxall was the first, taking silver in 1986—and the only non-German to win an individual medal after that until Megan did it. Hers was a very special gold, partly because the 2006 WEG was in Germany. I was part of the support team, assisting Emma with some odds and ends. I helped to coach Megan while she was growing up,

when she was kind of a little sister to me, so it was great to be there when she won.

The biggest letdown for me was in 2000, my last year in the World Championships, where I could compete on Van Dyke, my horse from home, with my own longeur. In the first round of compulsories, one judge had me ranked twenty-seventh, and every other judge had me first or third. Nothing could bring me back from that. I ended up with the bronze. It was disappointing, because I had so firmly believed that would be the competition where I finally would win gold.

Our National Championship was after that, my final nationals before I retired at age 24. They were in Santa Barbara, a place I knew and loved. I got to be on my own horse with my own person on the longe in my own home state. I had four of the most perfect rounds I'd ever had. It was a perfect moment. It was my ninth victory in a row at Nationals. At that competition, I was doing what I loved for the reason I loved it, and not for the gold medal.

Although I knew I wanted more for myself than just that sport, I am very grateful for the years I competed. It had taken me so many places, bringing opportunity into my life and teaching me everything—for example, how to prep for a routine, prep for a competition, manage a budget, multitask, balance school or training or work with other activities. That sport made me what I am today; I just knew that it wasn't the only thing for me.

For the first 10 years after I retired, I helped people in Pennsylvania and Virginia, trying to assist them in coming up to the level of California vaulters. That's always a challenge, with our country being so big and our sport being so small. Now I'm dedicated just to my career. Every once in a while, I'll go by somebody's practice, and if there's a horse around, I'll usually try to hop on it. Somehow, though, I don't find as much enjoyment in riding as I did in being able to move freely on the back of a horse.

DEVON MAITOZO

Staying in the Game

There are a lot of American vaulting "firsts" connected with Devon, a California resident who has devoted his life to the sport in which he earned seven World Championships medals.

At the World Championships in 1998, he became the first American vaulter to win an individual gold medal. In 2000, Devon founded FACE, Free Artists Creative Equestrians, as a hub for learning and artistic advancement for the sport of vaulting. FACE was the first U.S. team to win a World Championships gold medal at the Alltech FEI World Equestrian Games in Kentucky in 2010.

Devon, who rides dressage to train his horses, explains his organization's mission this way: "Our focus on craft, artistry, and horsemanship is the foundation of all we do, and we want to share this with our community and beyond."

Most people assume vaulting is for kids and that eventually, they move on to something else, but a trend is developing where people stay in the sport longer. There's a broader spectrum of vaulters competing at a later age than there used to be, and I seem to be the extreme example of longevity for a vaulting career. The evolution of the rules has allowed for that. I've been told by a lot of people that they felt empowered to continue because they saw me remain successful at a high level into my mid-30s and beyond. I've never considered leaving the sport entirely, although I've been faced with the challenge of continuing as a competitor when it sometimes

seemed beyond my grasp. Even then, I was always motivated to stay involved because it's such a huge part of my identity and I felt I wasn't finished yet. I figured that what I do for the sport might be even more rewarding as a leader and trainer than it has been as an individual competitor, so I stayed.

It's also why I transitioned from being an individual to being part of the team I was to coach for 2006 WEG. That was going to make the most of my experience and in turn, the value my role in the sport has for other people.

In 2010, after coaching and competing with the historic gold medal team at the Alltech FEI World Equestrian Games in Kentucky, my son was born. Being a father gave me a new perspective on how my role in vaulting could have an impact on others. I really believe the depth of value this sport can have on its participants is unmatchable, and this is why I'm invested in it on multiple levels.

My son, Nicholas Maitozo-Menn, has also dabbled in vaulting at a basic level since he was five. I don't want to be one of those dads who pressures his kid to follow in his footsteps, but I'm happy he's gotten at least a taste of it.

Vaulting started for me at a very young age, too. My mother, Roberta Crockett, thought it would be great for me to be exposed to animals, so she rented a home on a ranch in Santa Cruz, California, where the owners had Arabian horses and a 4-H club that offered vaulting. The day after we moved in, the landlord asked, "Is he going to start

The winner of the individual gold medal at the 1998 FEI World Equestrian Games, Devon Maitozo, on Whiskey 191.

vaulting?" I had no clue what that was. I had only been on a horse once on my sixth birthday when a simple trail ride took a traumatic turn after my horse decided to rear and gallop back to the barn. Luckily, my mother pulled me off just in time.

I learned quickly how vaulting can quell the anxiety a child might have around horses by the way he or she gets to interact with them. With vaulting, I was exposed to horses in a way that felt safe and comfortable, without the responsibility of actually directing them. I also liked the fact that it was a team sport.

All I had to do was walk up the hill from my house and there was the class at Seaview Vaulters with my first coach, Laura Jones. Suddenly, I was getting attention from older kids. I thought it was fun and it gave me a feeling of being unique. I wasn't especially fit or good at other sports as a young child. Vaulting was different. For the first four years, it was very casual, close to home, and a fun thing to talk about. I'd also go to competitions and often won. There weren't a lot of little boys competing, but it still felt great.

Four years later, in 1986, we moved to Los Altos Hills. In the neighboring town of Woodside was the Sundance Vaulters club run by Phoebe Hearst Cook, an heir of William Randolph Hearst. Vaulting was her pet project that she took very seriously. She wielded a lot of power with her wealth and interest in the blossoming international sport of vaulting, and I give her a good deal of credit for why vaulting became part of the FEI.

When I came to Sundance, I had slight delusions of grandeur from all my blue ribbons, but I soon realized I had a lot to learn. I was now in a club with 14 horses and an owner flying over the best vaulters from Europe to take part in the San Francisco Equestrian Festival she ran every year.

I had such inspiring coaches: Jeannette Boxall, who won a silver medal in the 1986 World Championships, and National Champion David Long, who

During an exhibition, Devon Maitozo performs a sideward facing stag handstand on Obra Prima de Banksy, an 18.1-hand Danish warmblood.

took me under his wing. I started training along-side my mentors, and David gave me the tools I needed to build a great foundation for a promising future.

Just 18 months after I moved to Sundance, I won the National Championships in my Bronze division. Then I went to a vaulting camp in Germany and watched the 1988 World Championships in Austria. I got to see David, Jeannette, and the best the sport had to offer. I was on fire after that; there was nothing stopping me at that point.

I was pretty good for a young teenager. In 1989, I won the National Championships at the Silver level, and by 1990, I had won Nationals at the top level, Gold. No one expected me to win Nationals at age 15.

At that point, I started vaulting with different clubs, but the rules at the time didn't allow anyone under age 16 to compete internationally. So when I turned 16 in 1991 and could compete abroad, it started me down the road of constant travel. I began competing regularly in Europe, and spending summers there while I was in high school. I may have been a young national champion, but I was still a far cry from the top of the sport.

I worked hard and wound up competing in the 1992 World Championships in Heilbron, Germany. It was a humbling experience to see where I stood in the pack at age 16, but by my first WEG in The Hague two years later, I had trained my way to being among the top few men in the world. A major turning point in my career came when I earned the individual bronze at the 1996 World Championships in Kapsovar, Hungary.

I moved to Europe after high school because the sport was so Eurocentric. I traveled around Germany, Denmark, and Austria, living most of the time in Germany. I learned German because many of the best vaulters were German, and I didn't like not knowing what they were talking about. That gained me respect. I got so much support from the vaulting greats and took advantage of that.

I was an expert couch surfer, staying wherever I could get good training and a place to sleep. I worked my way up the ranks on the international scene. I found horses through random connections, though sometimes that backfired. I had major horse troubles at the European championships in 1997, finishing last.

Later that year, I found an incredible horse named Whisky, and in 1998, I won the individual World Championship at the WEG in Rome on him with Marion Gottschalk on the longe. I was 23 and my ultimate dream had come true.

As soon as you win the World Championships, things change. You have something to keep, instead of something that you are trying to get. People expect a lot of you, so you have to prove yourself in a different way. A lot of luck is involved too, whether it's bad luck or good luck.

Just before the WEG, I graduated from the University of California at Santa Cruz. Through my college years, I trained at the Mount Eden club, where Emma Seely was the trainer. It was very consistent and I could count on it as the foundation to which I would add supplemental training in Europe.

Then I moved to Los Angeles, partly because I decided to pursue acting, but also as a way to forge a path away from my normal comfort zone. I continued to study acting and dance. Acting was a passion of mine, but I had no intention of dropping out of the sport. Instead of getting a job as a waiter as many aspiring actors do, I started coaching at the Barronsgate Vaulting Club in Agoura Hills. I thought this was the chance to have an impact as a coach and not just a vaulter. I had done a lot of coaching in the past to support myself, but that was for additional funds when my parents were still helping out.

After I got the gold, however, I was on my own financially. I realized I didn't want to start at the bottom as an actor, but rather, to maintain my connection to vaulting at the top. There was a horse

I'd seen named Mozart and I knew I could vault on him if I connected to Barronsgate. Here was my ticket to vault and make some money to get by. I could rent a little room and have enough money for gas and food. I traveled as an individual competitor and often brought students to Europe to compete. That enabled me to indulge a competitive career that otherwise would have been prohibitively expensive.

This obscure little club suddenly won the 2000 U.S. selection trials with me at the helm, and we traveled to the World Championships in Mannheim, Germany, flying over our horse, Mozart. He built everyone's confidence at every level. Due to a slip in the trailer on the way to the venue, however, he didn't pass the vet check. This misfortune was a blow after all we had been through to get him there.

The team ended up competing respectably on a Swedish reserve horse, and I ended up with a bronze medal on another American horse, Van Dyke, with whom I had relatively little experience. Considering the situation, I was very happy to come away with a medal at all. Having my former coach, Emma Seely, longe me was one factor that helped.

Two years after going to Barronsgate, and just after the championships, my vaulters and my friend and longeur Carolyn Bland branched off, and we organized Free Artists Creative Equestrian, or FACE. I got a new jump-start in vaulting when people normally would be ending their career in the sport. Competing as an individual was part of my brand as a coach. Being able to show others how to do it was important to me. I also simply had more I wanted to reach toward myself as a performer.

I earned another bronze in 2002 at the WEG in Jerez, Spain, on a German horse, Abu Dhabi, with Petra Reichelt on the longe. That WEG was a huge moment for recognition of our discipline, because vaulting was within walking distance of the other sports' arenas at the Games. The equestrian community got to see firsthand what we had to offer

Devon Maitozo was part of the silver medal team at the 2006 FEI World Equestrian Games Team in Germany.

and vaulting no longer would be overlooked.

Before 2005, vaulters were ineligible to compete on teams when they turned 18. That's why a lot of vaulters' careers fizzled out. When that changed, they added a rule that you couldn't compete both on a team and as an individual unless you were under 18. As a coach and choreographer, I was extremely motivated to field great teams, and now I could join those teams as a vaulter.

In 2006, I decided to co-coach a team with Emma Seely to represent the United States at the WEG in Aachen, Germany, and I vaulted on the team as well. We called ourselves FAME, an all-star composite of FACE and her Mount Eden club. It was a big year for Americans in vaulting. We were 0.002 of a point from winning the team gold at the World Equestrian Games, taking the silver. Megan

Benjamin, who was still under 18 and eligible to vault individually and on the team, became only the second American and first female to win individual gold at the World Championships.

That year, the team project became a big focus for me as a coach, although I still competed as an individual in the U.S. and some international competitions. That carried over through the 2008 World Championships in Brno, Czech Republic, as well. My FACE team qualified, and I also vaulted on the team there. After leading the pack with compulsories, we ended up with a bronze medal due to a fall during one Freestyle round.

In 2010, we decided to continue with much of the same group. I really wanted to vault as an individual again, but because of this stubborn mission of ours, I vaulted on the team. It was the only way I felt we could seriously have a chance to finally reach the very top, and it worked. At the WEG in Kentucky, we became the first U.S. team to win the gold.

Vaulting demands a lot of its athletes. If team athletes work together for just a year or two, it's a lot to expect them to go and win a World Championship, but it's something we often face in the United States. Teams need to have athletes of varying sizes, including a little person or "flyer," who is lifted up to 20 feet in the air. Borrowing horses from Europe for the largest events means the fortitude of a team must be rock solid.

There's a lot of responsibility there and not without its risks. Vaulting is inherently a very safe sport compared to some other equestrian disciplines, but when you push the limits, your safety margin narrows. Part of the reason why I decided to vault on my teams was also because I felt I could keep my flyers safe.

Our gold in Kentucky was won on my horse, Palatine, and longed by Carolyn Bland, who came back from retirement to join us for WEG. In 2007, I had found Palatine at a little facility in the former East Germany. WEG proved my goal of finding a dream horse to have been a success, but for team instead of individuals as I had planned.

In 2010 after WEG, I moved to Connecticut to be near my newborn son. The next year, having run out of money, I sadly had to sell my beloved Palatine. He was bought by Sydney Frankel in Woodside. Carolyn ended up staying at Sydney's home facility to manage that program, and I knew Palatine would be well-cared for. I still regret having to sell Palatine. Not many people today know I found him and was his first vaulting owner and trainer. He is still one of only two American-owned horses ever to win a gold medal.

In 2012, I moved back to California and started over. I performed pas de deux with ex-teammate Rosalind Ross that year, and we managed to be a fraction of a point away from the bronze at the World Championships in Le Mans, France.

After that, I focused on rebuilding the FACE club in the Los Angeles area, and have come to be one of the few people in the United States to make vaulting training their main career. At the age of 41 in 2016, I won the CDI Pacific Cup on my new Irish draught, Maximillion, and after training and competing on the team that represented the United States at the 2016 World Championships, I joined forces with teammate, coach, and vaulter Kalyn Noah. I'm proud to have joined Kalyn and her daughter Phoenix, with my son Nico, as a family, and continue to dedicate my passion toward FACE and the sport.

Now my focus is on pas de deux with Kalyn. This partnered double routine is a perfect way for me to continue my competitive career while emphasizing my strengths and minimizing the risk of injury. As a 43-year-old dad, it isn't worth it to risk the big dismounts I used to perform. I have spent a lifetime reaching for artistry within this unique sport though, and I still feel fit! Being able to continue as a vaulter, and no doubt as a coach, for decades to come is still the greatest of honors.

Photography Credits

All photographs by Nancy Jaffer except:

USET Foundation Archives: pp. v, vi, x *middle*, 13, 123, 124, 251, 255, 257, 258, 261, 262, 274

Rebecca Walton: pp. vii *top and bottom,* 9 *right,* 73, 233 *bottom,* 236, 237, 242, 245

Elaine Wessel: pp. 19, 37, 46, 189

Cealy Tetley: pp. vii *middle,* 43, 66, 80, 85, 97, 108, 132

Susan J. Stickle: pp. 25, 48, 98, 99, 183

Tish Quirk: p. 26

Courtesy of Margie Goldstein Engle: p. 36

Courtesy of Kent Farrington: p. 41

Karl Leck: pp. viii *middle,* 47, 70, 95, 101, 107, 109, 112, 113, 114, 117, 119, 120, 125, 147, 171, 173, 249, 252

Arnd Bronkhorst: p. 53

Shannon Brinkman: pp. ix *top and bottom,* 22, 65, 131, 221

Courtesy of Lauren Hough: p. 69

Annan Hepner: pp. 77, 79, 187, 190, 217, 223, 225

Terri Miller: p. 89

Courtesy of Phillip Dutton: p. 129

Lawrence J. Nagy: p. 135

Courtesy of Boyd Martin: p. 136

Fred Newman: p. 165

M. Kaiser Equine: p. 167

Bunny Milliken: p. 174

PicsofYou.com: p. 180

Courtesy of Chester Weber: p. 184 *top*

Ronnie Nienstedt: p. 184 *bottom,* 201

Courtesy of Suzy Stafford: p. 194

David Wharton: p. 195

Marie de Ronde: p. 196

Meredith Fetters: pp. ix *middle,* 197

Meghan Benge: p. 200

Krisztina Horvath: pp. 199, 203

Courtesy of Vicki Garner-Sweigart: pp. 207, 209, 210

Courtesy of Lynn Seidemann: pp. 212, 213, 214

Courtesy of Roxie Trunnell: p. 218

Courtesy of Becca Hart: p. 224

Courtesy of the US Equestrian Federation: p. 227

FEI Photo: p. 231

Taylor Rains: pp. x *top,* 232

Courtesy of Shawn Flarida: p. 238

Courtesy of Andrea Fappani: p. 241

Gore Baylor Photography: p. 263 *left*

Courtesy of Stagg Newman: p. 263 *right*

Phelps Media Photo: pp. x *bottom,* 267

Bob Langrish: p. 268

Alex Thomas: p. 270

Courtesy of Kerith Lemon: p. 273, 275

Courtesy of Devon Maitozo: p. 278

Blake Dahlgren: p. 279

Index

Page numbers in bold refer to photos and captions.